COLUMBIA COLLEGE

Y0-CAM-834

371.102⁷

APR '98

D

ENTEREDFEB 2 1996

The Ethnography of Empowerment

for Doug, Laura, Sara, Anna
and the baby in my palm

for Atso and transformation

The Ethnography of Empowerment:
The Transformative Power of Classroom Interaction

Heljä Antola Robinson

 The Falmer Press

(A member of the Taylor & Francis Group)
Washington, D.C. • London

Columbia College Library
600 South Michigan
Chicago, IL 60605

USA   The Falmer Press, Taylor & Francis Inc., 1900 Frost Road, Suite 101, Bristol, PA 19007

UK   The Falmer Press, 4 John Street, London WC1N 2ET

© H.A. Robinson 1994

All rights reserved. No part of this publication may be reproduced, stored in a retrieval system, or transmitted in any form or by any means, electronic, mechanical, photocopying, recording or otherwise, without permission in writing from the Publisher.

First published in 1994

A catalogue record for this book is available from the British Library

Library of Congress Cataloging-in-Publication Data are available on request

ISBN 0 7507 0367 9 cased
ISBN 0 7507 0368 7 paper

Jacket design by Caroline Archer

Typeset in 10/12 pt Bembo by
Graphicraft Typesetters Ltd., Hong Kong.

Printed in Great Britain by Burgess Science Press, Basingstoke on paper which has a specified pH value on final paper manufacture of not less than 7.5 and is therefore 'acid free'.

371.1023 R661e

Robinson, Helj"a Antola.

The ethnography of empowerment

Contents

Contents

Introduction

Kieffer (1981) observes that since empowerment is 'an interactive and highly subjective relationship of individuals and their environment', it demands 'innovation in qualitative/ethnographic methodology' and a 'special strategy to capture the intense experience of human struggle and transformation.'
(Seth Kreisberg, 1992)

Given all the criticism and pressure directed at education, it is amazing that there are still so many educators who are resilient and strong enough to go on (Levine, 1989). We are confronted almost daily in the media and professional journals with the decline of the educational system (Conner, 1989; Feldhusen, 1989).

Teachers, of course, are often blamed for the ills of education; but teachers themselves report that their situation is often untenable. Facing 'plateauing' or burnout, they feel trapped and driven to leave teaching altogether, to move to alternate levels within teaching, or to stick it out somehow by finding primary meaning and value in out-of-school experiences like vacations and hobbies (Kottkamp *et al.*, 1986; Levine, 1989; Milstein, 1990). Fifty per cent of all teachers leave their profession in the first five years of their teaching experience (Goodlad, 1990). Teacher prestige and status have never been lower than they are now (McCreary Juhasz, 1990). Many teachers are still convinced that what they are doing is of importance and meaningful, not only to them but to their students as well; but teacher stress under such societal ills as drugs, guns, teenage pregnancy, child abuse, and at-risk home environments seems to be on the rise. In the current social climate coercion, harsher punishments and tighter control seem to be the main way of coping with these ills (Neve, 1985; Glasser, 1990).

In a situation like this individual teachers feel that their voices are being drowned out; their creativity is stifled in an atmosphere of measurable efficiency and accountability (McCreary Juhasz, 1990). Schools are places characterized by academization and fragmentation and — even architecturally — more clearly resemble educational factories than places of learning and growth (Husen, 1989). Husen warns educators against stagnating and doing their monotonous duty, arguing that 'school pedagogy cannot avoid being strongly affected by fundamental changes in the surrounding society and that a mismatch can easily occur due to inherent institutional conservatism in the school'

(1989:13). But stagnation breeds stagnation, and suffocates all vision of new solutions to old problems. Even when offered as a methodological lifeline by colleagues or in workshops, the new often seems impossibly frightening; teachers still tend to teach the way they were taught rather than the way they were taught to teach (Jones, 1984).

And yet all is not hopeless. Good teachers not only exist, but abound. Sometimes they remain mavericks in schools run by tired, cynical administrators who either actively or passively hamper their best efforts. Even when supported by dynamic colleagues, administrators and appreciative parents, their spirits often flag under the barrage of blame and accusation coming from the media and the general public. But they go on teaching their children, fighting their uphill battles to provide a warm and exciting learning environment in overcrowded classrooms.

How do they do it? What is it exactly that they do? What constitutes good teaching, and where do good teachers find the energy and the enthusiasm to endure — even to grow? These are the questions that I set out to answer in this project. The answers surprised me.

My classroom experiences in Finland and in America had led me to believe that the crucial ingredient in the classroom is interaction — teachers with students, students with teachers — so I set myself the task of finding out what it is in interaction that facilitates good teaching. Perhaps, I thought, by studying how 'successful' or 'good' teachers and students interact I could map out the parameters of effective classroom interaction and so contribute to the expansion of solid teaching. In this way I hoped to show how some of the negative burden education is carrying could be changed or avoided. Is there something good teachers do in their interactions with students that other teachers might learn? Is there a particular interactive mode that is especially effective in learning environments?

In approaching these questions I opted for an in-depth ethnographic methodology that would enable me as a participant-observer to tap into the complexities of classroom interaction. Ethnography is especially beneficial in studying processes in education (Goetz and LeCompte, 1984), especially highly inter- and intraindividual processes like student-teacher interaction. William Louden's (1991) year long in-depth collaboration with one teacher in *Understanding Teaching*, for example, shows how much can be gained through researcher participation in a classroom: instead of erecting objectivist walls between the researcher and the research subjects, the ethnographer enters into interaction with her subjects, becomes a part of what she studies.

What surprised me about this research process was the way in which my participation in the classrooms I studied started changing me as a researcher — changed my thinking not only about good teaching but about good research as well. These changes worried me at first. If I was in fact entering into a changing interactive process and being changed by it, how could I reliably describe what I was observing? Traditional ethnographic methodologies are notably more sensitive to change than quantitative methods; but even ethnographic research as I had learned to conduct it requires a stasis or stability somewhere, some unchanging ground, for description to be reliable. On the other hand Noblit and Hare (1988) say that it is fairly typical for ethnographic research to discover a new topic during the immersion in field work. If the interactive process under study was dynamic, vital, changing, the researcher at least had to occupy a stable position in order to chart out the changes. But what if the researcher, by entering into the dynamic process, became part of the change as well? Was reliable empirical research even possible?

At some point in my field research I began to feel that interaction was too neutral a concept to depict the process I was studying. Interaction seemed to imply static interactive roles — teachers and students — that were played out by specific individuals in classrooms without significant change. True, there might be change in the *content* of the interaction — teachers teach new material, students learn things — but there should be no change in interactive roles. As my data collection progressed, I became increasingly convinced that this simply was not the case. There was a movement, a dynamism in the interactions I was engaged in studying that could not be explained through a static conception of interaction. Individuals in the classrooms I was studying not only changed roles more fluidly than I expected; their interactive fluidity was more directional than I expected.

What I experienced in the classrooms was what the four teachers in my study had experienced: a dynamic change and awareness, an increase of power from within, or what I soon began to call empowerment. It was not merely that good teachers interact successfully or effectively with their children, I found; it was that good teachers empower their children and are empowered by them. All four of the first-grade teachers I chose for the study had recently (within the previous two or three years) undergone a radical change in their thinking about and practices of teaching; but this change alone did not empower them. It was only in open-ended interaction with the children, in learning from the children as the children were learning from (and with) them, that the teachers began to feel empowered — and to feel that their personal empowerment was empowering for their children as well.

I found the transformative interaction I was calling empowerment most usefully discussed by Paolo Freire (1970), the revolutionary Brazilian educator whose term for the humanizing process he facilitates is not in fact empowerment but *liberation* — being freed from what he calls the banking concept of education. Freire impressed upon me the dialogical nature of empowering interaction — the ways in which empowerment or liberation is made possible by the interchangeability of teacher and learner roles — and also the directionality of good teaching, the channeling of everyone's experience in an empowering classroom from a sense of imprisonment and stagnation toward a feeling of freedom and life.

Another source that was published as I was writing this book is Seth Kreisberg's (1992) *Transforming Power: Domination, Empowerment and Education*, which confirmed my choice of Freire and the concept of empowerment as the best approach to my ethnographic data and methodology. He confirmed my understanding that although the term empowerment 'has an expanding presence in a broad range of fields and contexts, it has often been used as a rhetorical device without being carefully defined by its wielders' (1992:19). He also notes that in the context of educational usage 'it has begun to be drained of its critical edge' (p. 21).

What Freire and Kreisberg did not explain, however, was where I stood, or should stand, as researcher in relation to the exciting developments I was observing and participating in. Was it enough to stand back and describe what I was seeing? More to the point, was it possible — or honest — to stand back and describe what I was seeing? After all, in participating in the classrooms I observed, I was not only helping to facilitate the empowerment I was seeing, I was also feeling empowered myself. I was changing the classroom environment, and it was changing me. All my instincts as an empirical researcher told me that this was not a desirable thing, that my results would inevitably be skewed by the impact I was having on the interactions (would they have happened as they did had I not been so actively involved?) and by the impact they were having on me (would I have experienced things differently had I held myself more aloof?). And yet I also had a strong sense that it was desirable — that something very important was happening to me, and to everyone involved in those empowering interactions; and that a research methodology that led me to treat my own empowerment as undesirable was flawed. It became increasingly clear to me that somehow I had to adjust my methodological conception of what I was doing to account for the startling nature of my data: for the fact that everyone in the classroom interactions, including me, was being transformed, was being empowered while empowering others; and that my own inability to stick to my original methodological conceptions, rather than dooming my research to failure, was precisely the thing that made it work.

It soon became clear to me that there was very little difference between what I was doing as a researcher and what the teachers and children were doing as learners. They were learning: I was learning. They too, for that matter, were researchers. They felt empowered; I felt empowered. Why should my inquiry into classroom interaction be held at arm's length from a process in which it was immersed, and which it so strongly resembled? I resisted for a time the breakdown of the traditional gap between researcher and research subjects, between the describing *subject* and the *object* described — the gap that makes description possible — but tentatively, cautiously, I began to try on the notion of an *ethnography of empowerment*.

Just what I mean by the ethnography of empowerment can be suggested in a diagram (Figure 1):

Figure 1: *Dialogical relationships in interactive empowerment*

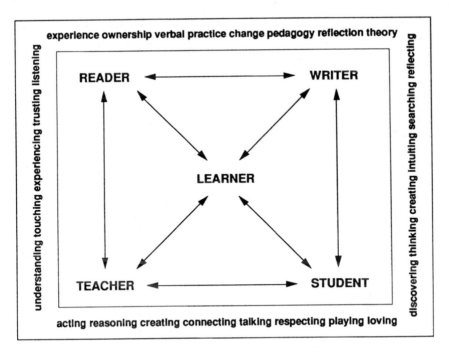

At first glance the diagram seems to be suggesting that there is in every classroom a person called the *teacher* (there is, after all, at least one person per classroom who is paid to play that role by the school district) and a group of people called *students*. In this traditional conception, the teacher is always an adult and students are typically children — either literal or (in secondary, university and other adult education) symbolic children. By setting teachers and students in dialogical interaction with other roles, however — reader and writer, and especially learner — the diagram stresses the interchangeability of these roles. When an adult in a classroom becomes a learner, most likely there is a child playing the role of teacher (or writer, or reader). A student in this conception is simply one who studies. Children and adults read and write, teach and study; everybody learns.

If we feed into the diagram only those participants in classroom interactions traditionally identified as teachers and students, then the empowering effect of open-ended dialogue is primarily pedagogical in impact; this would be the pedagogy of empowerment. The ethnography of empowerment begins with the realization that the ethnographer plays all these same roles in the classroom she is participating and observing in as well: she reads, writes, teaches, studies and, above all, learns. The ethnography of empowerment is grounded methodologically in the pragmatic perception that there is no fundamental difference between what ethnographers do and what teachers and students do. Learning is researching; researching is learning. Researching, a learning activity that involves reading and writing, teaching and studying, is something that everyone in an empowering classroom does.

But it is more radical even than that. The ethnography of empowerment recognizes that not only the writer of an ethnography but the reader as well enters into all these dialogical interactions. Like the ethnographer, the reader reads and writes, teaches and studies, and above all learns. Just as the ethnographer is empowered in and by dialogical interactions in the classroom, the ethnographer's reader is empowered in and by dialogical interactions in and by the book or article or conference paper. The diagram charts an expanding network of empowering interactions, so that, for example, the researcher empowered by interaction with adults and children in a first-grade classroom writes up a research study that empowers a reader in another university to enter into empowering interactions in local classrooms.

The aim of the ethnography of empowerment does become, in fact, less description than the transmission of empowering dialogue: passing on the experience of empowerment to other people. The goal is not so much *knowledge* about good teaching as it is the empowering *experience* of good teaching.

The original focal point of my study was to explore, in terms of teacher's self-esteem and teaching philosophy, the classroom interaction (both verbal and nonverbal) between first-graders and their teachers. The four first-grade classroom teachers chosen had made drastic changes in their teaching within the previous few years. Two of the teachers taught in a combination class, switching children for certain subjects. The teachers were from two different schools.

The study was conducted in the summer and fall of 1991 and January of 1992 in Northern Mississippi. In addition to my participant-observations in the four classrooms, I interviewed the teachers and their children, videotaped classroom sessions, dialogued with teachers through teacher-researcher journals, had the children draw pictures of their classroom experiences, gave the four teachers self-assessment instruments to fill out, and had two of the teachers make self-activated tape recordings of an entire day when I was not present.

The foreshadowed problems that initially gave direction to my study were the following:

- Teaching philosophy and change in teaching practices
- Teacher's self-esteem and interaction
- Importance of interaction in the teaching process
- Verbal interaction and the classroom
- Nonverbal interaction and the classroom

During the data gathering, as I began to see that the collected material started shaping into clusters of ideas that repeatedly rose out of my participant-observation, a major focus shift took place. The four teachers and their classrooms were different, and the roles I played in each were divergent to some extent, but something was similar in all of them. As my original conception of interaction as the basis of good teaching gradually shifted into the richer and more specific realm of empowerment, I did not abandon the idea of interaction; its role changed. It was no longer the end but the means, no longer my primary concern but the essential vehicle of my primary concern, which was empowerment. In refocusing the study from interaction to empowerment, self-esteem and the four teachers' teaching philosophies and the change in them took on new significance.

Keywords

Interaction refers to reciprocal face-to-face action. This can be either verbal, channeled through written or spoken words, or nonverbal, channeled through touch, proximity, eye-contact, facial expression, gesture, posture, appearance, environmental factors, and chronemics (use of time). Partly synonymous with interaction is *dialogue*, which contains in its etymological structure (*dia* as 'across') the role-interchangeability that is so essential to empowerment.

Teaching philosophy is a system of principles, conscious or unconscious, that a teacher has (or, since teachers have so little rational control of this, that 'has' the teacher) for the guidance of educational decision-making in a classroom context.

Self-esteem is a realistic respect for oneself and impressions and image of oneself.

Empowerment is a personal and social process, a liberating sense of one's own strengths, competence, creativity and freedom of action; to be empowered is to feel power surging into one from other people and from inside, specifically the power to act and grow, to become, in Paolo Freire's terms, 'more fully human' (1970:61).

Ethnography of empowerment is an ethnography that will not only record but actually lead to transformative and rehumanizing action in the world. The subject-to-subject relationship becomes the core of ethnography of empowerment.

Triangulation is the ethnographic process of studying and gathering data in a given culture simultaneously with the aid of a range of methods.

Intuitive discernment (Knape and Rosewell, 1980) refers to teachers' perceptual awareness of decision-making without an articulated teaching philosophy.

Banking concept of education is Paolo Freire's (1970) articulation of traditional teaching as depositing of information in the student's head.

Reflective thinking is the process of looking back and carefully considering one's thoughts, actions and decision-making.

Organization of the Book

Throughout this book I hope to convey the manifold layers of empowerment in an educational setting. By addressing the various pertinent layers of ethnography — the philosophical questions and reflection, the methodological questions, the researcher as a participant-observer, the teachers' classroom reality, the ethnography of empowerment and dialogical relationships born in empowerment — I hope to intertwine these layers and in this way show their interconnectedness. The different parts of ethnography — formulating a research idea and a focus, deciding on data gathering techniques, gathering the data, analysing, interpreting and reporting — are in constant interplay, so that a linear presentation of them does not adequately express the dynamic of ethnography. In each chapter I attempt to bring in a different layer in helping to gain understanding of ethnographic empowerment and to open up new tools to deal with educational empowerment.

Chapter 1 specifically addresses the research literature on empowerment and interaction as a springboard for philosophical reflections on the ethnography of empowerment. Chapter 1 attempts to chart a philosophical pathway through the issues that are of central focus in my study and that serve as a basis for understanding the methodological direction I take.

Chapter 2 discusses the specific methodological concerns and practices of this particular ethnography of empowerment. I discuss the three important ethnographies as a base for the ethnography of empowerment: holistic ethnography; ethnography of communication; and symbolic-interactionist ethnography. My research is *holistic* in that it focuses on a unified whole — interaction in the classroom — with all parts perceived as being interdependent (Mead, 1973; Jacob, 1988). The study uses ethnography of *communication* because it is interested in both verbal and nonverbal interaction. The study is *symbolic-interactionist* in that it gives a basis for understanding the teacher and children as forces in an interactive process where each defines and interprets each other's acts in a given situation (Jacob, 1988). Symbolic interactionism relies on the premise that humans act toward things on the basis of what meanings people assign to things. These meanings arise and get modified and interpreted in social interaction (Blumer, 1969). The ethnography of empowerment builds on these three by incorporating them into the transformative effect of dialogical interactions.

Chapter 3 is an analysis and interpretation of data gathered in this ethnography during the summer and fall semester 1991 and the beginning of spring semester 1992. The analysis is broken down into classroom portraits and empowering teaching practices (themes).

The last chapter outlines the pedagogical implications of the study. I discuss the impact of empowerment in relation to teachers' teaching philosophy and self-esteem in dialogical relationships. I develop a chart of attitudes and practices for empowering classroom interaction as opposed to the banking concept of education. I conclude with questions and further suggestions for study of empowering classroom practices.

Acknowledgments

My deep and heartfelt gratitude first to the group of professionals supporting me. With each of you I discovered new things about myself. It was Cindy Leigh who initially, in journal dialoguing, helped me get past my writer's block in a foreign language; you also introduced me to the excitement of brain-compatible learning and always found ways to challenge me to discover the undiscovered in my thinking. Your personal and professional innovation and enthusiasm directed me toward researching holistic learning in the first-grade classroom, and continued to sustain and empower me throughout the research. Peggy Emerson: you dialogued with me constantly, supportively, with great tolerance for tentativeness, on everything from teacher philosophy to physical and emotional exhaustion. Sherrie Gradin: you were aware of the importance of the political and the emotional in writing and research, you supported me as much with your sisterly caring as with your invaluable methodological and rhetorical suggestions. Linda Swindell: you helped me to understand the importance of methodological decisions and to realize what a long way I had come personally.

David Cox: your graduate seminar in breakthrough thinking and personal charisma provided one of the important seeds for this work, which I discovered all of a sudden, while not looking for it. Ken Bender: you believed in me and were always ready with an encouraging word. Margaret Talbot: you kept my spirits up. Kristen Sulser and Mitra Farshian transcribed my teacher interviews.

I want to thank my Finnish family for their support: Lämpimät kiitokseni vanhemmilleni Lahja ja Oskar Antolalle, jotka loitte elämäni edellytykset ja rohkaisitte rajojeni rikkomiseen. Isä: et nähnyt tätä kirjaa, mutta olisit ollut ylpeä Heljästäsi. Äiti: mihin minä ryhdyin, siihen minä pystyin, hiekkajyvä kerrallaan — kiitos kun kannustit minua. Kiitän rakkaita sisaruksiani (erityisesti Mirjami Hyttistä ja Marjatta Huhtaa), jotka antauduitte pitkäaikaiseen kaukotukisuhteeseen kanssani. My 'other' parents, Don and Berta Robinson and Jim and Ann Soo, and my 'other' brother and sister, David and Trina Robinson, all provided moral support throughout the writing of this book.

To Doug, my empowering spouse and love: it is with you I have learned to share my inner voice. Our long conversations about education and research methodology and life and caring helped me not only to formulate my ideas for the book but to find the courage in myself to see it through to completion. As you grew increasingly interested in pedagogy and I found myself reading theoretical works off your shelves, we grew together in both our professional and our personal lives.

To my daughters Laura, Sara, and Anna, in whose presence reality was renamed daily, and my exchange daughter Laura Tynkkynen, who in the future will see what it was all about.

To the teachers and children in my ethnography who search for and share the empowerment in their lives in the quest of becoming more fully human.

Life is pleasant but confusing and fearful.
Life is a blossoming in caring presence — yet unaware.
Life is trusting in continuity through changes.
Life is growing through pain.
Life is learning through connection and closeness.
Life is serenity and discovery.
Life is insecurity, hope and dynamic change.
Life is struggle, a leap into the unknown.
Life is now, complex, rewarding and full of questions.
Life is a celebration of love.
Life is being able to give up to make room for new growth.
Yesterday
   Tomorrow
      Now is here.

Chapter 1

Interaction and Teacher Change

To begin the process of empowerment, teachers must enter into a process of personal and institutional change that will lead to transformation of both the structure of schools within which they work and their relationship toward their colleagues and their students.

Teaching is an intellectual, creative, moral, and political endeavor.
(Kreisberg, 1992)

In this chapter I want to chart a philosophical pathway through the issues that are of central focus in my study and that serve as a basis for understanding the methodological and philosophical directions taken in this work. To do this I propose to review the pertinent literature on empowerment, interaction (verbal and nonverbal) and change in a fairly loosely structured way so as to move beyond mechanistic summary to a more dynamic, philosophical consideration of the thematic realm in which the study operates.

Empowerment is a term frequently seen in recent articles and research literature. It is used very generically, almost like a motto — a new buzzword that gives a title dignity and importance. As Weissglass (1990) points out, however, this generic dignification also has the effect of concealing or diffusing the concept of empowerment.

Let me begin by listing the implicit meanings of empowerment as it is found in the recent literature:

- a route to enhancing the teaching profession: the 'authority to teach with the professional standards that pertain to their work' (Mertens and Yarger, 1988:35);
- a more active and critical approach towards teaching (Goodman, 1987);
- the right to make decisions and to have a voice: 'There is a narrow line between empowerment and adopting a laissez-faire leadership style' (Foster, 1990:39; see also Sickler, 1988; Kanpol, 1990; Gitlin and Price, 1992);
- 'a positive force and literacy is the medium' — almost a synonym for learning, or for the practical real-world benefits of schooling, which teachers must help children to obtain (Fagan, 1989:572);
- letting go of feelings of victimization and recalcitrancy (Swart, 1990);

- when teachers 'begin to perceive themselves as the experts — intellectuals capable of shaping their professional lives and the profession itself' (Houser, 1990:58);
- internal control and individually divergent practices, solving problems independently (Glickman, 1989);
- releasing positive reciprocal processes (Cochran, 1988);
- a process of supporting people to construct new meanings and exercise their freedom to choose (Weissglass, 1990).

In these examples empowerment is seen as a solution to a perceived problem — a way of gaining something good and valuable that current educational practices are perceived as withholding, or of letting go of something harmful and restrictive that current educational practices are perceived as imposing. The difficulty I have in sifting through these uses of the term is that they are used almost liturgically, ritualistically, to invoke a dimly perceived problem and its solution without directly addressing either. There is a dearth of attempts at defining empowerment (Kreisberg, 1992); those who do tend to define it almost collocationally, by semantic association with a string of examples, so that, looking over my list of definitions above, I still feel unsure whether Fagan, for example, takes empowerment to be a synonym for learning as a process, or learning as an end result ('learnedness').

An exception to this variety of uses of empowerment is seen in Gitlin and Price's (1992) article in the *Association for Supervision and Curriculum Development Yearbook*. They define empowerment as a term linked with voice in the context of teacher evaluation — voice in terms of an awareness of power and domination and challenging the structures that cause unjust use of power. Kreisberg writes: 'Empowerment involves individuals gaining control of their lives and fulfilling their needs, in part, as a result of developing competencies, skills and abilities necessary to effectively participate in their social and political worlds' (1992:19).

Empowerment is individual and collective; it is power and freedom; it is external and internal, political and personal, a means to an end and its own reward. In order to see how the term can encompass all these attributes, we need a more capacious conceptual framework. Such a framework is offered persuasively and influentially by Freire (1970), who identifies the disempowering problem as *oppression* and its pedagogical method as the *banking* approach to education; the empowering solution as *becoming fully human* and its pedagogical method as dialogue, or the problem-posing approach to education. In banking education, students are perceived as passive receptacles into which knowledge can be poured by the teacher, the authority in the matters of knowledge. In problem-posing or dialogical or liberatory education, teachers and students work together to transform reality. Freire writes: 'problem-posing education involves a constant unveiling of reality. The former attempts to maintain the *submersion* of consciousness; the latter strives for *emergence* of consciousness and *critical intervention* in reality' (Freire, 1970:68).

Freire's larger critical framework for the discussion of empowerment is political: he identifies the oppressive forces that would thwart empowerment in teachers and students as the ruling power-holders and power-structures in society, and calls for concerted dialogical action-reflection for and among the oppressed to undo the dehumanizing, passivizing, disempowering effects of this oppression:

> It is not surprising that the banking concept of education regards people as adaptable, manageable beings. The more students work at storing the deposits entrusted to them, the less they develop the critical consciousness which would result from their intervention in the world as transformers of that world. The more completely they accept the passive role imposed on them, the more they tend simply to adapt to the world as it is and to the fragmented view of reality deposited in them.
>
> The capability of banking education to minimize or annul the students' creative power and to stimulate their credulity serves the interests of the oppressors, who care neither to have the world revealed nor to see it transformed. The oppressors use their 'humanitarianism' to preserve a profitable situation. Thus they react almost instinctively against any experiment in education which stimulates the critical faculties and is not content with a partial view of reality but always seeks out the ties which link one point to another and one problem to another.
>
> Indeed, the interests of the oppressors lie in 'changing the consciousness of the oppressed, not the situation which oppresses them'; for the more the oppressed can be led to adapt to that situation, the more easily they can be dominated.
>
> (Freire, 1970:60)

In this perspective, the contradictions in the various attempts to define — or even mention — empowerment in recent educational research stem from the writers' failure to seek 'out the ties which link one point to another and one problem to another'. As Freire says, this failure is normal and required in an oppressive educational system. If writers on empowerment focus on symptoms, like feelings of recalcitrancy or low social success, without making connections with the social forces that condition these symptoms, their potentially disruptive or revolutionary concern with empowerment can be defused or diffused into a series of local panaceas, technical adjustments that do not alter the structure of social interaction. Remove the feelings of recalcitrancy — improve students' chances at social success. This is especially true of writers who conceive of empowerment as the teacher's access to the channels of social power that perpetuate oppression: when the problem is perceived as the teacher's lack of authority or low professional standards, then empowerment becomes another word for oppression. This oppression Fromm

(1967) sees as a social push for conformity where a person has little initiative and everything in his/her environment is prescribed by the organization of the work itself, routinized and somehow prefabricated: 'They all perform tasks prescribed by the whole structure of the organization, at a prescribed speed, and in a prescribed manner. Even the feelings are prescribed: cheerfulness, tolerance, reliability, ambition, and an ability to get along with everybody without friction' (Fromm, 1967:163).

Freire doesn't use the word *empowerment* in his book — he prefers *liberation* — but I read *The Pedagogy of the Oppressed* as a discussion of and call for empowerment. Due to the centrality of Freire's ideas to my conception of this project, I have woven quotations from his book throughout this chapter; whenever his name or words appear, let them serve as a reminder that whatever my concern at the time — interaction, intuition, change — it is steeped also in the politics of oppression and empowerment.

Interaction

Learning occurs in a social context. The recent research on brain-compatible learning supports what Dewey (1944) and Vygotsky (Rieber and Carton, 1987) hypothesized: that learning occurs best in meaningful situations in an open and authentic environment, in interaction with other humans, in real situations that have a direct link to the experience or life of the learner (Neve, 1985; Hart, 1986; 1990; Nummela and Rosengren, 1986; Nummela Caine and Caine, 1991). To achieve 'mutual humanization' the teacher 'must be a partner of the students in his relations with them' (Freire, 1970:62).

Social relationships, including the teacher-child relationship, require reciprocity (Buber, 1970). The banking method of teaching, seen in many classrooms where the teacher is the authority and the knower, contradicts this. Buber insists that

> Whoever is overpowered by the It-world must consider the dogma of ineluctable running downs a truth that creates a clearing in the jungle. In truth, this dogma only leads him deeper into the slavery of the It-world. But the world of You is not locked up. Whoever proceeds toward it, concentrating his whole being, with his power to relate resurrected, beholds his freedom. And to gain freedom from the belief of unfreedom is to gain freedom.
>
> (1970:107)

Through the reciprocal act or interaction the children and adults engage in a dialogue that allows the exploration of previously unknown paths of knowledge. This means that at the heart of teaching and learning lies classroom interaction. In dialogical interaction the teacher becomes a resource of the learner's self-actuated development (Buber, 1970). Howe (1963) claims that education, relationships, and communication that are not dialogical — including much of traditional classroom teaching — are destructive and exploitative. This is very similar to Freire's (1970) idea of the banking concept of education, and his observation that education is used to manipulate and obstruct students from becoming fully human. Through this concept of education the following attitudes and practices occur:

- the teacher teaches and the students are taught;
- the teacher knows everything and the students know nothing;
- the teacher thinks and the students are thought about;
- the teacher talks and the students listen — meekly;
- the teacher disciplines and the students are disciplined;
- the teacher chooses and enforces his choice, and the students comply;
- the teacher acts and the students have the illusion of acting through the action of the teacher;
- the teacher chooses the program content, and the students (who were not consulted) adapt to it;
- the teacher confuses the authority of knowledge with his own personal authority, which he sets in opposition to the freedom of the students;
- the teacher is the Subject of the learning process, while the pupils are mere objects.

(Freire, 1970:59)

Dialogical interaction is collaborative and constitutes an invitation to become a person by allowing the I-Thou relationship to develop (Howe, 1964; Buber, 1970). Those who are capable of dialogical relationships accept themselves as total, authentic persons who can afford to be present for others. A dialogical person is open and disciplined in that she is capable of giving herself in dialogue, free to respond and initiate. A dialogical person is accepting of others and capable of responsible responses in the relationship (Howe, 1963).

This is no metaphor but actuality: love does not cling to an I, as if You were merely its 'content' or object; it is between I and You. Whoever does not know this, know this with his being, does not know love, even if he should ascribe to it the feelings that he lives through, experiences, enjoys, and expresses. Love is a cosmic force . . . love is responsibility of an I for a You.

(Buber, 1970:66)

Or, as he says a page later:

Relation is reciprocity. My You acts on me as I act on it. Our students teach us, our works form us. The 'wicked' become a revelation when they are touched by the sacred basic word [I-You, the dialogical word]. How we are educated by children, by animals! Inscrutably involved, we live in the currents of universal reciprocity.

(Buber, 1970:67)

Freire (1970) is eloquent on this reciprocity as well. 'Dialogue cannot exist, however,' he writes, 'in the absence of a profound love for the world and for human beings. The naming of the world, which is an act of creation and re-creation, is not possible if it is not infused with love. Love is at the same time the foundation of dialogue and dialogue itself' (Freire, 1970:77; translation slightly modified). Dialogue also requires humility; here Freire strongly recalls Buber:

The naming of the world, through which people constantly re-create that world, cannot be an act of arrogance. Dialogue, as the encounter of people addressed to the common task of learning and acting, is broken if the parties (or one of them) lack humility. How can I dialogue if I always project ignorance onto others and never perceive my own? How can I dialogue if I regard myself as a case apart from other people — mere 'its' in whom I cannot recognize other 'I's? How can I dialogue if I consider myself a member of the in-group of 'pure' humans, the owners of truth and knowledge, for whom all non-members are 'these people' or 'the great unwashed'? How can I dialogue if I start from the premise that naming the world is the task of an elite and that the presence of the people in history is a sign of deterioration, thus to be avoided? How can I dialogue if I am closed to — and even offended by — the contribution of others? How can I dialogue if I am afraid of being displaced, the mere possibility causing me torment and weakness?

(Freire, 1970:78–9; translation slightly modified)

Dialogue requires that persons take a 'daring plunge into the experience of union' (Fromm, 1967:171). Heaney likewise notes that

dialogue or interactive communication is the means by which knowledge leading to critical consciousness is created and shared. This process actively involves all partners in liberatory learning: teachers, administrators, community persons, and learners themselves. Process is difficult to distinguish from content. It is more than the method by which content is taught. It is the whole network of interactions and relationships which comprise learning, including methodology — the latter being far less significant than other factors.

(Heaney, 1982:16)

Berliner (1984) stresses the astonishing complexity of teaching: he reports that teachers engage in about 1500 interactions daily, with different children and issues. Interaction is an extremely complex and difficult process, but it is also the part of teaching that many teachers say they enjoy and value the most (Levine, 1989). The interactions in a classroom weave in and out of the classroom climate that the group together establishes. This collective element in interaction is crucial: children, too, are active participants in the shaping of classroom climate (Woolfolk and Galloway, 1985).

The classroom climate or atmosphere is conducive to learning when it allows errors and is based on freedom, warmth, and sensitivity to others (Nigro, 1940; Neve, 1985). Currie (1988) was able to show that, by heightening awareness of students' emotional needs and consciously increasing 'affect time' in the school (consciously increasing hugs, eye-contact, holding children in teacher's lap in a rocking chair), teachers were able to bring about a 46 per cent decrease in aggressive behavior in the course of a four-year period. Not only teachers but parents and other community members were taught the importance of affect; the climate of warmth thus extended beyond the boundaries of the classroom into the child's total life environment.

Currie does not mention this in his report, but it seems that as more positive attention is directed to the emotional development of children, the school atmosphere changes for the better, becomes more 'successful', since children's needs are better met and they can be more effectively encouraged to be themselves and to explore all of their capabilites. In this sort of climate children are also seen holistically, rather than as entities that only possess cognitive (usually linguistic and mathematical) capabilities, as they are in many of the nation's schools (Gardner, 1985; Currie, 1988).

The relational quality of feeling reverberates through interaction (Cahn, 1990). A feeling of threat will perpetuate itself through the interactions that make up a relationship, laying down new myelinated pathways and firing patterns in the brain cells and effectively shutting down openness to change and learning. Conversely, a climate of warmth and acceptance will proliferate, generating an excitement and enthusiasm that fosters risk-taking by allowing mistakes and promoting open-ended explorations of diversity.

The relational quality of these interactions is channeled through verbal and nonverbal contacts in a classroom. Verbal interaction has received much attention in the teaching process; the impact of nonverbal communication in the classroom has not been recognized widely (Gillespie, 1988).

Verbal Interaction

Speech is used in classrooms to teach. In fact, teaching is often equated with talking — the verbosity, narrative style, and banking method of education Freire (1970) talks about. Yet words — language — are the essence of dialogue (Giroux, 1988). They are the agent of an individual's transformation in education. In dialogue words include two dimensions, reflection and action; and

when a word is deprived of its dimension of action, reflection automatically suffers as well; and the word is changed into idle chatter,
into *verbalism*, into an alienating and alienated 'blah'. It becomes an
empty word, one which cannot denounce the world, for denunciation
is impossible without a commitment to transform, and there is no
transformation without action.

(Freire, 1970:75–6)

On the one hand teachers use speech in a classroom to direct, guide,
instruct, suggest, and persuade the students to do different things. On the
other hand teachers use speech to silence students, deprive them of their own
words and keep them locked in silence. In many classrooms silence is valued
above all else as a signifier of important learning going on. But people 'are
not built in silence, but in word, work, in action-reflection' (Freire, 1970:76).
Research done on cooperative and brain-compatible learning supports the idea
that it is essential for students to be able to formulate their thoughts in dialogue with other people (Hart, 1983; Johnson and Johnson, 1991).

Besides speech, the verbal messages themselves, teachers use prosodic
signals like timing, pitch and emphasis to clarify their verbal messages. All
paralinguistic signals, messages independent of the content of speech such
as emotional tone of speech (hurt, excitement), are present in interactions.
Nonverbal signals are used when attitudes, experiences and emotions are not
so expressible by words (Argyle, 1988).

When there is a contradiction between the words and body language,
nonverbal messages are believed (Ross, 1989). 'To say one thing and do another
— to take one's own word lightly — cannot inspire trust' (Freire, 1970:80).
Freire talks about teacher talking as 'alienating verbosity' as the teacher 'fill[s]
the students with the contents of his narration — contents which are detached
from reality, disconnected from the totality that engendered them and could
give them significance. Words are emptied of their concreteness and become
a hollow, alienated, and alienating verbosity' (1970:57). This kind of verbal
onslaught on children is often thought of as 'real teaching' — which matches
with what Freire says about education as an act of depositing. In reality
'knowledge emerges only through invention and re-invention, through the
restless, impatient, continuing, hopeful inquiry people pursue in the world,
with the world, and with each other' (Freire, 1970:58; translation slightly
modified). This invention and continuing process of enquiry requires the whole
person, including emotions that are reflected in nonverbal interactions.

Dialogue and true interaction cannot exist without the basic elements
of love, humility, faith in people: 'Founding itself upon love, humility, and
faith, dialogue becomes a horizontal relationship of which mutual trust
between the dialoguers is the logical consequence' (Freire, 1970:80). 'Only
dialogue, which requires critical thinking, is also capable of generating critical
thinking. Without dialogue there is no communication, and without communication, there can be no true education' (Freire, 1970:81).

Interaction requires listening to students. Weissglass (1990) differentiates several forms of listening:

- active listening, which involves paraphrasing or interpreting the heard communication;
- passive listening, no talking but eye-contact and other nonverbal signs that signify listening;
- inattentive listening — no attempt to respond, listener continues own activity, such as reading;
- pretend listening — maintaining false nonverbal signs while the person is thinking about something else;
- conversational listening — talking and responding is expected and encouraged;
- argumentative listening; looking for flaws in talker's verbal communication;
- informational listening, listening with a purpose of extracting certain information;
- constructivist listening: listener communicates interest, caring and acceptance. Constructivist listening includes both cognitive and affective processing in interaction.

This last lies at the heart of empowering dialogue:

> Interest is communicated by maintaining eye contact and asking thoughtful questions; caring, by facial expression and, when appropriate, by holding a hand, or touching an arm or shoulder; acceptance, by not criticizing, giving advice, or interrupting one's own story, and by reassuring that it is beneficial to express feelings.
>
> (Weissglass, 1990:356–7)

Nonverbal Interaction

Although a good deal of research has been done on various aspects of nonverbal communication, that research has had little or no impact on teaching (Woolfolk and Galloway, 1985) — possibly because it is so difficult for teachers, or anyone else, to become aware of their nonverbal communication and go on behaving normally. And yet nonverbal communication is integral to classroom climate or atmosphere, which in turn forms the context in which the interactions between teacher and students take place. Teaching as it is usually understood is almost exclusively verbal — conscious, rational, articulate, the teacher talking to the students — despite the fact revealed by research that only about 35 per cent of interaction happens verbally (Ross, 1989). Another estimate is that 35–90 per cent of communication is channeled through nonverbal communication (Bennett, 1990). In the traditional classroom children signal their boredom to the teacher nonverbally, by fidgeting, getting up to go to the bathroom or to sharpen their pencil, talking to their neighbors, or otherwise 'disrupting' the 'classroom' — which means, of course, disrupting the flow of the teacher's talk. Instead of reading these nonverbal signals correctly and changing their own behavior, traditional teachers typically escalate 'discipline', attempting to restore 'order' in the sense of frozen nonverbal communication. The teacher talks, the children sit silently and listen. The teacher's body does not communicate to the children nonverbally — which is to say, the children are not to notice or 'read' the teacher's nonverbal communication, are to act as if the only relevant communication in the classroom were verbal. The children's voices are to remain silent until they are called on by the teacher; and while they are waiting to be called on, their bodies are to remain perfectly still, so that the teacher too can pretend that nonverbal communication is irrelevant, even nonexistent. As Woolfolk and Galloway (1985) suggest, paying more attention to nonverbal interaction might transform the very idea of teaching.

Ellison (1990) has noted the striking impact of brain research on educational theory and practice: we now know, and can prove physiologically, that nonverbal communication is integral to learning. New scanning technologies allow us to trace the neurological changes in the brain when people find themselves in nonverbally conditioned atmospheres of threat, domination, and fear — the neocortex shuts down, thinking becomes almost impossible, learning out of the question — or of warmth, caring, and support — the limbic system operates more efficiently and facilitates not only complex thought but memory as well. And yet, as Ellison also points out, many educators still remain ill-informed about how the brain works and the implications of brain functions for teaching. Neurological research can, in fact, help explain many educators' resistance to talk of brain-compatible classrooms: the myelination of neural pathways makes it difficult to change deeply ingrained habits and assumptions, and it is always easy to justify and rationalize the refusal or inability to change by ridiculing brain-compatible pedagogy as merely 'the latest fad'.

Nonverbal communication, as I will show more fully in Chapter 3 when I describe students' and teachers' responses to their environments, is of enormous importance in the social and affective life of the classroom — its rules, norms, expectations, groupings, climate, distribution of power, emotional mood or climate — and is influenced by the physical milieu (Woolfolk and Galloway, 1985). It consists of unconscious body movements, expressions, gestures, the use of personal, social, and public space, appearance, touch, and the way we view time and environment (Hall, 1965; Argyle, 1988; Ross, 1989). It also serves many functions in a classroom. Patterson (1983) suggests that nonverbal behavior provides a social channel for providing information, regulating social interaction, expressing intimacy, exercising social control and facilitating service. Argyle (1988) lists other functions of nonverbal communication: expressing emotion, communicating interpersonal attitudes, accompanying and supporting speech, self-presentation and rituals (greetings, classroom rituals).

Teacher communication can be intentional, for example when directing children through a transition; it can also be unintentional, when treating children indifferently without meaning to do so. Whether intentional or unintentional, however, the teacher's ingrained attitudes guide her or his behavior. For example, children of the opposite sex or those with frequent behavior problems may be treated adversely because of the teacher's conditioned assumptions. Brophy and Good (1974) found that children for whom the teacher did not have very high expectations, or with whom they did not want to have to deal, were placed further away from the teacher. These students were paid less attention unless they misbehaved — and in fact students typically read such placement as an invitation to misbehave. This behavior in turn retroactively justified the teacher's nonverbal (and often unconscious) treatment of them.

Figure 2 shows different aspects of nonverbal behaviors, or nonverbals that have direct relations with classroom interaction.

Figure 2: Nonverbal communication in a classroom

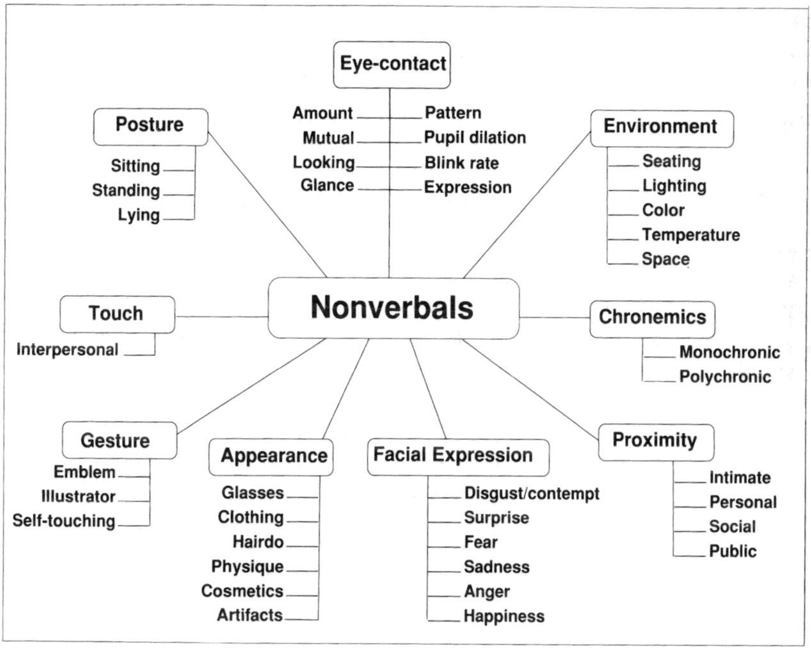

Touch

Miller (1988) calls white American culture a typical 'low-context culture', in which social interaction is not as crucial as in 'high-context' cultures like those in southern Europe or the Middle East. It is characteristic of low-context cultures that physical contact is not encouraged — and the normative pro-gramming that is started in childhood regarding touching carries over to the classroom. Many classrooms that I have observed (outside this study) show a very low occurrence of teacher–student touching. In fact, in many schools classroom rules state: 'Keep your hands to yourself'. One reason for this could be the publicity that child abuse cases have received. Teachers have become careful in showing affection and warmth through body contact: fear of being misread thus exacerbates the touch-me-not atmosphere that is already norma-tive in our low-context culture. On the other hand, in states like Mississippi and twenty-two others, unlike in other western and eastern industrialized countries, physical punishment is allowed (Newsletter of the Committee to End Violence Against the Next Generation, 9/1993), so that the only physical contact that is tolerated is abusive in another way, causing pain rather than pleasure, distance rather than closeness. Another reason for avoiding physical contact and touching could be found in factors like fear of AIDS, contracting lice, etc.

But there is no getting around the importance of a loving touch in class-room interaction: patting, stroking, holding, embracing, and tickling. As Currie (1988) shows in his study of a small rural school, verbal interchanges are supportive of classroom climate but they cannot replace physical contact:

> A commitment to family and the goal of openly establishing affective relationships with children was made three years ago. The beliefs outlined above were paramount in creating a warm and loving at-mosphere at the school. These first had to be communicated to the staff along with some procedural safeguards, designed to protect all involved. Then the program had to be communicated to the parents and the community at large.
>
> Initially, touch was reintroduced through the example of the principal. Hugging and patting became an everyday occurrence in the hallways of the school. Children began to respond in hordes, often nuzzling their way into the principal's path. It was quickly apparent that many (more than 50 per cent) were needing daily contact both physical and verbal.
>
> (Currie 1988:85)

During the three-plus years that the school's experiment had been in place when Currie studied it, 'incidents of aggressive behavior decreased by 46 per cent' (1988:86) — including, one presumes, aggressive behavior (defined as 'discipline') on the part of teachers. Gillespie's (1988) study of US and foreign teaching assistants suggests that nonverbal aspects of teaching may relate more significantly and directly to teaching success than is generally recognized. On the basis of her study she recommends analysing nonverbal behaviors in con-junction with verbal behaviors.

In the quotation above, Currie mentions the role of touch in creating 'a warm and loving atmosphere' — and warmth is often mentioned as one of the most important byproducts of loving touch. A warm atmosphere can partially be generated verbally, through teacher praise (Barrow, 1984), but when verbal praise is not backed up by touch (and other physical signals), it may be perceived as hypocritical, false, even cold. Warmth has to be felt — not just heard. Some of this 'feeling' is culturally determined: a child raised in a low-context culture may feel the warmth of a teacher who never touches students, while to children raised in a high-context culture that teacher might seem cold. A teacher can also touch students without feeling warmth toward them, and that touch may then be felt as cold or threatening or even violent. Thus it is the child's concept of teacher warmth that is critical in developing a working relationship (Rohner, 1986). The ability to demonstrate warmth can be learned: Blase (1986) found that students have a humanizing effect on their teachers, and older teachers often are more sensitive to their students.

Proximity

Proxemics, the study of people's use of space, is indebted to Edward T. Hall (1965) who, in his seminal work *The Hidden Dimension*, classified the space people use informally into four categories:

1 Intimate distance (touching to eighteen inches) is for protecting, hugging, comforting, and close relationships.
2 Personal distance (one-and-a-half to four feet) is used with friends. This distance indicates you discuss subjects of interest and involvement.
3 Social distance (four to twelve feet) is used in traditional teacher-student interactions, between strangers and business acquaintances.
4 Public distance (twelve to twenty feet or more) is normally used in one-way communication such as lecturing to a big crowd, or addressing the whole student body in the cafeteria, or monitoring children on the playground.

In interpersonal relationships distance is a critical factor. Manipulating distance is a form of social control; teachers and students can show feelings of rejection and acceptance through choice of distance — often unconsciously (Argyle, 1988). Teachers have this freedom of choice in a classroom; students lack this freedom. Moreover, cultural differences are notable in the usage of distance. For instance, African Americans stand further away and take up more space than white Americans by moving around more (Argyle, 1988). In some cultures (as in Latin America and Arab cultures) people stand very close together when interacting with each other (Ross, 1989). Within each culture, including the classroom culture, there are rules (spoken or unspoken) which allow certain variations but also set limitations for usage of space in the classroom.

Eye-contact

Looking, or gaze, is one of the most important aspects in human social behavior (Argyle, 1988). Gaze is used for sending signals and messages and for giving cues in conversations as to when to stop and when to give a turn to the other person. The amount of gaze (length and fixation) may tell a teacher, for example, how interested a student is in the issue the teacher is addressing, or it may signal a wish to initiate interaction. Mutual gaze, eye-contact, is a sign of liking, openness and intimacy. If people expect positive reactions from others they gaze more. Gaze can also be interpreted as expressing negative emotions, as in various 'hate stares' ('if looks could kill . . .'). A prolonged stare can be interpreted as very threatening (Argyle, 1988). Teachers use a prolonged stare to silence misbehaving children and to show disapproval. In the right circumstances it can also be interpreted as sexual attraction.

Intensity of emotions is expressed through gaze. Tomkins and McCarter (1964) found the following cross cultural emotions expressed through eyes: interest/excitement: (eyebrows down, eyes track and look); enjoyment — joy (smiling eyes, circular wrinkles); distress/anguish (cry, arched eyebrows); fear/terror (eyes frozen open); shame/humiliation (eyes down) anger/rage (eyes narrowed).

In verbal exchanges with others, people use visual cues to let others know about their personal intentions. Eye-contact is used to let others know you want to keep or relinquish the turn to talk (Ross, 1989). Gaze can be used as a substitute for proximity. In a classroom, instead of talking or walking up to a child, a teacher may make eye-contact. Since teachers work with groups of children it is hard to make eye-contact frequently with each individual; but Hills (1986) points out that direct contact with each student is essential.

Facial expressions

Faces are the most important channel for nonverbal interaction (Argyle, 1988). Feelings, attitudes, intensity of emotions are expressed through frowns, movements of eyebrows and smiles. Ekman (in Argyle, 1988) lists emotional expressions that have been found in most studies of human facial expressions: happiness, surprise, fear, sadness, anger and disgust/contempt. There are also others: interest, shame, pain, startled, puzzled, amazed, questioning.

Children are very adept in figuring out how their teachers are really feeling, despite all attempts to conceal anger, disgust or aversion. Ekman and Friesen (1982) differentiate three kinds of smiles: false, felt, and miserable. Many children walk into classrooms with the teacher smiling falsely at them — their eyes and cheeks not involved in the smile. This was found to be related to the teacher's need for self-presentation. A false smile communicates that teachers are trying to portray a role that does not necessarily coincide with their authentic feelings and thoughts.

Individual and gender differences have been found in facial expressiveness, which can be explained through parental styles, a person's experiences and the socialization process (Argyle, 1988). Understanding facial expressions is connected to skill in empathizing: 'By imagining what we would feel like if we adopted the facial expression, we imagine what it would feel like to be the other person' (Argyle, 1988:138).

Jecker, Maccoby and Breitrose's (1965) study revealed that many teachers were incapable of interpreting children's facial expressions when considering whether they had understood the material or issue at hand. Another result uncovered by their study was that teaching experience did not much improve the ability to interpret nonverbal cues.

Gestures

There are wide cultural variations in using gestures. Gestures can be emblems, illustrators and hand movements connected to self-touching (Argyle, 1988). Emblems are signs, nonverbal acts or hand signals, such as the OK sign with the thumb up, for which people of the same culture share the same meaning. Emblems have three components: the place to which attention is directed, the shape of the hand and movement of the hand.

Illustrators are movements that are directly tied into speech, for instance, gesticulating while teaching or talking on the phone. Illustrators add to the information given through speech. A teacher folding a paper boat with children will say: 'Take this corner and fold it half-way down towards the center.' Without seeing which corner the teacher is pointing at you cannot follow the directions accurately.

Self-touching includes fidgeting and moving hands and feet. Self-touching is a common channel for the expression of emotions, such as extreme inhibition (withdrawal movements, stereotyped movements, hair gesture, general motor unrest, unnecessary movements), depression (slow and few movements, hesitations, use of hiding gestures), elation (fast movements, rhythmical, spontaneous, empathetic and self-assertive), and anxiety (hiding the face, wringing and interlocking hands, gestures involving the hair, opening and closing of fists, plucking eyebrows, scratching face, pulling at one's face, and aimless fidgeting) (Wolff in Argyle, 1988).

Posture

Every culture has its socially acceptable postures for different cultural contexts. If someone does not adhere to the rules he/she will be thought of as strange, rebellious or eccentric (Argyle, 1988). In a traditional classroom the socially acceptable posture is to sit straight in your seat, keep your gaze forward and be quiet. This social expectation in schools carries the term 'seatwork'.

The main human postures are standing, sitting, squatting, kneeling and lying. Postures communicate interpersonal attitudes and emotions. Postures communicate liking and openness through immediacy, which consists of leaning forward, gazing, touching, and having proximity and direct orientation. Emotions like relaxation, agitation and tenseness also show in body postures (Argyle, 1988). Students give teachers many postural cues. But how well do classroom teachers observe children and change their pace when they notice several children in the body posture of boredom?

Posture is affected by the person's body image, which is an essential part of self-image. Emotions are conveyed through the way people show relaxation or tension in their bodies (Argyle, 1988). Through observing their students' body posture, reading the cues of boredom or excitement, fatigue or concentration, teachers can make changes in their teaching — moving on to a new activity when they notice signs of boredom or fatigue, lingering longer on an activity when they see their children are engaged.

Appearance

Clothes affect how we are seen by others totally, socially and professionally. Although many things cannot be changed about personal appearance, many others can. Teachers can control the way they dress. Argyle (1988) points out that the choice of clothing communicates many things besides keeping warm and conforming to conventions. The social meaning of clothing changes; for example, something that is seen as fashionable may later appear strange, even appalling (length of skirts). Clothes communicate different aspects of social meaning. Formal and informal occasions, membership in a group, attractiveness and fashionability are features we express through the choice of clothing. Through choice of colors people can express moods or their personality as well (Argyle, 1988).

Many studies have shown that people who dress neatly and respectably are portrayed by others as more reliable and acceptable (Ross, 1989). Formal, fancy dress (dresses and hose for women, jacket and tie for men) and casual, comfortable dress may not only affect the way students perceive a teacher; because one's dress also affects one's perception of self, it may also affect the way a teacher actually behaves, more formally and stiffly in formal attire, more casually in comfortable attire. A nicely or professionally dressed teacher may be unwilling, for example, to get down on the floor with children, for fear of getting dirty; this will contribute greatly to the teacher's classroom interaction.

Environmental factors

The choices schools and teachers make about how space is used, decorated and organized are part of the nonverbal communication through which classroom teachers influence their students. As teachers change the arrangement of furniture from row-and-column work areas to more informal settings this communicates to children that the room belongs to everyone in it, that you share space and that you are invited to cooperate with others (Palmer, 1971).

McPherson (1984) made an interesting discovery that in row-and-column classrooms teachers actually have a harder time controlling the classroom because children have to choose between academic interaction with the teacher and social interaction with peers. Row-and-column classrooms also increase student problems and preclude the interaction that is essential for learning.

Lighting influences the way people become motivated to do a task. Bright lights are an invitation for energetic listening, while a dim light helps an informal atmosphere to emerge and facilitates conversation. Temperature can be a deterrent or a stimulant. In classrooms that are too hot or cold, the sharing of meanings becomes difficult if not impossible (Verderber and Verderber, 1986), at least for those children whose learning style prefers a certain temperature (Dunn and Dunn, 1987). Some children learn better in warmer, some in colder environments. In the South schools are sometimes closed because of high humidity and heat in school buildings with no air conditioning.

Verderber and Verderber (1986) also found that colors in the classroom can encourage learning. Yellow is interpreted as being cheerful, red exciting, blue peaceful, soothing and comfortable.

Chronemics

Chronemics deals with the perception and use of time. This perception is very culture-bound (Argyle, 1988). The Anglo-Western sense of time is monochronic, which means that everything is planned to happen at a certain time in a linear way. Schools function this way: there are structured times, periods, scheduled lunch, PE., music, etc., hours that need to be observed for the school to run smoothly. In more high-context cultures perception of time may be polychronic; the flow of activities more closely follows the natural events of that culture. Ross (1989) points out that the sound of the bell in schools breaks the natural flow of events and hinders flexibility in organizing activities according to their nature.

Although some nonverbal communications (like refined measurements of hand movements, fast-moving gaze-shifts and voice quality) are almost impossible to study outside of the laboratory, most interaction requires naturalistic situations. In these cases, a qualitative study can tap the complexities and the context of what is being observed in interaction (Argyle, 1988). Some researchers see interaction more atomistically and propose that it is possible to form a realistic picture of the classroom interaction and climate through labeling and counting certain behaviors and their nature (Flanders, 1970; Sugai and Lewis, 1989). These measures can be helpful, especially in becoming aware of certain details in teaching, but they do not give a holistic, dynamic picture of

the teaching process, and, in fact, tend to block out the very nature of interaction, its context and its meaning. Fraser (1989) suggests that researchers
look into combining quantitative and qualitative studies rather than regarding
them as mutually exclusive.

Change in Education

Change is an integral part of our society. Education, often considered the
stabilizing force in society, is part of that change. Whenever the nation has
been at risk, education has been blamed and vigorous attempts have been
made to reform it (Goodlad, 1990; Goodlad, Soder and Sirotnik, 1990).
However, Goodlad and others suggest that many of these reforms have brought
about little improvement in education. In the eye of this educational storm is
the teacher, who is trapped and scrutinized incessantly. Jones (1984) and Smith
(1986) note that change is difficult because many teachers keep teaching what
they were taught as children rather than what they were taught to teach. This
causes a vicious cycle that is hard to break. Breaking out of the cycle is
possible — but it requires a radical transformation of attitudes and thinking.

Genuine change occurs in a classroom only when the teacher changes
(Nias, 1987). If changes are initiated outside the teacher, say by the administration without the teacher's consent, he or she may go through the motions
of superficial change, but things will probably remain the same within the
classroom walls (Nias, 1987). In a larger sense genuine change occurs only
when collective dialogues change: between teachers and students, teacher and
teacher, students and students, teachers and students and administrators and
parents. An example of teacher change is an English professor's change in her
teaching and thinking about learning. Jane Tompkins writes: '. . . I can never
fool myself into believing that what I have to say is ultimately more important to the students than what they think or feel' (1991:27).

In the everyday life of the school, Lortie (1975) concludes that in their
careers and thoughts about education, most teachers resist substantial changes
in educational practices or school-wide reforms that change their daily lives.
However, as a result of some impasse they feel they have reached in their
teaching, many teachers do nevertheless gravitate naturally — or out of necessity — towards change. As we will see in this study, teacher change results
in a more open and inquisitive, perhaps more complex way of seeing the
classroom. This is not to say that change in schools is unidirectional and
hierarchical, with administrators or professors changing teachers and teachers
changing children; rather, a dialogical model of change would suggest that
everyone in a school setting — especially, perhaps, the children — is ready for
change, is constantly inviting change, and a willingness in one or more participants in the dialogue to change brings about a responsive, interactive change.
Teachers who are empowered to experiment with more open-ended, dialogical
classroom practices are themselves already responding to an openness to change

in their children, and the children in return respond to the teacher's new openness to change. Change is relational, dialogical.

One byproduct of this process is more energy and direction in classroom life and in the personal lives of teachers and students as well. In his book, *The Meaning of Educational Change*, Michael Fullan (1982) notes the primacy of personal contact and interaction in change. He stresses that teachers need to find *meaning* in change for change to have an effect. The search for that meaning is often clouded by the fact that 'the depth of the relationship between feelings and educational change is rarely acknowledged by most educators' (Weissglass, 1990:351). Weissglass stresses that educational change requires change in people's beliefs, attitudes, and types of relationships, which are all tied in with how people — teachers and students, parents and administrators — feel about themselves and other people in the school community. Traditional teaching assumptions, especially the behavioristic orientations, typically focus on the products rather than the processes of learning (Smith, 1986; Garrison, 1988).

Professional growth requires change. Growth indicates that teachers are still learners themselves. But many traditional aspects of education conspire against teachers' growth. Lortie (1975) looked at the organization of teachers' work and the sentiments they have about everyday routines, and found that 'schooling is long on prescription, short on description' (Lortie, 1975:viii). He insists that 'teaching is unique' (Lortie 1975:244) — unique in the sense of being always different, always fresh, ever changing — but teachers do not always perceive it that way. Teaching often feels stagnant, boring, stale, like more of the same. The reality in many educational settings, as Troen and Boels (1988:690) note, is that 'schools are organized in a way that prevents collegial interactions'. 'Isolated teachers in isolated classrooms feel tethered in place and stuck in jobs that never change' (Troen and Boels, 1988:688). Teachers work long hours, they take their work home, their thinking and actions are closely monitored. Teachers 'are prevented from exercising their own knowledge with respect to the selection, organization, and distribution of teaching material. Furthermore, teachers often operate under working conditions that are both demanding and oppessive'. (Giroux, 1987:25)

What makes the difference is a willingness to enter into openended interaction with young people — precisely what prescriptive pedagogical conceptions of the teacher's authority and discipline typically preclude. Because a teacher's students are different individuals from year to year, and even the same individuals in any given year are different from day to day — mood shifts, environmental changes, experiential variation — a teacher who interacts openly with her or his students will partake dialogically in that difference, that freshness, as well. 'To expect teachers to contribute to the development of their occupational knowledge seems reasonable,' Lortie (1975:245) writes; 'to the extent that they do, their future standing and work circumstances will benefit.'

As a person the teacher takes active steps towards self-fulfillment. The teacher performs a caring role, caring not only for the children in her class but for her own professional self and taking responsibility for life-long learning as well. This growth 'is a never-ending process; when one ceases to grow, one ceases to live and begins only to exist' (Heck and Williams, 1984:1). Yet many schools systematically block teachers' personal growth through administrator demands (Johnson, 1990), with the result that many teachers plateau or burn-out (Milstein, 1990). A Teacher Health Survey (Humphrey and Humphrey) estimated that 23 per cent of teachers admit to poor or fair ability in coping with stress. The results showed that 'teachers averaged four-and-half days of absence each year because of illness, with 33 per cent of such absence related to stress' (1986:11).

The essence of teaching is the dynamic process between the students and the teacher, and this is also the key to fighting plateauing and burnout. We cannot force anyone to learn (Rogers, 1961), or even to interact, but it is possible for teachers to facilitate learning — to create a classroom atmosphere that promotes learning. It is even better when the teacher models learning for the children. Paolo Freire (1970) suggests that through the dialogue that is central to education each 'teacher-of-the-student' becomes a teacher-student and each student-of-the-teacher 'becomes a student-teacher':

> Dialogue is the sealing together of the teacher and the students in the joint act of knowing and re-knowing the object of study. Thus, instead of transferring the knowledge *statically*, as *fixed* possession of the teacher, dialogue demands a dynamic approximation toward the object.
>
> (Shor and Freire, 1987:14)

Teacher's Philosophy and Self-esteem

A personal philosophy or a world view is essential for teachers in situating their actions in the totality of the classroom environment. A teaching philosophy helps teachers interpret classroom actions in relation to their experience. Questions like: What is knowledge? How are teaching and learning related? What knowledge is most important? are reflected in the thoughts of teachers as they make daily decisions. It is these basic beliefs about teaching that guide the teacher's decisions. Like the natural use of our facial expressions in daily interactions with people with whom we are connected, the teaching philosophy of teachers is sometimes apparent, well-understood, and articulated, but sometimes unconscious and hidden. Teachers are forced to consider issues that require ethical and value judgments because they form the very basic

fabric of educational process. It seems, therefore, reasonable to expect teachers to have some understanding of the nature of these judgments, the linguistic functions they perform, how, or whether they can be justified, and so forth. There is little consensus among moral philosophers on these issues, to be sure, but teachers nonetheless need to resolve them to their own satisfaction in order to provide a consistent rationale for their professional judgments.

(Carbone, 1991:322)

What is a teaching philosophy? Does every teacher need one? According to Dewey:

> Philosophy is thinking of what the known demands of us — what responsive attitude it exacts. It is an idea of what is possible, not a record of accomplished fact. Hence it is hypothetical, like all thinking. It presents an assignment of something to be done — something to be tried. Its value lies not in furnishing solutions (which can be only achieved in action) but in defining difficulties and suggesting methods for dealing with them. Philosophy might almost be described as thinking which has become conscious of itself — which has generalized its place, function, and value in experience.
>
> (Dewey, 1944:326)

Knape and Rosewell (1980) hypothesize, in the absence of research, that in terms of philosophy there are three kinds of classroom teachers: teachers with educated discernment (teachers who have themselves adapted some philosophical theories or adhere to a philosophical school of thought); teachers with intuitive discernment (lack of education in philosophy but have developed a working educational decision-making that serves as a philosophy); and teachers of non-discernment (teachers mechanically carrying out actions, often reflecting contempt towards theories and philosophy). In this book I am concerned with the movement from nondiscernment, and especially the feelings of burnout and dissatisfaction that go with it, towards educated discernment.

Dewey (1944) notes that often homespun philosophies are genuine and adequate for teachers. Teachers with intuitive discernment are individuals who have done some thinking about their teaching practices and are able to reflect on their own thinking and teaching. As Bonnett and Doddington write, the essence of philosophical reflection is to 'work out our own attitude towards the content of our existence and human existence in general. In this way our knowledge acquires subjective weight — the significance of what we know is brought home to us' (1990:121).

Dewey's term *reflection* was forgotten for half a century; but as educators have increasingly grown tired of the simplistic technical view of teaching based on the demand for accountability — especially since the early eighties — many education theorists have begun to resuscitate it as a focal term in describing successful teaching practices (Bonnett and Doddington, 1990; Colton, 1991). Reflective thinking is essential in terms of being able to understand the connections one makes in the teaching process and in the process of developing and molding one's future actions. Critical reflection is an attitude of mind that leads into inquiring about one's environment rather than accepting issues and questions at face value (Bonnett and Doddington, 1990:116). A teacher's personal philosophy of teaching is expressed through this attitude and manifested in values and assumptions about children, learning and teaching.

In reflective teaching practices Sparks-Langer and Colton (1991) see three components that aid teachers in making decisions in the classroom: the cognitive, the critical, and the interpretive. The cognitive element entails the teacher's use of knowledge, processing of information, and decision-making; the critical element includes a concern with values, beliefs, goals and experiences bearing on teaching; and the interpretive element involves the teacher's own reconstruction of knowledge, experiences and actions in context through personal narratives. What is the force or element that holds these together in practical classroom situations? My working assumption in this study is that teachers' cognitive, critical and interpretive decision-making is guided and shaped by dialogical interaction in the classroom, and that it is of critical importance for their teaching philosophy.

Teachers with intuitive discernment are open to thoughts and feelings — their own and others' — and are willing to reflect and act upon them. Susanne Langer (1951) calls intuition the immediate awareness of an entity or the method through which we become aware of that entity; and since in the classroom the entity which the teacher must intuitively discern is a group of human beings, children, each with the complex totality of his or her experiences, intuitive discernment is a primary ingredient in dialogical interaction. Indeed the manifold roles of teachers (Heck and Williams, 1984) — the teacher as person, colleague, nurturer, administrator, facilitator of learning, etc. — require that teachers extend this dialogical intuitive awareness beyond classroom interaction to the entire school environment and reaching the community beyond.

In this research teachers were asked how they felt in these roles as teachers. When is this awareness reflective, and what makes it so? Does a teacher with intuitive discernment operate through the cognitive, critical, and interpretive elements of reflection — and if so, how? If an intuitively discerning teacher reflects intuitively upon her or his teaching, for example, by writing the teacher narratives Sparks-Langer and Colton (1991) discuss, does this reflective articulation constitute a philosophy or can it be said to remain intuitive? Where is the boundary between philosophical and intuitive discernment — and what would be the value of drawing it clearly?

Eisner (1979) calls the teacher's intuitive engagement in the classroom, with goals and intentions fluid and flexible enough to change as needed, the artistry of teaching. It will not suffice for a teacher to master all the techniques and methods of teaching and employ them mechanically — this is non-discernment. Teaching begins in interactive dialogue with students, which requires precisely the intuitive and artistic fluidity Eisner describes. This suggests that what Knape and Rosewell (1980) praise as adherence to a philosophical system may in fact generate non-discerning teachers; but it does not imply that effective teachers should resist articulate awareness of their own intuitive discernment. In order to improve their intuitions about complex educational interactions, teachers need to educate themselves about those intuitions, work toward an articulation of them, or perhaps even a fragmentary and endless series of such articulations. The implication here is that teacher growth should move from intuitive discernment to philosophical articulation rather than vice versa; but also that 'intuition' and 'thought' should be in a dialectical interrelation that is ongoing. Louden's (1991) work indicates that long-lasting, meaningful teacher change is a slow process and very much woven in with the personal history and life experiences of an individual teacher. This ongoing, long-lasting, dialogical process calls for openness to change (Kirk, 1986), or lifelong learning.

While this dialectical movement from each teacher's intuitive discernment to educated reflection and articulation (and back) precludes universal contents for teaching philosophies, Lynch (1989) suggests that effective teaching philosophies must have at least the following characteristics: respect for everyone (including the students); communicative sensitivity; acceptance; involvement; moral engagement; a commitment to human rights and democratic process; a determination to provide creative environments and facilitate more complex and sophisticated thinking; and engagement with both ends and means.

It is a truism that teachers play an extremely vital role in fostering the child's self-esteem, alongside the home environment and significant others in the child's life. Nias (1986) points out that for 200 years the field of education has attached great importance to the idea of knowing and catering to the individual child, but has paid little formal attention to the concept of the individual teacher — especially, as McCreary Juhasz (1990) notes, the teacher's self-esteem. Yet self-esteem is a crucial element in the way teachers themselves construe their jobs (Nias, 1986).

Some work has in fact been done. Lortie's (1975) research on teachers shows that personal dispositions are not only relevant but at the very core of becoming a teacher. Henjum (1983) argues that schools need teachers who demonstrate traits associated with what Maslow (1968) calls self-actualization, such as enthusiasm, participation, emotional stability, self-assurance, love of adventure, strong will-power, and nonfrustration. According to Tonelson (1981) high self-esteem teachers treat students with dignity and encourage their self-acceptance, serving as facilitators in allowing students to be themselves. This suggests that the best way to get teachers to facilitate student learning is to promote their adult growth (Johnson, 1990). Glasser's (1990) insistence that basic needs (survival, power, love and belonging, freedom and fun) must be satisfied in a quality school requires an awareness of these needs and validation of the students as worthwhile persons. McCreary Juhasz (1990) underlines the dilemma of teacher self-esteem through teachers' triple role of facilitating student learning, participating in organizational planning, and developing themselves as professionals. Lerner (1985) shows that self-esteem in both teachers and students is a product of learning and is based on high tolerance for frustration, the ability to care for others, a willingness to work hard, and perseverance in the face of obstacles. Johnson (1990) describes outstanding teachers as those who are self-sufficient learners.

Ongoing learning through life and evidence of growth helps teachers to fight burnout and plateauing — the feeling of stagnation and emptiness that daily classroom life often brings. Some research (McIntyre in Schwab, 1983) suggests that teachers who evidence more feelings of burnout are those with a more external locus of control in the form of administrator rewards and punishments. Lifelong learning, however, extends growth into a 'never-ending process; when one ceases to grow, one ceases to live and begins only to exist' (Heck and Williams, 1984:1). As Sarason (1971:166) asks, 'If teaching becomes neither terribly interesting nor exciting to many teachers, can one expect them to make learning interesting or exciting to learners?' At the heart of teaching lies the dynamic interaction between a student and a teacher. Can the mere presence of a teacher and mechanized interaction in the classroom become revitalized? The ethnography of empowerment shows that it can.

Chapter 2

The Ethnography of Empowerment

By virtue of subjectivity I tell the story I am moved to tell.
(Alan Peshkin, 1985)

General Method

This study is an ethnography focusing on single classrooms rather than larger cultural systems. The methodological base for my study is bricked together from three different types of ethnographies: holistic ethnography, ethnography of communication, and symbolic interactionism. My research is holistic in that it focuses on a unified whole — interaction in the classroom — with all parts perceived as being interdependent (Jacob, 1988; Mead, 1973). I conducted the intensive fieldwork required by a holistic approach through participatory observation in four first-grade classrooms in the fall semester of 1991; I collected the supplementary informant perspective on teachers' own classroom interaction that is also required by holistic ethnographies through interviews and researcher-teacher journaling.

My study is also communicative since I am interested in both verbal and nonverbal interaction in the classrooms, two primary preoccupations for communicative ethnographers. What messages do teachers and students convey to each other in the course of their classroom interaction? Focus is on the speech community, the classroom, and individual speech, especially in the case of the teacher (Saville-Troike, 1982). Saville-Troike notes that the ethnography of communication focuses on the one hand on the particular description of communication in a cultural context, on the other on how a theory of human communication could be built on understanding and forming concepts about communication (Saville-Troike, 1982).

Communicative competence, the ability to be understood in a speech community, is central to the ethnography of communication. It is embedded in cultural competency, which is the total set of knowledge and experiences that a person brings to any situation. When children come to a classroom for the first time, they have a new language to learn that is interwoven with the culture of the classroom. Once the school setting becomes familiar to the children, they have yet another language to learn every time they go to another teacher and a group of different students. Similarly, when a classroom has a substitute, children need to make adjustments to a person who has different interpretations and expectations for the classroom as a social setting.

The focus in the ethnography of communication has shifted over the years from a more issue-oriented emphasis to an attempt to understand the whole speech community. Saville-Troike points out that in ethnography of communication observed behavior is seen as expressing deeper patterns in the life of a culture, and 'culture is what the individual needs to know to be a functional member of the community' (1982:8). The ethnography of communication is concerned with the ways in which communicative units are patterned in a speech community, and in which they are interwoven with other aspects of a given culture (Saville-Troike, 1982).

Due to the evanescence of nonwritten communication, I backed up my observations of classroom communication by videotaping classroom interaction and performing secondary analyses of the communicative situations on tape.

Finally, this study is symbolic-interactionist in that it strives to understand the teacher and children as forces in an interactive process where each defines and interprets the other's acts in a given situation (Jacob, 1988). Symbolic interactionism works on the premise that humans act toward things on the basis of the meaning they assign to things. These meanings arise and are modified and interpreted in social interaction (Blumer, 1969). Blumer, who constructed the concept of symbolic interactionism, talks about the 'root images' that symbolic interactionism is based on: 'human groups, or societies, social interaction, objects, the human being as an actor, human action, and the interconnection of the lines of action' (1969:6). Interacting with others, associating with others requires taking another person into account. As Blumer says, people (such as teachers) who deal with other humans on a daily basis learn to take them into account in far more complex ways than by simply acknowledging their presence or responding to them or their actions:

> Taking another person into account means being aware of him, identifying him in some way, making some judgement or appraisal of him, identifying the meaning of his action, trying to find out what he has on his mind or trying to figure out what he intends to do. Such awareness of another person in this sense of taking him and his acts into consideration becomes occasion for orienting oneself and for direction of one's conduct. One takes the other person into account not merely at the point of initial contact, but throughout the interaction.
> (Blumer, 1969:109)

In using the symbolic-interactionist approach in ethnography one also supposes that persons act toward each other as subject-to-subject, instead of as subject-to-object or object-to-object. This is, in fact, the behavioral and attitudinal core of taking others into account. In an ethnography the researcher does not recede into the background or become an objective onlooker, but, in the process of creating the story of the culture under study, assumes an active role as a participant-observer in the naturalistic setting. Thus the methodological significance of intersubjectivity, of the subject-to-subject relation: treating people as subjects who relate to other people as subjects (as opposed to the abstract demographic objects studied by quantitative methodologies) is more than an ethical virtue; it is a crucial stance that facilitates the research. To strive to understand the life of classroom culture is to 'develop a different attitude, a different way of being in the world', an attitude that is not passive but receptive, an attitude that 'allows the scene to speak' (Eisner and Peshkin, 1990:99).

This eclecticism is, I believe, essential to a truly holistic ethnography. But I want to go further and argue that these three approaches should not only be combined eclectically — a little of this, a little of that — but also actively integrated into a deeper level of empirical knowing. I would like to call this deeper ethnographic level an *empowering* approach: one that will not only record but actually lead to transformative and rehumanizing action in the world. And this is where the subject-to-subject relationship becomes the core of the ethnography of empowerment.

One of the reigning assumptions of scientific inquiry is that the researcher merely observes — he does not effect change in the environment studied. In fact, that is precisely what one is supposed to avoid as much as possible. The researcher stands behind glass or otherwise in a qualitatively different world from the research subjects, whose world is (or should be) absolutely beyond the researcher's reach. Ethnographic methodology has successfully challenged this assumption in its insistence that it is impossible ever to stand outside the reality one studies; one is always an interactive part of that reality, and as researcher is merely slightly more self-reflexive than other parts (Eisner, 1991). Self-reflection in ethnographic research is a significant contribution that ethnography has made to educational research — and awareness of one's writing and its impact on others is central to the self-reflexivity (Atkinson, 1990; Atkinson and Delamont, 1990). 'The fully mature ethnography requires reflexive awareness of its own writing, the possibilities and limits of its own language, and a principled exploration of its modes of representation' (Atkinson, 1990:180).

What I want to suggest, however, is that ethnographic research still remains timid about this interaction — unwilling to rock the boat of 'neutral' observation too violently, and so also unwilling to question the nature and above all the purpose of participant-observation. Why should we observe anything? What do we hope to gain from it? What do our research subjects gain from it? Is our only purpose more knowledge, more and more accurate descriptions of the field under study? I began this study more or less convinced that descriptive knowledge was enough; but as I interacted with these four teachers and 110 children I increasingly felt that this conception of what I was doing was inadequate. All four teachers had fairly recently felt locked into a teaching style and philosophy that worked well enough but did not satisfy them; and then, through collaboration with people in the Department of Curriculum and Instruction at the University of Mississippi, had made pedagogical breakthroughs that excited them, filled them with enthusiasm, and in so doing transformed their classrooms. *This* interaction with researchers was empowering for them and for the children in their classes. Was my task simply to enter into their already empowered interactions and describe it? I found the teachers' enthusiasm contagious; I too felt empowered by my interaction with them and their children. Was it possible that I was not only picking up the energy of their empowerment, and so being personally transformed, but also passing it back to them, enhanced by my own enthusiasm?

This possibility intrigued and excited me — also, perhaps, alarmed me a bit, so deeply has the ethos of neutral description been drummed into my head. But I reasoned: what better purpose for a research project than the empowerment of teachers, students, *and* researchers? I enter into the classroom as a researcher, determined to take something out of it for my own purposes, perhaps for the purpose of science, of knowledge — what do I give back? And then if I come out of the classroom feeling personally empowered but do not pass that empowerment on to my readers, am I not squandering it, letting it dissipate uselessly as I sit before the computer?

My methodological aims in this ethnography of empowerment, then, include the following: a commitment to participation in and facilitation of an ongoing process of change in all relevant interactions (teacher-student, student-student, teacher-researcher, researcher-student, researcher-reader, etc.), and specifically to change from disempowerment to empowerment; a concomitant commitment to dialogical interaction as the transformative scene of empowerment; a commitment to developmentally appropriate and brain-compatible practices not only in the classroom but in research as well; liberation from conformist expectations (the accepted blueprint for ethnographic research on the teaching of reading and writing, for example) and entering into a caring community; and the grounding of all theory in empowering practice and of all practice in empowering theory, along the lines of Charles S. Peirce, who insisted that 'the end of thought is action only in so far as the end of action is another thought' (Carpenter, 1955:96).

In each of these areas I take empowerment to mean a liberating sense of one's own strengths, competence, creativity, and thus freedom of action; to be empowered is to feel power surging into one from other people and from inside, specifically the power to act and grow, to become, in Paolo Freire's terms, 'more fully human' (1970:42). An empowered person is one whose self-esteem enhances and is enhanced by enthusiastic interaction with others — whose energy and joy of life is contagious, flows out to and back from others, and who is thus the polar opposite to the candidate for burnout (Milstein, 1990). This individual aspect of empowerment is socially born, since

> in communicating among ourselves, in the process of knowing the reality which we transform, we communicate and know socially even

though the process of communicating, knowing, changing, has an individual dimension. But, the individual aspect is not enough to explain the process. Knowing is a social event with nevertheless an individual dimension. What is dialogue in this moment of communication, knowing and social transformation? Dialogue seals the relationship between the cognitive subjects, the subjects who know, and who try to know.

(Shor and Freire, 1987:13)

Taking empowerment as my fundamental methodological aim means in practice that the test of value for any research practice is, ultimately, how empowering it is — for the teachers and students (with) whom I interactively study, for you, my reader, and for me, the dialogical link between the empowered and empowering classrooms in North Mississippi and the empowered and empowering classrooms (or other forums) in which you teach and learn. In deciding whether to include or exclude a specific analysis — say, a discourse analysis of a videotaped classroom interaction — I invariably refer my decision back to this basic question: how meaningfully transformative is this? What difference will this make for the lives of all the subjects of my research — including my own as its author and yours as its reader?

Research Population

I chose the four teacher informants for my study through purposive sampling. The research was conducted in two North Mississippi school districts; teachers were chosen for it based on the following criteria: the teacher teaches first grade; had a recent history of major change in her teaching practices (change in teaching philosophy); was able to articulate the changes made; and demonstrated interactive ability with children. Looking back at the process of choosing the four teachers, I would say that there was an additional criterion at work here, although at the beginning of the study I was not aware of it — an intuitive sense that I needed to have good teachers for my study. In the course of the study I was able to describe what it was that made these teachers good. The common denominator is that the teachers were empowered, although each in her personal, unique way.

At the outset I discussed the study with each teacher, explaining the purpose and methods of my study. I expressed my wish to observe but also participate in their classroom activities as they saw appropriate. Each teacher read and signed a voluntary consent form explaining the procedures of the study.

The changes the teachers had undergone in their practices were what Fullan (1982) calls voluntary as opposed to imposed change. These changes emerged through dissatisfaction with and a sense of the intolerability of their current situation, a feeling that 'something *has* to be done'. As you will see in the portraits of the teachers' changes and their personal transformation, the way these teachers came to a new approach to teaching allowed for a more open way of 'naming the world' that Freire talks about. The teacher changes were changes from the banking approach (children as receptacles of learning) of education toward a more transformative idea of education. Their change was a change from unaware conformity to a more aware, active, responsible and holistic view of their teaching. The crucial impetus in their change was Andrea from the University of Mississippi (I have changed all names in this study), in dialogue with whom they were able to explore and take steps in the direction of change. A grant written by Andrea facilitated some of the changes they made. Their changes involved becoming more aware of their own thinking and teaching philosophy; becoming more interested in reading professional literature; finding out about research; and making things work within the confines of their classroom. Their changes made them reach outside their classrooms as well, to other professionals and teachers trying to make similar changes, and so becoming more alive in their own classrooms. In Chapter 3 each teacher herself talks about the experience of her change and its impact on her teaching practices.

The teachers chosen were:

- *Patricia*, 55 years old, twenty-six years of teaching experience, six years in school A.
- *Gloria*, 40 years old, seven years of teaching experience, four years in school B. Experiences from K-6.
- *Christine*, 35 years old, thirteen years of experience in the same school and grade with the same teacher partner.
- *Jasmine*, 50 years old, twenty-one years of teaching, of which nineteen have been in school B.

Once I had settled on these four first-grade teachers for the study and had obtained their consent to conduct my research in their classrooms, I sent voluntary consent forms to their children for the fall of 1991, for the children's parents to sign and return. This procedure proved to be much more tedious and time-consuming than I expected and forced me to begin the observations a month later than I had originally projected. In all the classrooms parents were reminded several times about the consent form. In Patricia's room I talked to the parents at their first parent meeting on September 9. The number of children in all four classrooms was 110. All parents signed the consent form, two parents only after a telephone discussion. One parent had simply forgotten to do it. Rick's mother did not want to sign it at first because she thought this project had something to do with speech therapy. Once this misunderstanding was cleared up, she sent the form in.

Specific Procedures

Ethnographic studies are based on field work and call for triangulation or multimodal strategies — a variety of different approaches to data-collecting

(Pelto, 1970; Denzin, 1978; Goetz and LeCompte, 1984; Van Maanen, 1988). Multimodal strategies also ensure that the meanings conveyed by an informant are understood in the frame of reference of the informants (Hirsjärvi and Hurme, 1984). As Denzin notes, 'no single method ever adequately solves the problem of rival causal factors. . . . Because each method reveals different aspects of empirical reality, multiple methods of observations must be employed. This is termed triangulation' (1978:28). The different elements of data gathering through triangulation are visually expressed in Figure 3.

Figure 3:   Triangulation in relation to the research design

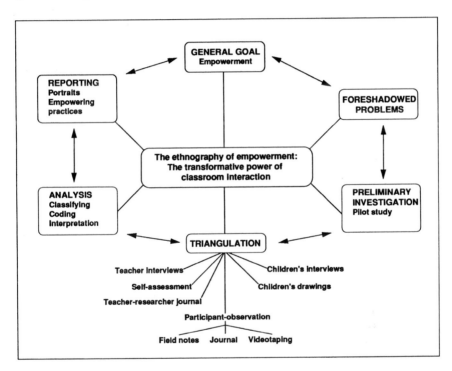

In an ethnographic study the formulation of questions, gathering of data and analysing of data all overlap. Even writing this book to report on the study works the same way: I find myself working like a quilt maker, putting pieces together to support all sides while keeping in mind a general but constantly shifting sense of the overall color scheme and design, and directing all my efforts to the aim of making something that will engage and warm you as my reader. Perhaps this simultaneity and working back and forth is what Van Maanen calls 'unruly, conflict ridden and always problematic' (1988:139).

Issues of Reliability and Validity

Reliability involves the extent to which a study can be replicated; validity is concerned with whether a researcher is investigating the phenomenon under investigation or something else (Goetz and LeCompte, 1984; Wiersma, 1991).

Reliability

Reliability is a form of authenthicity, but not in the sense of fidelity to the 'completeness' of an experience. The chosen analysis invariably represents an arbitrary stopping point, since cultural phenomena can always be divided and categorized into smaller units. Since as an ethnographer I deal with naturalistic settings, my study will be vulnerable to the problems of replication. In attempting to enhance the external reliability (the extent to which consistent results can be obtained by independent researchers) I am confronted with the following problems. I need to be especially aware of, and precise in recording the development of, my own status in the groups I am studying. This I attempted to do by keeping a participant-observer journal on the aspects of my role in the course of the research, to facilitate the observation and interpretion of shifts and changes occurring in my social role. This proved to be fruitful during the course of hectic data gathering — although I often wished there was a faster way of recording the data. During the participant-observation I was sometimes able to make field notes that enabled me to write more specific entries in the participant-observer journal; twice several days lapsed before I could write down the story of a particular observation, which meant that the description of that particular observation lost some of the vividness of detail that the actual experience had. A good way of alleviating this problem would be to record the first impressions from a particular classroom observation in the car before entering any other responsibilities, which tend to confuse the immediacy and significance of the classroom experience.

I attempted to alleviate reliability problems raised by the selection of informants by providing the criteria used to choose the key-informants as well as careful description of research subjects. This is done in describing the teachers as well as in the teacher portraits in the analysis section (Chapter 3).

Social situations and analytic constructs are a critical concern for external reliability. What informants feel to be appropriate to reveal in research situations can color the data collected. I have attempted to circumscribe this problem through triangulation, which is described earlier in this chapter. Since information was gathered over the course of six months, it was likely to be more reliable than a one-time effort would have been.

The choice of terminology used and definition of central terms is important. These I refined and developed during the course of the research, and these refinements required that I carefully record the times of change for the purposes of analysis and interpretation. To ensure reliability, methods of data collection must be explicit and well-defined, so as to give other researchers a stronger possibility of replicating the research (Goetz and LeCompte, 1984). The methods of data collection — participant-observation, videotaping, teachers' and children's interviews — are described in specific procedures earlier in this chapter.

Internal reliability is concerned with how well individual observers in the same study would be able to extract similar observations (Goetz and LeCompte, 1984). I was the sole observer in my study but did use videotaping of classroom activities and tape recording of interviews to extract verbatim accounts of my own observations and the key-informants' descriptions, which helps mitigate this problem. However, in using mechanically-recorded data there is a problem of the mechanical recordings masking problems that occur in real situations (Goetz and LeCompte, 1984). This was evident in the case of videotaping the children drawing in Gloria's room with me as the teacher. The observation in the videotaped situation offers another interpreting tool. Videotapes of classroom interactions and audiotapes of interviews will not alone suffice. However, in conjunction with the information from the classroom participant-observations and teacher interviews about the teachers' philosophical and professional choices, the different methods of data gathering form a reliable base for interpreting the cultural setting in these four classrooms.

Validity

External validity is concerned with generalization of the research results (Wiersma, 1991). External validity can be strengthened through multisite studies. Reporting the differences and idiosyncrasies of the sites will reveal limitations to the generalization of the results. The study was conducted in two schools in different school districts, and in three classrooms, in one of which two teachers taught in close collaboration.

Internal validity, the question of whether I observed what I set out to observe, studied what I set out to study, had its problems. Because ethnography occurs in a natural setting, there is no option of control. The naturalness of the data enhances internal validity (Wiersma, 1991). Perhaps the gravest threat to internal validity when looking at it from the viewpoint of the quantitative paradigm is participant-observer effects. But in the ethnography of empowerment participant-observer effects are its strength. In dialogical relationships in the classrooms the transformative effect of the teacher on the researcher and students, the researcher on the teacher and students on the researcher, etc., are the core of the dynamic interaction that accounts for empowerment.

Goetz and LeCompte (1984) suggest that the researcher spend enough time in the field to ensure that the interpretation of data supports the experiences of the informants. Triangulation is also used to help increase internal validity. The process of triangulation is described earlier in this chapter. Since as a participant-observer I went into the classrooms on a regular basis, the children did grow accustomed to my presence and responded mostly in their natural ways to classroom activities and other people in the group.

The Process of Triangulation

In this study, classroom interaction, both verbal and nonverbal, was investigated in four different ways: 1) through classroom observation and participation in classroom activities (teacher-child-centeredness, climate, cooperation, etc.), which were 2) recorded on videotape and in fieldnotes; 3) through analysis of children's drawings of teachers and classroom activities; and 4) through interviews with children related to their perception of classroom activities and climate and their teacher as a person. Teacher self-esteem and teaching philosophy was investigated through 1) teacher interviews, once before school started, again after the participant-observation ended; 2) teacher-researcher journals, in which I asked them questions reflecting my participant-observations and they responded; and 3) teacher self-assessment instruments (BrainMap, 1989; MindMaker6, 1991).

Participant observation is one of the central ways of collecting data in qualitative studies (Overholt and Stallings, 1976; Booth, 1987; Jacobs, 1988), and one of the keys to its success is fitting in, becoming part of the group — establishing an accepted social role as a participant in the interaction being studied. In my case it was thus essential for me to join the classrooms observed, become one of the adults the children (and the teachers!) were used to seeing in the classroom.

Since it is impossible for even a team of observers to observe everything that is going on in a classroom, following some of Goetz's and LeCompte's (1984) suggestions, I used the following questions to focus my observations:

1 Who was in the group? What were the individual identities and characteristics of the people in the group?
2 What was happening?
    a What were the regular and irregular behaviors, routines, events and activities? What were the social contexts within the classroom?
    b How did people in the classroom behave toward each other? What was the relationship between the students and teacher in the group? What roles emerged from the group? How did decision-making occur? Was there a pattern to interactions in the classroom? What attitudes did the interactions reflect?
    c What was the content of the conversation in the classroom? What beliefs did the content of the conversations reveal? Who talked and who listened? What nonverbals were used and in what context in the interactions of the students and teacher? What was the relationship between verbal and nonverbal messages?

3   How were the identified elements connected in the classroom context from a participant's point of view or the researcher-participant's perspective? What rules (established or unconscious) governed the classroom interaction? How did the classroom group relate to other classroom groups and/or teachers in the building?

4   Why did the class operate the way it did? What are the meanings that students and teacher attributed to what they did? What values and beliefs were found among the people in the classroom?

In between participant-observations, then, I reviewed these questions, drawing on my memory of the observation to fill in gaps that the more structured list of questions revealed in my understanding of what I had just experienced. The shifting, changing, energizing relationships between me and the informants, and between the teachers and children, guided my inquiry in the classrooms. My experiential and attitudinal background and these questions formed the framework or lens through which my data was sifted, the reason why I included what I did, and why I left out what I did. Thus my researcher lens has filtered data in two phases: first, in the selection of what I did observe and record in the classrooms, and second, in the selection of descriptive data included in this book, my report of the ethnography.

To investigate the elements of teacher philosophy and self-esteem, I engaged the four teachers who participated in the study in researcher-teacher journal writing over the course of the research time frame. Journal writing is a way to reflect on one's personal and professional growth to clarify and voice problems, and to serve as catalyst for change (Holly, 1989; Wibel, 1991). In my study the journal writing was dialogical, with my entry — observations and questions — on the left side of the word-processed paper and room on the other side for the teacher to respond by hand to my observations and other things that happened during the videotaping session. (I wrote up my side of the dialogue after each videotaped session and gave it to the teacher in question.) My choice of dialogical double-entry journals with the teachers was influenced by the concern that the amount of work and busy schedules the teachers had would hinder them from contributing long, involved descriptions and reflections without any questions on my part in their journals.

Participant-observation

I kept a participant-observer journal to describe my experiences in the classes, my personal thoughts about my role as a participant-observer, and my shifting sense of how my role evolved in each classroom. I used my recollections and field notes done during the participant-observation as a basis for making these journal entries.

The immersion of a participant-observer in a culture varies in studies anywhere from blitzkrieg ethnography — relying on two or three days of field-work — to years of intense involvement (Goetz and LeCompte, 1984:18). A researcher as an ethnographer gets deeply involved with her experience in the field. On the subjective-objective continuum, ethnography is placed toward the subjective end (Wiersma, 1991). Through these subjective pictures, and images that an ethnographer sketches on the basis of the participant-observations and other experiences, the reader can look (read) through an album of photographs, snapped through verbal descriptions of classrooms and here constituting part of this report. 'Ethnography does not masquerade as a neutral approach; it does not pretend to generalize or predict' (Chiseri-Strater, 1991:xxi). An ethnographer immerses herself in the lives of her informants in ways that enable her to build a holistic picture of the informants' experiences. Elisabeth Chiseri-Strater suggests looking closely at the lens through which an ethnographer approaches the task as she pursues answers to the questions. The lens through which I am attempting to weave a tapestry of the four teachers and their children's lives is more specifically described in Chapter 3 after the teacher-classroom portraits.

Field Notes

During the participant-observation I took as many notes as I could, describing what was going on, recording the length of time each activity took and who was involved in what I was observing. These notes changed drastically in indirect proportion to how much I participated. The more I participated the fewer notes I took; the more I wrote the less I participated, becoming then more of an observer.

These field notes formed the basis for writing in the participant-observer journal when I went home and entered the day's observation in my computer. The field notes also had question marks next to notes that called for further clarification. This is the source of most of my questions for the teachers in our double-entry partner (teacher-researcher, T-R) journals.

Videotaping

I used videotaping as a means of triangulation. Audiovisual documentation allows 'vicarious revisiting' of the audience of the research at later points in time (Erickson and Wilson, 1982:40). Ethnographers generally agree that video-taping is best done in conjunction with field observation:

> Because settings of social life are so complex and their details are so numerous, the ability to revisit an audiovisual record enables us to compensate our limited human information processing capacities and to discover, after the fact, new aspects of meaning and organization that we did not realize at first.
>
> (Erickson and Wilson, 1982:40)

If videotaping were to be made the central or focal record of field work, one would need a full-time camera-operator. In the classrooms I visited, so much was going on that it might even have been helpful to have two or more video cameras: one or more focusing on specific local interactions, another shooting the overall scene. Since I considered my videotapes more of a secondary backup than a primary record, I did not strive for this sort of coverage. As positivistic research moves through the ethnography of description toward the ethnography of empowerment, the importance of quasi-objective recording instruments like the camera eye diminishes; it becomes perceived as increasingly inadequate, as a kind of dead, flat, two-dimensional rendition of a lived experience, and is increasingly displaced as a primary research tool by interactive, intersubjective records like dialogical journals.

And so, while I did videotape every classroom session I observed (with the one exception, when I arrived without a blank tape), I mainly left the videocamera in one corner of the room, taping away on its own — although in each room I changed its place from one time to the next, so that each room was taped from different angles. (Occasionally, when the teacher addressed the entire class at once, I went behind the camera and zoomed in on the teacher and individual children.)

Erickson and Wilson (1982) call this approach to taping 'maximally neutral documentary'; it can, as they say, be a mixed blessing (1982:42), since human interactions do have their constantly shifting emphases; videorecording from a stationary position does not necessarily allow for this. Taping in the self-contained room, where there was little or no extra room to park the videocamera, was especially problematic. Once (10/3/91) I thought I was taping classroom interaction for thirty-five minutes before I realized someone had kicked the cord out of the socket. From then on I taped from a different corner (there were only two electrical outlets in the classroom). As activities changed I would go change the camera angle, but in general tried to avoid standing behind the camera, since this seemed to be distracting for some children.

Prior to this data gathering I had had experience in using a video camera taping university students teaching small groups of children, and, in my previous job, taping large group presentations and activities.

The sound quality of the videotape is usable, but some interchanges, and especially children's voices, are hard to hear, especially in activities that were shot from further away. In the three classrooms in school B, where the classrooms are connected to other pods through hallways, the microphone has picked up the background noise of the other classrooms — something that I as an observer blotted out as soon as I walked in the classrooms.

The initial impact of me walking into the classrooms with my camera was varied. Since a videocamera isn't something that children usually see in their classrooms they were naturally curious. They had questions like: 'Why is the lens there? Are you the newslady? Where did you get that thing?' (Field notes, 10/15/91). Especially the first videotaping sessions were full of children's questions.

> The camera caused a commotion. There were several children who moved in front of the camera to make faces, introduce themselves, etc. Patricia told me after school that it had been a very busy, different and 'one of those days' . . . Mrs. Hawthorne's [assistant teacher] final comment on the day was: Video camera is all this group needs!
> (Participant-observation journal, 10/3/91)

All through the observation period children's interest in the gadget would occasionally perk up. In some ways the video camera was like another person that they wanted to have contact with. They personified the camera, talked to it, sought contact. The autofocus lens moved in and out, and some of the children were intrigued by how that worked; they seemed to behave as if the motion of the lens actually was the camera responding to their talking. In fact, the animism of six-year-olds could be seen in their relating to the camera. For example, Earl (Videotape, 11/19/91) jumps up, looking into the camera lens, and Niki stops a few yards from it in front of it, hands in her pockets, moving her lips but not making any sounds as if she was the newsreader on television.

I let the children examine the camera so it would not be a stranger to them:

> The children are coming back from lunch. They are very interested and inquisitive about the camera. I get many questions: 'What are you doing here again?'
> 'Why is the lens of the camera moving?'
> 'Are we going to be on TV?' etc. Towards the end of my observation the children were so intrigued by the camera I decided to let them look through the lens. I lifted up some 8–10 children to see what they could see through the lens. Elliot, Drew, and Jacob are very interested in finding out about my purpose of being in the room. It almost feels as if they hadn't noticed me all those previous times.
> (P-O journal, 10/10/91, Christine's room)

In Christine's and Jasmine's classroom there had previously been some videotaping, and Jasmine, I quickly learned, tolerated the camera but was not very eager about the technical device in her room. 'It just changes me,' she mentioned several times during my participant-observation. This made me more careful about asking for her assistance and also resulted in my being more of an observer than a participant in her classroom. Once I walked into her room when the children were out and the two teachers, the assistant teacher and the student teachers were talking about that very problem:

> I came back at 1:05 to interview some more children in Jasmine's and Christine's class. I just walked in with the two student teachers, assistant teacher and the two teachers talking (children came back from lunch at 1:10). Jasmine exclaimed: 'We were just talking about you.'
> 'I see, what were you saying?'

'Did you just come or did you wait outside and listen to what we were saying?' 'I'm just now walking in,' I said.

'We were talking about you in the classroom and the others are saying the children don't change when you come in with the camera and I am saying they change when you get here.'

'That's interesting. I could come in without the camera if you'd rather have it that way.'

'Oh, it's all right,' Jasmine said, and our conversation stopped because the children started streaming in and there was a shift in focus and activity.

(P-O journal, 12/9/91)

Lortie (1975) describes interruptions in classrooms as unwanted, unproductive and irritating to the teachers. Knowing this and the fact that teachers' time with their children is already very fragmentary due to the scheduling, different special classes, and business with the school office, I attempted to be as fluid and flexible as possible and to adapt to the routines as best as I could. With Jasmine my presence with the camera, especially whenever I first walked in — even though she always knew I was coming and had agreed to my visit — caused 'erosion of work flow' and led me to behave less comfortably in her classroom (Lortie, 1975:178).

Christine and Jasmine, two of the teachers in my study, have adjoining classrooms, a pod that they have shared for the last twelve years. In the beginning I decided to observe the teaching partnership simultaneously. This was changed in October because I felt I was not concentrating on either room sufficiently. It felt as though I was being too superficial, although one aspect of this observation was extremely fruitful and interesting: the way in which Christine and Jasmine communicated with each other through their daily activities. 'This might be difficult,' I wrote late in September. 'How can I possibly observe them both and give full attention to everything I want to notice? . . . I want to explore how their communication works across the room so in a way I think I need to observe the two classes simultaneously' (P-O journal, 9/26). These are the kinds of decisions that an ethnographer runs up against constantly during data collection; the decision one does finally end up making will inevitably result in different kinds of emphasis in the descriptions of the cultural settings.

In all of the classrooms observed children write journals about what happens in their daily lives. The videotaping experience was strong enough to end up in a journal entry. This particular entry Ken read during sharing time after the children had stopped writing in Patricia's room: 'A guest is here and she is taping. We are writing in our journals and the visitor is [long pause . . .] Heljä Robinson. I like it when she comes. She is nice to us' (Field notes, 10/15/91).

The videotaping was used to analyze nonverbal interaction as well as to strengthen the participant-observation and other methods of triangulation.

Visual records are excellent in recording the complexity of human interactions and conveying its reality (Pelto, 1970). As I suggested earlier, however, the use of videotapes has its limitations. It works like cosmetics: it hides the rough edges and sometimes conceals the reality which the actual experience brings. The experience I had in Gloria's room, having them draw for me, was one of these experiences. My feeling about the interaction was a sense of frustration, similar to what I had seen Gloria experience with her group of children:

> 12/12 Gloria's room. Children drawing for me. Gloria left the room to take care of some things in the office. I gathered the children on the carpet. We talked about giving Ms. Wilkinson a gift of their pictures and their names in a photo album. They got little slips to write their own names and a message they wanted to give her. They drew for me something about their classroom and Ms. Wilkinson. Everything went well till a couple of children said they didn't feel like drawing. I took the three children aside while others were drawing and explained to them about my study and how important it would be for them to draw me something. They agreed to do it and went ahead to work.
>
> After drawing the pictures children started losing interest. Many needed individual help in spelling, choosing a color, finding a crayon, a new paper to replace a wrinkled one. I felt the same frustration Gloria does when everyone is wanting to act and react simultaneously. I could feel a thought entering my mind: 'I wish Gloria would come back and handle this situation.' It's a feeling of a lot of tiny things going slightly out of sequence. Nothing is really terribly wrong but nothing feels right either. I had never had an experience quite like that with a group before. I think talking with Gloria about it and trying out different things might change the situation — or else not.
>
> (P-O journal, 12/12/91)

We talked about this situation afterwards and analyzed it as well as we could, but we both felt frustrated — we felt, in fact, like novice teachers. We could not put our finger on what was going on in the group. But then as I watched the videotape of this particular day I was amazed, even shocked. The turmoil and frustration that I had imprinted as an image in my memory of this particular event could not be compared to what I saw on tape. Instead of a woman just on the brink of losing her cool, the me that the videotape showed was competent, calm, and knew what she was doing. Which was the reality of 12/12 in Gloria's classroom? Why did Gloria and I share the same perception of it — while the videotape (or my view of the tape) disagreed? More than reality, we are talking about the perception I had that day in the classroom and the perception of the videotaping of that same event weeks later.

Perceptions of individuals are always unique, including people doing research whether quantitative or qualitative. Ittelson and Cantril discuss perception as a factor one has to be aware of:

Even the scientist studying transaction enters it as a participant. He does not somehow stand outside the transaction and observe it from some remote and inaccessible height. There are as many points from which the transaction can be entered as there are participants. Each participant observes and acts from his own *personal behavioral center*. Perceiving is always an activity by a unique participant from his unique position, providing him with his own unique world of experience. To the extent that two persons' positions overlap, including not only their orientations in time and space but also their interests and purposes, they will tend to have common perceptions and common experiences. And it is these common aspects which make social activity possible.

(Ittelson and Cantril, 1967:211)

Since the video camera can only shoot a certain section of the room at any given time, this further narrows down its usage as a total representation of what happens in an actual event. A way to alleviate this would have been to have several videocameras and trained personnel to use them, but in the context of my study this was not practically possible.

Besides concealing, the videotaping also reveals. Things that I as a human observer block out or choose not to see can be seen on tape. The videotapes show a number of child-child interactions that I as the participant-observer did not see or was not aware of at the time of my actual experience. These are reasons why triangulation really gives a more complete picture of the culture under study.

Interviews

Teacher interviews

Interviewing teacher informants was a way of learning to understand the teachers' thinking, experience, education, motivation, values, beliefs, changes in teaching, feelings of worth, self-perceived strengths and weaknesses, self-perceived emphases in teaching, professional image and growth, cooperation in the classroom, image of children as learners, teacher as a learner, thoughts about parent involvement and its importance for the classroom.

I interviewed the four teachers twice: first, in the beginning of the study, before classroom observations started, in July and August; and second, after classroom observation was completed, in the beginning of January. The first interview focused on information about the teachers' backgrounds, their professional growth, their concept of teaching, their self-esteem and self-image. The second interview included elements about interaction and teacher roles and sought confirmation of observations I had made during the fall semester in their classrooms. In conducting both sets of interviews I used a nonscheduled, standardized, but open-ended interview format (Goetz and LeCompte, 1984). I tape-recorded the interviews and transcribed them for analysis.

All teachers were used to using audiotape in their classrooms so the taping of these interviews did not cause as drastic a change as did the video camera. Still, the interviewees and I both experienced some discomfort, especially in the beginning of the interviews, before the recorder was forgotten. Here is my own disclosure about such a moment:

> I noticed both of us changing our talking mode as I switched on the tape recorder, as if a third 'presence' was there monitoring what we were saying. This feeling wore off as the interview progressed and at the end of it we seemed to be quite at ease with each other — the tape-recorder totally forgotten.
>
> (P-O journal, 8/22/91)

According to Patton (1980), interview questions typically deal with six clusters of questions: experience and behavior; opinion and value; feeling; knowledge; perceptions; background; and demographic questions. I incorporated all six types of questions into the teacher-interview schedule. Before the study began I contacted all teachers, discussed their involvement in the study, the degree of commitment it would take, and, in the beginning of the first interview, had each one sign the voluntary consent form.

Interviews are most effective in conjunction with participant-observation (Pelto, 1970). Participant-observation may strengthen interpretations of an interview or contradict the interpretation of action seen in the classroom. The transcribed interviews were especially helpful in gaining background information and information on issues like teaching philosophy and interaction, and in exploring how the teachers' values and beliefs were reflected in their classroom interactions.

The interviewer-effect on the key-informant is often perceived as a potential problem in ethnographic research: 'a friendly relationship will inevitably create a style of interaction and a shared set of attitudes and tendencies that may significantly color the information given by the informant' (Pelto, 1970:97). This is, however, only a problem insofar as the ethnographer sees herself as striving for 'colorless' description. With a focus on dialogical or intersubjective empowerment, coloring — having an impact on others, letting them have an impact on you, coming to see things in new ways, through other people's eyes — becomes an integral part of ethnographic methodology. For example, having lived in the community for only two years when I began the research, and having come there not only from a different region but a different country, in many ways I remained an outsider. But in our communications in the classroom, as the teachers and I became more familiar with each other, and as we increasingly discovered how convergent our thinking was on educational issues, a good deal of mutual caring and support began to emerge, and the outsider-insider dichotomy broke down. This breakdown was possible only because the teachers and I were willing to let each other's experience color what we said and how we interpreted what the other said.

Four of the interviews were conducted in the teachers' classrooms after school, three on the university campus, and one at the researcher's home. The interviews varied from thirty minutes in the second round of interviews to two hours in the first round of interviews. The formal school setting elicited more specific child-related stories than the informal settings.

The children's interview

In interviewing children there are special problems to consider. Concrete thinkers that they are, children frequently give radically 'local' answers to questions, answers reflective less of general attitudes than of whatever they happen to be looking at, what they have done previously, or what they are just about to do. The consistency of answers varies. I interviewed three children twice (the first time by accident — a girl assured me I had not interviewed her) with several weeks in between and observed that environmental and experiential factors have a lot to do with what children talk about. Some answers changed drastically. After that first accidental duplication I decided to try it again to see if the answers varied as much. They did, but, as it turned out, only in the examples the children gave; the basic attitudes (liking the classroom, the teacher, and learning) did not change.

The children's interview focused on how they perceived the classroom and the teacher, especially in terms of what they liked about their classroom. Their interview was a nonscheduled standardized interview (Appendix B). I conducted the children's interviews gradually during the months of November and December. I kept a list of children in each class and marked down whom I interviewed when and how long each interview lasted. There was no particular order in which I did the interviews. I interviewed children between their activities, trying to avoid major disruptions of their normal classroom life. I sat down next to the child to be interviewed or across from him/her and wrote his/her answers down verbatim. This worked with all except Lisa, who talked so fast and so much that I could not keep up with verbatim statements. Instead I paraphrased some of her answers. In one of the 110 interviews a child found the activity a waste of his time, invented silly answers, and generally displayed a hostile attitude. Paul (11/21/91) in Jasmine's class took the questions as 'questioning' or testing. To questions concerning how he felt about his teacher and showing anger in the classroom he said: 'I don't know that one', as if there was a correct answer to the question that he couldn't think of. Most took talking with me as an interesting task, and eagerly awaited their turn to be interviewed. ('Do I get to come next?' was a question I heard often) Apart from some isolated cases, they seemed to enjoy the individual attention they got through the interview. Jake was disappointed after the interview was over. He looked at me with his big blue eyes and said: 'Ask me *one* more question.' So I asked him what he wanted to become when he grew up. 'A paramedic!', he said without hesitation and left, waving his hand with a grin on his face (Child interview, 11/19/91).

The children's interviews are important in the alternative picture of classroom life they can provide. The children and their learning is, after all, the purpose of them all being there, and they are participants in classroom interaction, their perception of their classroom and their evaluation of their teacher.

Christine mentioned that it was nice for me to have some one-on-one time with each child because often teachers feel they have too little time for individual talks with the children with so many of them in the classroom. All the teachers were interested in finding out what the children had said so they could use the information to change their classroom to better meet the needs of the children. This could be perceived as another byproduct of the ethnography of empowerment.

The children's interviews were also important to me as a participant-observer. They helped complete the picture of classroom life in my mind. True, it's deceiving to talk about a complete picture because the classroom culture with interaction in the focus of it is always in the process of changing. Also depending on which part of my involvement in the interaction I am thinking about, the image of the classrooms shifts. The children's interviews emphasized how important children are in the interactive empowering classroom dialogues. Teachers do not deal with just groups of children but with individuals who have important personal contributions to make in the classroom community. When someone is absent, all feel it. When someone suffers, all take part in it. When someone has a joy to share, all are filled with wonder.

Here are two different accounts of children's interviews, clarifying their place in the triangulation process and also showing the anxiety that the open-endedness of ethnographic study can cause the researcher:

> I worked with several children interviewing them . . . It's a big project to interview each child but really gives me a good feeling and a more in-depth understanding of how their classroom works. It looks like true triangulation. I feel like I have some concrete information from the children about how they view their life in the classroom. Maybe this is the quantitative researcher in me that relaxed once I got material that can be put into graphs and tables if need be, who knows?
>
> (P-O journal, 12/9)

> Participant-observation, Gloria's room, 10:40–2:50. Today I felt like things were coming together. I participated and observed in Gloria's room and also interviewed children as they had pauses between their activities. Talking to each of the children separately gave me a much better sense of who they are and what they are about in the classroom

community. I almost wish I had done this earlier to have gotten a better sense of the children earlier. The interviews took anywhere from four minutes to fourteen minutes, the average being around 6–7 minutes, depending on how willing the children were to express their opinions and able to articulate their thoughts.

(P-O journal, 11/19)

Teacher Self-assessment

The teachers were asked to self-administer the BrainMap (1989) self-assessment profile, which illustrates the way the teachers' brains create their personal and professional worlds. The BrainMap is one of the first biologically based educational testing instruments devised. It demonstrates a whole-brain approach to thinking about thinking and is based on insights in the neurosciences, psychology, philosophy, cultural anthropology, artificial intelligence, linguistics, and cognitive science (Using the BrainMap; Interpretations and exercises). In this instrument the answers are calculated and summed up into four scores — anterior, posterior, right- and left-brain scores — on the basis of which a profile is drawn on a visual image quadrant chart of the brain. The chart then gives descriptions of the test taker's ways of thinking.

The teachers also self-administered MindMaker6 (1988), a values and beliefs instrument. The MindMaker6 profile is based on Clare Graves' 'biopsychosocial' theory of human values and beliefs. After answering questions and adding up six scores, each related to a worldview (kins-person, loner, loyalist, achiever choice-seeker or involver), the test taker may draw a profile that gives descriptions of her concept of reality and human nature, her personal inner reality, assessment of situations, preferred organization types, environments and possible limitations and strengths.

Two of the teachers were so interested in their scores they figured it out themselves. There are drawbacks to these instruments. The teachers received the instruments with mixed feelings: with enthusiasm in getting a chance to find out about their thinking processes and with doubts about how they were going to answer all the questions and when. All teachers mentioned that some of the items were constructed in ways that really did not give choices that they felt comfortable with. They had to choose the least conflicting choice which really was not a choice they would have chosen in real life. Some items were constructed in ways that called for a more flexible answer like 'it depends on the situation'. Since that was not possible, the teachers ended up having to make forced choices. These instruments were used to provide additional data on the teachers' thinking. In distributing them to the teachers I told them to answer as best as they could — giving each question an answer close to something they could live with. This, they mentioned, was difficult to do in filling out the instruments. The teachers completed these instruments at their own convenience.

Children's Drawings

Children in all classes drew pictures of their experiences in the classroom. To prepare the children for the activity I had them close their eyes and imagine a day in school and then figure out what they wanted to express about their experiences in a visual form. I specifically asked them to include their teacher and themselves in the picture. All 102 children present that day participated. I also gave them an option to write about their picture — which twenty-seven of them did. All but one child produced a drawing. Dean looked at his paper, wrinkled it up and pierced the paper with his pencil, and threw it on the floor.

Reading and playground activities were the most popular topics for the children's drawings. The teacher and child were drawn together in fifty drawings, the child alone in seventeen pictures. Thirty-one children drew other things: something they had learned about (space, internal organs in the human body); the school building or a physical place in the school (reading loft, cafeteria, playground, outside scenery with trees and sun); or about their experiences (church, approaching Christmas). Two children drew me, one with my guitar and one with me holding hands on the playground. All the pictures where the children drew visible faces feature smiles — smiles on the teachers' and children's faces.

Additional Data

In addition to these methods of gathering information two of the teachers, Gloria and Patricia, carried a voice-activated tape-recorder one full day from the morning till the children went home from school. These tapes provided information on interactions of teachers from morning till the children went home.

I also accumulated handouts, children's writing samples, letters to parents, other written materials and photographs of classroom interaction during the course of the semester to provide additional information on classroom activities and interaction.

Pilot Study

I performed a pilot study with one first-grade teacher who was not included in the research, to uncover problems in the interview schedule designed for the teachers. This was done before the teacher interviews, on July 18th, and resulted in changes in the sequencing of two interview questions.

The child interview was piloted on October 27 with a first-grader not participating in the study. No changes were made at this point. However, after interviewing most children in Gloria's room some additional questions emerged that I added to the question roster for the rest of the children in the three other classes: Why is learning important? Does your teacher get angry? How? How do you know when she is angry? Does your teacher hug you? How often? Do you hug her? What is your favorite place in the classroom?

Data Collection

The data were collected according to the following schedule:

- July and August, 1991: First teacher interviews.
- September–December, 1991: Classroom observation, participation and videotaping: classroom contact with each classroom every other week for one to three hours at a time, depending on classroom schedule. Observation at different times of the day, on different days of the week. I talked and played with children during recess and lunch time in order to familiarize myself with their interactions in a more non-teacher-directed situation.
- November, December, 1991: Children's interviews.
- December, 1991: Children's drawings.
- December, 1991: Voice activated tape-recording of whole day's inter-action in Gloria's and Patricia's classrooms. I did not ask the other two teachers to do this because of the pressure I felt I was putting on them at a busy time of the year with the extra Christmas duties and work-shops they were giving outside the school (and because of Jasmine's negative reaction to the presence of the video camera in the room throughout the fall).
- December, January, 1992: Self-administering of MindMaker6 and BrainMap.
- January, 1992: Second teacher interview.

Analysis Procedures

The accumulated raw data include approximately sixty hours of participant-observation, forty hours of videotapes, eight hours of teacher interviews (208 pages), twelve hours of teacher talk and interaction in the classroom, four notebooks of fieldnotes, sixty-eight pages of teacher-researcher journals, fifty pages of participant-observer journals, completed teacher values and beliefs instruments (MindMaker6), completed self-assessment profiles (BrainMap), 102 children's drawings, assorted collections of children's written work and journals, pictures of classroom activities, and other materials like children's drawings, notes and teacher notes to parents.

I began to analyze the data by reviewing my original proposal from June, 1991, at which point I noted changes that had taken place during the course of the study. As I started the data gathering process, clusters — or analytic units — began emerging, which I used as tools for organizing the description of the data. Goetz and LeCompte (1984) stress that in qualitative research all stages of research are interdependent, as Figure 3 illustrates (see p. 41); thus data are in fact invariably analyzed throughout the research process. Since data were collected over a period of time, the previous participant-observation would always give either an idea, a more focused question, or approach for my next participant-observation. The first observations were a more global attempt to find out about what was going on, whereas the subsequent ones gave details to the picture, filling and making the whole picture more substantial. Each time spent at the computer after a class visit was a mini-analysis of what I had seen and experienced, analysis for which I needed supportive data in the future visits to understand more fully. These mini-analyses also prompted me to go back to look for more background reading on the basis of which I found a larger perceptual base to take to the classroom. The concept of empowerment is a major example of going back to the very beginning of my assumptions and theoretical framework.

This interdependence is perhaps the most exciting as well as the most frustrating and confusing element in undertaking an ethnographic study. The amount and variety of data requires that an overarching goal be kept in mind; otherwise you can drown in the sea of details, with no land in sight. However, the authenticity of an ethnography arises out of the difficult dialectic between this sort of structure and openness to the details and the flow of the material — between planning and flexibility, or between a clearly defined pathway and a willingness to deviate from that path when the data demand a detour.

In organizing, describing and interpreting the data and making inferences from it, I employed constant comparison and analytic induction. Unlike quantitative studies, where you start with a more structured and limited idea and cling to that structure from beginning to end, ethnographic data can hold surprises. As a researcher I frequently found myself in a state of self-doubt because of the constant questioning, comparing, scrutinizing and analyzing of all parts of my research design simultaneously. One day I thought this is what the data seemed to be leaning towards and the next day something different and previously unobserved emerged. This shifting of focus gives a researcher a richer view of the life in a classroom and an understanding of how even small details add to the experience that the participants have in a classroom context. Data analysis in qualitative research follows four different stages: summary presentation of data, interpretation of data, integration of findings within broader interest areas, and significance or application of research findings (Goetz and LeCompte, 1984). In this report I intertwine the presentation and interpretation of the data in Chapter 3, in an attempt to describe the collective context of classroom life by offering classroom profiles — including teacher description, self-esteem, teaching philosophy, and changes made in their teaching practices, the context, social network, climate, and verbal interaction in conjunction with nonverbal interaction in the classrooms.

Chapter 4 attempts to integrate the analysis and discuss the applications of the research findings. Qualitative theorizing requires one to frame the research questions in a broad, open manner so as to make it possible for the analytic units to emerge from the data rather than specifying variables a priori, as in quantitative research (Overholt and Stallings, 1976). I first analyzed my written materials, color-coding those clusters of descriptions that had emerged in the framework of my imposed participant-observation. For example, I used red for *interaction* (I) with subcategories of management, self-esteem in relation to interaction, feelings in interaction, and the following dialogical relationships:

teacher-student (t-s);
teacher-teacher (t-t);
teacher-assistant teacher (t-ta);
teacher-researcher (t-r);
teacher-parent (t-p);
teacher-university professor (t-u);
teacher-outsiders (t-o);
researcher-parent (r-p).

The other clusters of descriptions included the following categories: *personal portrait* (P, green), *thinking* (T, purple) with subcategories in concept of teaching, nature of knowledge, evaluation and self-correction; *nonverbal behavior* (N, black); *participant-observation* (P-O, yellow); *sharing and personal disclosures* (S, orange); *empowerment* (E, pink).

Initially I had descriptions that did not fit in the categories discussed here, and marked these with question marks. A closer comparison of these resulted in labeling these *descriptions* (D, blue) of activities and explanations of what happened in the classroom for me to gain a better understanding of my observations.

The teacher interviews and participant-observer journal entries were similarly coded. The answers to the children's interview questions were categorized according to the questions and used as supporting material for other data gathered.

The analysis and categorizing procedure can be characterized as comparing, contrasting, and ordering. Working inductively and generating statements of relationships (Goetz and LeCompte, 1984) or through abduction (leap into the unknown on the basis of intuition) (Peirce, 1958) I discovered linkages and relationships in the gathered data. The data gathering phase and connections that emerged took the study in an entirely new direction. Instead of detailed, quantitative analysis of verbal and nonverbal interaction, empowerment emerged as a new focus.

A holistic approach includes the description of clusters emerging from the data as well as verbatim statements of teacher-informants. Verbatim statements are especially valuable in helping the reader to make his own decisions about the interpretative claims I have made. The verbal description of analyzed data is central to reporting because 'interpretation is not merely "conveyed" but actually constituted in our writing. Our methodological reflection and critical self-understanding, therefore, calls for disciplined awareness of our own practices as writers' (Atkinson and Delamont, 1990:122). This I am attempting to do by critically assessing my role as a participant-observer and by addressing the biases that my life experiences have on my study. The participant-observer role is addressed throughout this report because it is important for the reader to be aware of my awareness and of the lens through which I am looking at my data. It is through the rhetoric of writing that an ethnographer convinces the readers of the authenticity, plausibility, and factual status of her or his research (Atkinson and Delamont, 1990).

Chapter 3

Portraits

Mature love is union under the condition of preserving one's integrity, one's individuality. Love is an active power in man, a power which breaks through the walls which separate man from his fellow men, which unites him with others, love makes him overcome the sense of isolation and separateness, yet permits him to be himself, to retain his integrity. In love the paradox occurs that two beings become one and yet remain two.

(Fromm, 1967)

My intention here is first to give the reader a sense of myself as the participant-observer and each classroom, with a biographical sketch characterization of myself and each teacher, her change and teaching philosophy, and issues of self-esteem. Throughout the chapter I make use of data from all sources: participant-observation, teacher interviews, videotapings, self-assessment instruments, children's drawings, and other materials.

Heljä

I place my self-portrait here with the classroom portraits in order to under-score the inevitable blurring of the boundaries between subject and object, and between the lens and the object viewed through the lens. The people involved in my study — the teachers, the children, and I — were not so much isolated subjects or objects as interactive participants in intersubjective relationships. Having initially, in accordance with traditional ethnographic research procedures, revealed my personal background and bias in the methodology chapter, I have since come to feel that those revelations most obviously belong here, in the chapter that portrays the various adults that played a significant role in the study. In the empowering dialogical relationships schematized in Figure 1, I am as much a reader and writer, teacher and learner as the other four people portrayed here.

To 'create an impression that my accounts are credible' (Wolcott, 1990:133) I as an ethnographer am letting the reader see, on the basis of verbatim statements and through revealing the lens through which those observations were made, what actually happens in the four first-grade classrooms.

The outsider-insider dilemma that characterizes my adult life as a mother of three bilingual and bicultural children probably steered me to this particular topic for my study. I wanted to know more about what goes on in my children's classrooms. As a Finnish high school student I studied John Dewey in school — I remember his motto 'Learning by doing' from a psychology or history class. I remember thinking, 'This person has interesting ideas — I would like to know them better.' In the university (still in Finland) I grew even more excited about Dewey, and staying for two years on the West Coast (now in the United States, with preschool-age children) I was able to see some of his thought in action.

Eight years later, however, my family moved to Mississippi and a new cultural adjustment began. My children were now in school and I was their concerned parent, eager to find out what kind of an education they were receiving. The political climate in the country had changed; the region was very different from the America I knew. The wounds of history in the South were barely scabbed over, the language was different, the weather was a shock. I was a graduate student and an outsider teaching multicultural education to juniors in the university. Yet as a white woman I was also more easily accepted by white female students than some of my black fellow students and colleagues. The schools felt strange, yet at the same time strangely familiar, since all through my childhood I was involved and entangled with schools and students at the very doorstep of our house. I lived my childhood between two schools a hundred yards apart — a boarding school of 100 adult students, and a middle and high school with 500 students — as the daughter of the man and woman who between them ran both (my father as principal and my mother in charge of the offices and finances).

What were my thoughts about Mississippi schools? I found them authoritarian and full of rules — the rationale and origins for which nobody really knew (four pages of rules merely for taking a school bus ride!). There seemed to be an emphasis on numbing the body so the mind would flourish. The children had only one or two recesses a day, and even these could be (and often were) taken away from an entire class if a single child misbehaved — or was perceived by the teacher as misbehaving (talking too loudly, not staying in line in the halls, etc.). The teachers seemed to think that children could go on forever with no fresh air, no movement, no change from the monotony of identical daily schedules. (In Finnish schools our schedules were different every day, from the first through twelfth grade. Finns get used to studying different things on different days of the week and I found the repetition of the American schedule oppressive at first.) I didn't see much understanding of or sensitivity to the children's needs, especially their physical, emotional and social needs. In fact, talking was forbidden and no free time was allowed, so my children were actively hindered in making friends.

The problem with focusing on the intellect, achievement, testing, and academic minutes, of course, is that the brain lives in the body and can't function without the body's cooperation. In my children's schools constant and rigorous emphasis was placed on seat-work, staying in line, being quiet, being nice, being polite — even if tears were in your eyes from boredom or a teacher's harsh words. Somehow the conflict between, on the one hand, idolizing the body through advertisements and spectator sports and, on the other hand, abusing it by neglecting it in schools — of all places! — did not make sense to me. My worst shock came when I heard that corporal punishment was not only legal but actually used in schools — in the twentieth century in a civilized country! I was thinking: is this the same country whose educational values so excited me in school — the same country where the Dewey of learning-for-life and valuing meaningful experiences lived and thought, wrote and taught?

My first year was an experience colored by cultural shock and adjustment. To me it seemed as if the schools I was introduced to were marked by what Carol Mattson (1985) calls the 'non-success settings' characterized by these features: convergent orientation; lack of individual attention; silence valued and maintained whenever possible; peer pressure to conform; rigid classrooms; traditional seating plan; closed-system thinking (only one answer correct); emphasis on left-brain thinking; authoritarian discipline; focus on teacher; bound to lesson plans; piecemeal curriculum; legalistic emphasis; and correctness the ultimate concern.

In my graduate courses I learned that many people — parents, teachers, education graduate students, and children alike — shared my concerns and shocked feelings, and through my teaching and student-teacher supervision experiences I saw many more settings that provided a different kind of an atmosphere. I became interested in seeing closely how some teachers were able to work in a system that restricted them in many ways but could not prevent them from teaching in ways that they believed in.

Perhaps through all this I was idolizing Dewey and making too much of his influence in America. Perhaps much of my initial negative response to education in Mississippi came from my own culture shock, my reluctance to leave Finland, the intensity with which I respond to suffering children. In any case, these are my biases, the background features that largely shaped or conditioned my approach to this study. As the reader it is essential that you be exposed to them, that you bear them in mind, as you read and reflect upon my specific procedural choices.

Fortunately — and this was the impetus that finally led to my decision to study empowering interaction in a few first-grade classrooms — I was exposed to other kinds of classroom situations as well, places where excitement could be seen on children's faces. What made the difference between the rooms I described first and these others — where school was not only a place to be every day, but seemed to be a joyous event for both children and teachers? I wanted to find out — and so chose teachers from this second kind of room for my study, teachers that I have since come to think of as empowered and empowering.

These four teachers were never a sample of some larger population about which I wanted to be able to generalize; they were teachers who were doing exciting things in their classrooms, teachers whose teaching (it often seemed to be at once more and less than that) was wildly successful in ways that I wanted to learn more about — for which reason I wanted them in my study.

Participant-observation is an interesting experience: time-consuming, sometimes uplifting, sometimes very disheartening. It requires keeping close track of what you are doing, when and where, and an attempt to keep the different experiences separate. Sometimes I found this hard. I would have participant-observations so close together that in my mind some experiences ran together. Twice it was impossible for me to write about my participant-observation until a few days later. Those entries lose the immediacy and vitality that the more immediately written ones have. In the beginning I took more notes. In all of the classrooms children do a lot of writing, so it was pretty natural to have someone sit and write close to them. As I became more familiar with the groups, I wrote less and participated more. It is interesting that in Patricia's group, where I participated the most, my field notes were the most sketchy, but my impressions and recollections most vivid.

An involvement with a group of even half a year gives a researcher a chance to feel the ups and downs of field work. It feels exciting when you start seeing that what you collect is not just an amorphous mass of materials (which is what it felt like at first) that you frantically try to keep in order on shelves, in binders, notebooks, file folders, and boxes, but an ongoing record of experience that actually takes on meaning in the framework of the participant-observation. Here is a description of a beginning participant-observation:

> Gloria welcomed me to her class by suggesting a shared reading time. Before I sat down on the carpet next to the children Lionel said: 'Tell those kids to quit bothering me' while organizing himself next to me. I suppress a smile. I am doing it now, I think. I am really observing and participating! This is it! This is going to be fun but I need to learn to know the kids' names fast, not to mention learning to know them otherwise, too. Children are pretty curious about me. They ask questions about who I am and soon start asking for help. In journal writing they ask my help with spelling.
>
> This feels like a long, long day for the kids. I haven't been here but a few hours and I think: they need to get out and about, get refreshed, so they can start all over again! Gloria's assistant teacher was gone so she was glad I was there although I really didn't do much besides being with one of the groups doing rhyming words.
>
> (P-O journal, 9/4/1991)

This experience is an example of how my bias as a teacher from a different background and experiences finds herself looking at a situation that in my informants' cases seem to be normal and perfectly to be expected. The interpretation I make in the classroom situation about children having a long day is based on my own expectations of needing breaks more often and being allowed to change pace (physically anyway) when I need to do so.

The human slips show up as well: fatigue, memory lapses, and the like. Here is a description of one of my most frustrating experiences:

It certainly wasn't my day today. I videotaped and evaluated my university students all morning and one of them did not have a videotape along so I let her have mine. My car was being fixed and didn't get done for me in time to drive to the school so I got a ride from my colleague. I got into the classroom, dripping from the rain, hauling the equipment, plugged the cord in and reached for my videotape. Alas, no videotape in the bag! 'I can't believe it! How could I forget I was coming to videotape today! I wasn't supposed to give my only tape away!' I berated myself. I lamented my busy day, felt like turning right around to get one, but I didn't have my car . . . So I swallowed my disappointment, curled up the cord, and reached for my field notes. My thinking processes were stuck, I didn't pay attention to the interaction in the classroom. In the process of trying to hurry to do my data gathering I acted in a way that made the very thing impossible! I had a myriad of irritable thoughts in my head. My body was there but it didn't do me any good!

Gradually my interest picks up again and since I can't change what happened I start coming alive from the stupor of my hurried existence. I circle around the room to help children with their writing, asking about their pictures (they were drawing their favorite season). Nicole came to ask me what I was doing as I was sitting down writing notes. I told her I was writing in my journal. I showed it to her. She went away and came back later to ask if I had written anything more. I told her I wrote about her coming to me to ask about my writing. She smiled and said she wanted to show it to Ms. Jurgens.

Leaving the building I was a comic sight — still stewing inside. I left the building carrying my bag of cords, field notes and transformer, my purse on my right shoulder. I was pushing the videocamera on wheels with a tree trunk tucked under my left arm (for my early childhood science class borrowed from Gloria on impulse) and branches of bamboo sticking up from my left middle finger. I can't believe this! All this after a carefully planned day.

(P-O journal, 11/5/91)

Many of the 110 children were aware of my foreignness. I could no more hide it than they could their southern accents. Children showed a lot of interest in where I was from, who I was, why I was in the room, and what I was doing. Here is a description of one such incident from my field notes:

After sharing books with each other Latory walked over to me fifteen minutes later and said: 'Do you speak like that, you know, Chinese?'

I said I didn't speak Chinese but I do speak Finnish. 'Well, speak it,' he urges and I say: 'Tältä se suomi kuulostaa.' [This is what Finnish sounds like]. He looks at me, giggles, turns around and skips away.
(Field notes, 10/28/91, Christine's room)

As time went on in the fall the children became more familiar. I saw them in the store, school playground, etc. When I walked into a classroom, some children would come and hug me, tell me about something that happened to them, or describe what they had done in the classroom.

Because of my foreignness I became a resource person on Finland in the rooms. Before Christmas I told them about customs in Finland and taught them a dance around the Christmas tree. In one class I shared my country more as they were studying different countries around the world. I helped Patricia find other people in town from different countries to come and share their experiences with children.

Patricia

Patricia Farnsworth teaches in a school with self-contained classrooms. Her class has twenty-five children, twelve boys and thirteen girls. The children come from all socio-economic levels. Half of them are entitled to free lunches. Patricia's group has seven African American and eighteen white children. Patricia works with Julia Hawthorne, an assistant who is with her for the first year.

Patricia has short curly grey hair; she wears glasses and earrings. She wears skirts more often than not. Often you see Patricia's face in a thoughtful, pensive expression that breaks out into a wide smile that reaches the eyes and triangulates up toward her nose. This frequently happens when she sees that a child has discovered something, crossed a hurdle, or solved a problem. Typical positions for her in the classroom are leaning over a table where a group of children is working, sitting down with a group of readers or in the child-decorated author's chair with children standing around showing and discussing their work with her. Patricia's voice is expressive; she talks fast with a rich Southern accent. Patricia enjoys talking, reading, sewing and being with friends.

The classroom has a row of windows on one wall which makes her classroom very bright. The classrooms are situated along a long hallway. Patricia uses the outside hallwall of her classroom as a 'teaching wall' where children display their work from thematic units to share what they have learned with others. In the fall, for example, they displayed full-size bodies with the different body parts and functions shown as colored cut-outs. After studying they wrote in their journals what they had learned. All the children wrote a page or more about what they had learned. Here is Michael's journal entry: 'The skull protekcs your very important brain. The heart pumps blood and keeps you alive. The liver is like a gint warehouse. The lungs help you breth. The kidneys clean your blood. Intestines give off waste. The muscles work with your bones. Bladder gives off licwid waste' (Undated journal entry). Charlotte writes: 'The brain tell the heart what to do. The heart pumqs bloob' [The brain tells the heart what to do. The heart pumps blood.] (Undated journal entry).

Other displays on the teaching wall during my study included Columbus' ships going to America, a Christmas scene, and the study of foreign countries. Patricia's room has no desks. She has replaced them with brightly painted tables found in the school building. Her chairs are mismatched: some are wooden, some plastic with metal legs. They come in different colors: red, blue, yellow, green. As you walk into the classroom, directly in front of you is a reading loft. Next to it there is a table introducing the author of the week, with his/her books on it. Children's journals, which they write in daily, are in plastic bins underneath the blackboard. Julia's and Patricia's desks are back-to-back in front of the long window wall. In front of them is a shelf (blocking the view from the desks to the rest of the room) full of materials like math manipulatives, rods, and boxes with children's names on them for mail going home at the end of the day. Behind the teacher's desk there is a half-moon-shaped table for group work. At this table an adult can sit in close contact with all the children sitting around the table. Julia uses it frequently for reading activities. There are cubbies for children's coats and other belongings. As you walk in, there is a carpeted area towards the left of you in front of which the author's chair is situated. The author's chair is white with children's felt tip drawings and writing on it. AUTHOR'S CHAIR is spelled across the top. Whenever the class shares their writing the children take turns sitting on it; otherwise Patricia uses it herself during large group time. At the far end of the room there is a long countertop with a sink and a fish tank, behind which there is a bulletin board. A red easel stands in front of the fish tank.

All children but one reported they like the way their classroom looked; Charlotte did not care for the way it looked because 'it's messy' (Interview, 12/3/1991). When I walk in the room, I am struck with a feeling of vitality, of people doing things actively — could this be what she means by 'messy'? It does not look sterile; it looks like a place where people are using things and they have a purpose. Children know where materials are in the classroom and they are able to get them when they need them. There is a lot of walking and talking in the room — usually with a purpose (going to get a journal, washing hands, sharpening a pencil).

The reading loft is the children's favorite place in the room. A couple of children said they liked all the places in the classroom 'except for the real, real old toys but I love the toys that look real new to me' (Michael, 12/3/1991). Megan liked to be 'by Mrs. Hawthorne because I can see the fish' (Interview, 12/3/1991). The fish tank has an observation journal next to it so that anyone who is interested in observing the fish for a period of time may do so and record observations in the log which the group occasionally shares.

The children like Patricia. All but one child — who said he didn't know how he felt about her — said they felt 'nice', 'happy', and 'good' about her. Holly added that she 'felt sorry for her for all these children because she has to do so much' (Interview, 12/2/1991). Learning is exciting for Patricia's children because 'it is fun' (Children's interviews — 21 answers). Michael likes learning because 'it helps you learn more and you can help other people to learn more' (Interview, 11/21/1991). Learning is tied in with how the teacher makes children feel. Hannah mentioned that she likes learning 'because my teacher is nice to me and teaches me good stuff' (Interview, 12/3/1991). Charlotte portrays her teacher as a princess, or a queen out in the yard.

Drawing 1:   Charlotte's drawing of Patricia

In Patricia's classroom sharing thoughts with peers is an important ingredient of learning. Patricia stresses the importance of the ability to communicate with others, to help each other learn, to understand what they have learned and to feel good about it. Anthony said he liked learning 'because you get to talk a lot and you understand. I just like it because it's fun' (Interview, 12/3/1991).

Patricia uses graphic organizers (Venn diagrams, webbing) to help children think about what they have learned. For example, as they were studying trees they made a web of experiences the children had about trees and what they knew about trees, and another web at the end of the unit about what they had learned in the course of studying them. By visually comparing these two webs it was easy to see the change in the knowledge gained. When I walked into the classroom the children would always, sooner or later, come and show me what they had made or learned since they had seen me last, explaining the process of what they had done.

Patricia has a group of unique children; they are active, talkative, they have varying interests. The class as a whole enjoys sharing their thoughts and experiences and reading — the activities that Patricia is most enthusiastic about. Since the room is organized in a way conducive to group work, a lot of what goes on is done cooperatively. In cooperative groups children learn together and they are also responsible for each others' learning (Slavin, 1991).

In the group there are some strong friendships between the children but the sociogram based on the children's own perception of who they like to be with shows that children feel they have many friends in the room, or, as Lassandra puts it, 'we are sisters and brothers in this class'. This does not mean that there are no conflicts in the classroom. There are some children who find themselves in conflict more often than others, especially Quinnus, Edward, and Ken; occasionally Patricia has an 'unusual' day when everything seems to 'fall apart' (Second interview, 1/10/1992).

What do Patricia's children like to do in and outside school? With no exceptions and with no hesitations all the children listed two or more of their favorite things to do in school. These activities included playground and recess activities, reading and working with books, and centers. Other favorite things to do in school included homework, which often was superstar math. Children also listed as the things they enjoyed to do in school art activities, projects, writing journals, eating, games on rainy days, working on dodecahedrons, partying and talking, and playing with friends. When I asked Edward what the best part of school was for him, he said: 'Well, that's hard because I like everything' (Interview, 12/3/1991). This characterizes the general atmosphere in the classroom. The above list of activities and the manner in which children responded to questions about school showed that school for all the children in Patricia's group is a place where good things happen; they look forward to coming there each day.

There is overlap between school and home activities. Interaction with people at home is important. The majority of children (twenty-two) reported playing with their little sister/brother or their friends and doing something related to school work like reading, homework, math. Seven children reported enjoying watching TV, and children also mentioned working on building models and 'projects on the computer' (Edward, Interview, 12/3/1991). What is the significance of pointing out these things? The way children talked about their home and school lives did give me the impression that the two worlds were connected in the children's experience. Perhaps this is also illustrated by the fact that parent nights are popular and requests for parent involvement or support with the classroom activities are easily filled. The class had an authors' night where the majority of parents and children came to hear the children read the books they had made and illustrated. In the authors' party there was a familial atmosphere where parents sat in a big circle with their children while one child at a time sat in the white author's chair brought from the classroom to share his/her book with the group. Although the readings took a long time, parents, first-graders, and siblings sat through the night with anticipation and pride. I presented the class with a photo album of the pictures I had taken during the fall while in their classroom.

During the spring unit of studying China the parents arranged for the class to go to a Chinese restaurant in town. 'Parents have been absolutely phenomenal,' Patricia says. 'I have been so fortunate with wonderful parents who just . . . do anything. I get a 100 per cent response with homework' (Second interview, 1/10/1992). Patricia sends the parents a letter every week telling what is happening in the classroom. In a letter on 10/1/1991 she explained to parents how their children will learn to write using invented spelling, and how to best support their writing at home. Invented spellings are children's approximations of writing words the way they hear them. Children progress through stages of invented spelling, first hearing only initial sounds, self-correcting as they have more literacy experiences. Reading and seeing words written, and hearing adults and other children model reading and writing children gradually naturally move toward conventional spelling of words (Cambourne, 1988). She concluded the letter by expressing how important each child is in the group. The letter is signed by both Patricia and Julia.

Patricia views herself as loving learning, being organized, although not in an ideal sense of the word (in 'a scatterbrained way'), and flexible. Here is her description of herself as a teacher:

P: [I am] scatterbrained sometimes. I cannot stand sameness and I guess I'm random. I always have, I know, when someone would look at some of the things I do, they might think it is more random than it really is because . . . I know exactly what I want to come out of it. But when I start it lots of times I deviate from the original way because of things that come up. But I always wind up in the place I want to be, usually. You know I don't ever just start out something without having clear objectives in my mind of what I want out of it. So I'm organized, very organized in my way of organization but . . .

H: Who are you comparing yourself to when you say 'in my way of organization?'

P: Well, somebody told me one time that they were very structured and we were talking about [it] . . . and she was saying some children do better in a structured class than in that kind of free environment that you have and very unstructured. And, you know, I said I really get kind of uptight when I hear that. I said because my room is probably more structured than what you considered structured because it is structured . . . I spent a lot of time planning and pulling materials together and all that. I said, I don't consider structure sitting in your desk all day doing workbook pages and work sheets and passing 'em in and going from this activity to this one and I don't consider that structure . . . I think we've got structure all mixed up. To me, structure is when you know what you're going to do and you have end results that you have in mind, but you're going to let the children do a little bit of the guiding along the way and you're going to deviate and maybe something you've got doesn't really gel out, but maybe something they come up with does and you go off on that, but yet, you've still got that basic overall idea. And I think that I'm very flexible and that comes from being in a lot of classes where it was not flexible . . . So one day we saw the bluebirds fly by [and] . . . we stopped because it was so exciting . . . So we stopped what we were doing and we talked about how they're leaving Mississippi and that we really ought to do something about it if we can. So we wrote letters to the PTA and asked them for money for bluebird boxes and so the PTA wrote us back and had someone come in and talk to us and I think it was soil conservations, but we have ten bluebird boxes now. We have a bluebird trail for the whole school that all came out of that because we stopped what we were doing, we weren't talking about birds but this was a teachable moment and we stopped and took it. So we have a lot of teachable moments where I'm not going to let something pass by and come back to it later when it's not going to mean anything. I don't care what we're doing . . . if it's related in any way. If I think that's an important thing or if the child sees something and he or she thinks it's important, then we're going to stop. And we're not going to lose that time. So that part is not structured but . . . I really wish that people could see that . . . Things to me, things just don't happen. You know, you've got to be there guiding and you've got to plan it, you've got to know, you can't just start out and say I hope they're going to learn such and such. You're going to have to provide avenues for them to learn it even though they're going to make choices along the way and they're going to cause you to go off on different avenues . . . you're still, basically you know what you want to come out of that and lots of times it's nothing but just loving a story, you know, just loving the sound of language and being able to hear that author and feel like you know him because of the things he writes about; like *Owl Moon*, how wonderful that was to feel what that little boy felt when he was out in the woods. And to feel cold because the author shows you pictures that are cold and gives you words that make you know the cold hand on your back that makes you shiver and if you're sitting in a hot room or whatever — I'm not thinking about the structure really.

H: I guess flexibility and some of the things you mentioned you would also consider . . .

P: Flexible, yes. And I love learning myself, and I love books myself, I cannot remember a time in my life when I didn't love books and if I don't have a book that I'm reading, I just feel a big void there. I've got to have, I don't know, there's just a compulsion with me there's got to be a book somewhere that I'm reading. Lots of times it's professional books, much more since I started being interested in whole language.

(First interview, 7/19/1991)

This excerpt of our conversation illustrates how important Patricia thinks the children's contributions are to the learning process. Although she herself has a strong general idea, a vision, or a plan of what she wants to happen, she invites the children to create the direction and content and allows the dialogue between herself and the children to generate the excitement of learning. These teachable moments and 'avenues' that children choose and fill with significance in connection to their own experiences are the most valuable moments in the classroom. There is heightened interest and a real experience; no use waiting for a time months later when it says in the curriculum it's time to study bluebirds. The bluebird incident and the teaching wall show how the learning within a classroom gets shared with the larger school community. Sometimes Patricia also lets go of an idea when it doesn't take off, or when she does not feel like teaching it, when her own attitude is not the best (Second interview, 1/10/1992).

Patricia's children have reading pals in kindergarten for whom they have made books and with whom they occasionally share reading. The previous year they shared a play with other classes that they wrote, made props for, and acted in themselves. As a result of my involvement in the classroom the children got penpals from Finland in a first grade taught by a former colleague of mine. Patricia's children wrote letters; I translated their letters into Finnish interlinearly and showed them to the children so they could see what the Finnish looked like; the letters were sent, and their Finnish penpals answered them back. (The Finnish children will be starting English in two years, in the third grade; this is a good way to get them seeing the reason for studying it). Another first grade, Ms. Dover's class, shared the experience of visitors from Finland and other foreign countries with them. I taught them a Finnish folk dance, showed pictures and slides, my exchange daughter and I talked in Finnish, and they learned to say some Finnish words. The teaching wall had a journal entry by Ricky (January, 1992) after they studied Finland.

It snws a lot. It is cald the land of the Med night sun. They lev clos
to the nrtpol. They have dans. They lev clos to the are dik srcol. [It
snows a lot. It is called the land of the Midnight Sun. They live close
to the North Pole. They dance. They live close to the Arctic Circle]

Patricia's interview remarks also show the emotional investment with
which she is capable of charging her words. In the PTA meeting where Patricia
was talking to parents about writing as a tool for learning, this excitement was
communicated to the parents. 'Joy, fun, and beauty of the language' come
before learning to read; if you have these there is no problem in learning to
read (Parent meeting, 1/21/1992).

Some days are not as good as others. In terms of Figure 1, the dialogical
relationships are not always empowering. Things happen: feelings change,
relationships shift, both in the room and outside on the playground, both at
school and at home; children and adults alike bring problems and attitudes and
emotional grids into the classroom from their lives outside it.

Patricia thinks that children should feel that whatever they come to school
with, whatever they do at school, their teacher still cares about them — that
there is forgiveness in the classroom. When things go wrong and children
make unwise choices, they know that they get to start all over again and there
won't be grudges held against them. Sometimes Patricia herself brings an
attitude to the classroom that starts things going in a direction nobody ends
up enjoying. 'You have to take the responsibility some time. When things go
wrong that day because of something inside you . . . those days I don't feel
like I communicate as well because things are not right with me' (Second
interview, 1/10/1992). By admitting her feelings and communicating them to
the children, Patricia sets an example of how they might act in a similar
situation.

Patricia's self-assessment instrument, the BrainMap, shows that she is an
explorer, a visionary, and a searcher. She is a right-brain thinker with a dom-
inant 'explore' profile, which typically deals in possibilities, is at home with
life's complexities, and responds to and insists on variety (BrainMap, 1989).
In her MindMaker6, her three top value codes identified her as a loyalist, an
involver and a choice-seeker. While the loyalist's key concern is: Does this fit
my beliefs, the involver's question is: Is this fun and can I share? The choice-
seeker's concern is: Does this make sense? This strongly comes out in everything Patricia does in the classroom, with the students, with the parents, and
even with the administration. Patricia is more group- and future-oriented than
oriented towards self and the past.

Patricia's experiences in school as a child were not particularly happy, but
the experience of learning to read and write made a significant difference in
terms of understanding what she wanted from life. About reading Patricia
says that it was 'like opening a whole new world to me that I didn't know
about' (First interview, 7/19/1991).

Change

The changes that all four teachers have been through are changes from more traditional teaching practices to whole-language teaching, from stagnation to dynamic change, from mere imparters of knowledge to being learners themselves. As they have become convinced that the changes they have made work in the classroom, they have started grounding larger areas of classroom activities through whole-language philosophy. Instrumental in this change was the dialogical relationship between the teachers and Andrea, the university professor who had been visiting their classes, and who applied for and won a grant for planning innovative changes in local primary schools.

The way Patricia changed brought an important focus shift into her teaching. Instead of focusing on isolated skills and predetermined detailed knowledge she needs to give the children, she changed into viewing teaching more holistically.

> In the beginning I felt like everything had to be in black and white. These are the skills. I didn't know about the rest of the stuff that goes along like the learning skills. I just did not know that it is the whole child that you have got to get to, not just making sure that they make that K sound.
>
> (First interview, 7/17/1991)

She was looking for the secret of reading in every class she took, only to find that the secret was not in the tricks at all, but in the opening up to understanding the whole child and being willing to participate in a dialogical relationship with the children (Second interview, 1/10/1992). Katz and Chard (1989) point out that in classrooms where the focus is on academic instruction at the expense of a concern for the whole child, much of what goes on is governed by instructions, directions, and other forms of behavior management. 'The less capable we believe our students to be, the more likely we are to structure their learning' (Rosenthal, 1990:17).

Patricia's change entails moving from thinking about teaching as a banking concept to thinking about it in terms of more self-directed, flexible and unpredictable endeavor. Patricia knows her students better now than before and trusts their experiences to give direction to classroom activities.

Philosophy

Patricia has changed her teaching from a more traditional approach to whole language teaching. In her teaching philosophy she believes in encouraging children to feel with conviction that whatever happens, they are secure, they have another chance, they are important. Conversely, 'If you've convinced a child they can't do it, they can't do it' (Second interview, 1/10/1992:9). High expectations will be met; children blossom in an atmosphere of trust and encouragement where they feel they are accepted.

Because of her own experiences as a child in school Patricia is determined not to do the things that made her uncomfortable. 'I will never do some of the things I had done to me. I'm not going to make children do those things I don't want to do as a teacher. I'm not going to ever let a child just sit around because I can't find anything for them to do when they're through with what they've got to do' (First interview, 7/19/1991). She teaches her children as she would like her own children to be taught: with a sense that they are valuable, their person counts, they have feelings and expectations too.

Patricia thinks it important that school helps children get along with each other, see what meaning learning has in their lives, and gradually become independent learners. This is especially important for her because sometimes school is the only place children can learn these things. 'I think that children ought to be able to get along in this world and that starts with being able to know how to get along with children' (First interview, 7/17/1991). The nurturing of good feelings in children is apparent in everything Patricia strives to do in the classroom, on the playground and with parents. It is important to ensure that children are learning, but 'you don't want to keep them from coming to conclusions on their own. Sometimes when you do not have enough time, you have to be careful and realize that tomorrow is coming and you don't have to do everything today' (Second interview, 1/10/1992:10). The important thing that children need to be able to see is that 'their learning has to do with their life' (First interview, 7/17/1991).

Self-esteem

Self-esteem is connected to learning in that if people 'have self-esteem they feel like they can accomplish tasks, they do not feel like they have to run and ask someone else every step of the way. They have the confidence in themselves to experiment, to take risks' (Second interview, 1/10/1992). Patricia has a rule in her class that before asking the teacher, children need to ask three other people first. This encourages social support networks to emerge in the group and encourages children to find out about each other's learning and discover how important it is to care about each other's experiences.

Knowing oneself is important for a teacher. Patricia says that 'knowing myself makes me a better teacher and I know myself a lot better than I used to' (Second interview, 1/10/1992). Earlier it used to be important to know what other people thought about her, but now she has a lot more confidence in what she is doing in the classroom. But self-esteem and self-knowledge are never isolated from other people. Knowing and esteeming the children, and becoming known and esteemed by them, plays an important part in Patricia's teaching as well. She often asks children about their experiences and tells them about her own, and uses these experiences as a basis for starting anything new in the classroom. As the various individuals in the room — children and adults alike — get to know each other better, the interest they take in each other's lives builds collective and individual self-esteem, or what might be called dialogical self-esteem. Latasha, who is in Patricia's class for the second year (after being retained), has 'just blossomed' this year as a result of this ongoing dialogical process; Patricia has made a conscious effort to support her development and interact with her mother (Second interview, 1/10/1992). Patricia is more herself now than she used to be as a teacher. Earlier she felt she had to try to be something that she was not:

> I used to try more than I do now . . . I used to have an idea how I ought to be, and when I finally realized I am not going to be what I ought to be 'cause I'm very hard on myself — not as much as I used to be — I think I have let up on myself a little bit, because I do not agonize about things . . . that I don't feel that I have done a good job of. I just feel like now I have to do the best that I can and accept that. That is the best that I could do at that particular time and if I make mistakes, I can maybe try and correct them, but I cannot do it over . . . at that particular time and I've got to learn from things that I do and go on and not be so hard on myself.
>
> (Second interview, 1/10/1992)

Patricia feels confident and empowered inside her classroom and empowered in her relationship with the assistant teacher, the student teachers, and parents. Life in a school has its tough sides, too. Those relationships that limit the feeling of being oneself, of being respected and trusted, are likely to create hurdles in everyday interactions within the school:

> as a colleague, I think I get along well with the other teachers, [though] we are not always on the same wavelength . . . We do not plan together, but we cooperate real well together, you know, as far as I know; there is never any friction or where anybody is not speaking to somebody or mad at somebody . . . We have never had any of that *per se*; sometimes, some colleagues do not put out enough effort to go along as others, but for the most part, we have a . . . If we could ever decide on a philosophy and work together on it, our personalities fit together enough that we would be wonderful, it would be unbelievable what we could do.
>
> My frustration has been not being able to share some of the things that I know to be true in a way because you have to be so careful that you do not come off sounding like you know it all so I can't do that. Now, that is something that I wish I could. And I wish if there were new teachers I could do that. With my student teachers I love that, because I'm able to share, so that is all I can do.
>
> (Second interview, 1/10/1992)

Although empowerment is brought about by dialogue, relationships can be disempowering as well (Kreisberg, 1992). An example of hindrance to empowerment is

> the administration. And . . . sometimes you have people who would like to see you fail and do things and say things that shouldn't be and it's the negative part of people. Very seldom do I have a problem with a parent, very seldom. Most of the time parents, especially at this age, they want their children to do well. Most of them, especially the poor parents, want their children to do better than they were able to do and if you make the parents feel important, then they'll help you so much. That's the positive, but it's just the way some people are that you have to deal with — the negativism and this, you know I don't want to change so I don't want anybody else to change kind of thing.
>
> (Patricia's first interview, 7/17/1991)

'I've learned that we get along better when I don't make suggestions,' Patricia says, suggesting that her voice really has no place outside her classroom walls (Discussion, 3/16/1992). 'Sometimes I feel like when I close the door, I close out the world' (7/17/1991). This is a situation that describes the reality of many teachers, the problematic situation with administration, the *power over* relationship instead of the *power with* (Kreisberg, 1992).

Patricia's wish for education would be to have administrators 'who have a vision' and who could be as 'happy and joyful as the kids and the teachers' (First interview, 7/17/1991). With the vision the dialogical relationships within the school community would hold it together as opposed to the present situation where 'we're all too fragmented' (7/17/1991). More than anything else Patricia wishes for spirit, something that you can not touch or classify: 'Camaraderie' (7/17/1991).

Reflection on participant-observation

My role quickly took the shape in Patricia's classroom that it remained through the duration of the study. I had anticipated that in each teacher's classroom my role would be different depending on how an extra person in the room could find a niche, be accepted. It soon became evident that, because of the extra hands I was able to provide, Patricia welcomed me to take part in everything that was happening in the room:

> P: You fit in with us very well, because you have the same philosophy and you know what we are doing and so when you come in and the kids are all over the room or whatever you just fit in with them.

H: Well, I felt comfortable coming to your room because I felt like you are always [saying] 'Oh yes, please, another adult!'

P: Well, you were able to help when you were in here. You know, just watching you interacting with the kids and watching you becoming a part of the class . . . it has just been having someone else in here, it has not been disruptive at all.

(Second interview, 1/10/1992)

My first visit was met with curiosity:

Children arrive from recess. No adults in the classroom. Four children recognize me from their vacation Bible school. I sit with the children and one of them, Edward, introduces me to the class. They ask who I am and I tell them I am a mother, a teacher, and a student. Patricia points out that I will be coming in their class and they will have an opportunity to be my teachers as I take part and observe their classroom activities. As I leave Patricia asks if I know any publications about doing a portfolio. I promise to take a copy of an article to bring her. (Took it the next day)

(P-O journal, 8/27/1991)

This was a visit without the videocamera, since I did not have all the voluntary consent forms available. The first visit with the videocamera caused a major disruption because it was such a new experience for the children. They made faces in front of it, introduced themselves, and talked to the camera as if it were a person in the room.

On October 15th my participant-observer journal has another entry about how the children feel about the camera. 'The children seem to be more at ease with the camera. Occasionally they come and say: "Is it on? Are you taping now? Can I show my face?"' It seemed that the camera was more of a disruption than my own presence in the room. With Patricia herself, it didn't seem to matter whether the camera was there or not.

Sometimes I would observe the children's interaction and activities, take part in their discussions, or answer their questions. Usually I just picked one of the groups to work with or an individual that Patricia suggested I work with:

Working closely with Heather and Hannah got me very excited about what they are learning! As I was working with Heather she had several sentences starting with a small letter or capital letters in the middle of a sentence. As we worked through she started noticing those by herself. She said: 'I'm going too fast in my little self' and added after a while: 'My mother calls me a fasty.'

(P-O journal, 10/23/1991)

Ken and Peter are looking for a *word*. I am wondering what is happening. [There are several dictionaries and books in front of them] Ken says: 'He is looking for a word: renegade.' Peter says: 'I'm just looking for a *good* word for my book. I'm writing for my kindergarten friend.'

(P-O journal, 12/17/1991)

These two times, my experiences brought home to me just how important attitudes towards learning are; like all human beings, children need to believe that what they are doing is significant, enjoyable, and worthwhile. Even without a teacher always telling them what is right and what is wrong, children learn to correct their own work; and because they discover mistakes and misunderstandings themselves, what they learn stays with them much longer.

Gloria

Gloria Wilkinson shares a large room with a second-grade teacher. The room is divided by tall bulletin boards and bookshelves that block off the other classroom visually. They share the classroom sounds and noises, and the classroom teachers try to be aware of each other's activities so as not to disturb each other. Gloria's pod is connected to another pod by a hallway, which means that in practice there are three other classes Gloria is aware of and connected with while teaching. Gloria has twenty-eight children, fifteen boys and thirteen girls. One moved away from the school district, and one child moved in during the semester. One fourth of the group is African American, three-fourths white. There are four retainees in the group. Gloria's children are typically middle-class. Seven children are entitled to free lunches. Twelve of Gloria's students are children of teachers or assistant teachers.

Gloria's classroom is shaped like a pentagon. The room does not have very much natural light but has plenty of fluorescent lights, so it looks light and colorful. The bulletin boards, which function as walls between the second- and first-grade rooms, are made by children. They work on them in connection with other projects done in the classroom. This is one way of making the children feel the classroom is truly theirs.

> H: In my interview with the 21 children today I asked if they liked the way their classroom looked. Everyone except one said they liked it. The favorite place was the loft and what really had impressed them was their ability to make such a nice bulletin board with Pilgrims and Indians. Asked why they liked the bulletin board activity. One said: Because we worked so hard with it. Another said: cutting is so fun! With everything else that you do in the classroom do you think you have enough time for children to do art activities as much as they want to?

G: I have always done a lot of art. I am not artistic, but I encourage
    the children to add details, color. We talk about illustrations in
    books. I have had less success with Group I projects in class this
    year. I think they are too loud. (We disturb the other classroom)
    and don't share as much as I would like (They fuss over markers,
    etc.). But yes, I feel that my children do enough art, because we
    plan art activities and then allow them to participate in art as free
    center activity.

                                                    (T-R journal, 11/19/1991)

The bulletin board activity proved to be the second favorite thing for the
children to work on in the classroom. The loft is by far the favorite place for
the children to be in the classroom (Interviews, 11/1992).

As you walk into Gloria's classroom you pass the assistant teacher, Ms.
Schaeffer's desk; there is a table on the right for small group work and another
table on the left for a center. She has the children's desks facing the board in
rows of six. Between the board and the children's desks there is a brownish
rectangular rug where children gather during large-group time. Gloria has a
well-used comfortable blue chair for herself. To the left of the desks there is
another worktable and behind it racks for hanging coats. To the right of the
blackboard there is a movable stand for a book and behind it Gloria's own
desk. The desk is in front of a blue reading loft behind which, in the far corner
of the room, there is an outside door. Children can read up in the loft. The
computer is under the loft. There is a small storage area between the loft and
the outside door in the far corner of the classroom.

Most of Gloria's children like the way their classroom looks. Three children did not because 'There are too many things on the walls' (Patrick, 12/4);
'I don't like when they run around' (Mary, 11/19). Theresa perhaps (11/19)
expresses her position in the classroom community when she says: 'I'd move
everybody's seat — then I'd be in the middle.' In the interviews I asked each
child who their friends were in school. Theresa mentioned three names and
her teacher but nobody in the group mentioned her as being their friend.
Friendships in the classroom vary. More than children's interpersonal relationships in the group, the activities going on in various contexts determine
who spends time and talks with whom (Gloria, T-R journal, 12/12/1991;
Field notes; Children's interviews).

Gloria is medium build, average height with short brown hair; she wears
slightly tinted glasses. She is very expressive verbally and nonverbally: in her
favorite activity, reading, she uses her voice (pitch, stress, tone) to channel the
excitement of a story to the children, and her eyes to express surprise, sus-
pense and humor. She is very mobile in her classroom, walking from group-
to-group and from child to child. She dresses comfortably so as to be able to
immerse herself in the classroom activities. She hugs children a lot, touches
them while passing or talking to them, makes eye-contact even when not
interacting with a specific child, as a way of creating a dialogical space with

several children at once. She is admired in the class. Gwen wants to come to school and learn because 'you might get to be a teacher' (12/4/1991), and to be a teacher would be to be like Gloria. Lisa's drawing of herself and Gloria shows the affection felt by the children in her class.

Drawing 2: Lisa and her teacher, Gloria

Gloria's excitement about children learning and little details about teaching (finding a good book, hearing about a new idea) is very contagious. Even so, the group she has now exhausts her: 'I start off fresh in the morning but I am usually frustrated by 1 p.m.' She communicates empowerment with her presence, her lively hands, the way she moves and talks and looks at people.

How did Gloria end up in teaching? Gloria became a teacher after majoring in business and realizing that was not what she wanted to do. Her sister's choice of career in education gave her the final push: 'So it was something that was buried inside me that I had always wanted to do but I just thought, well, I can't do it right now but I finally did' (First interview, 8/22/1991). She has taught at various grade levels but feels most at home with the lower grades because of the strong background she got in them during her teacher education. Her area of emphasis is language arts and she says she has to make herself do math in the classroom, a fact which she would like to change in the near future. This does not hinder the children from enjoying math in the classroom.

Gloria's children like her. In interviewing them they responded to the question 'How do you feel about your teacher?' with words like 'good', 'nice', 'fine', 'OK', 'terrific', or some derivation of 'I like her because she is nice', 'She nice. She do good things to us' (Shakatha, 12/4/1991). Positive feelings about the teacher like 'I love her 'cause she teaches good' (Paul, 11/ 19/1992) are evident in the room, although there was an exception to this. Lucas' answer was a sullen 'Bad', in the same vein as all his other answers the day I interviewed him (11/19). Some children gave reasons for liking their teacher: 'she does a lot of fun stuff with us' (Earl, 11/19); 'she is important to the kids to have' (Jeremy, 11/19), 'I feel like every time I need to talk to somebody I can' (Lisa, 11/20).

Gloria's perception of herself as a teacher is very positive:

G: I think that I am a warm teacher . . . my children are not afraid of me and they love me and . . . they get lots of hugs and I'm a positive teacher. And I wasn't a screamer until this year — no, I'm teasing. I'm real patient with the children . . . I think I plan activities, I choose things that the children are interested in and we do lots of hands-on things. I have a strong background in child development, in the kinds of activities that are appropriate for children. And then I put those into practice in my classroom.

H: If you think about those strengths, patience and flexibility . . .

G: I'm very flexible.

H: And do you know how they emerged? Did you always have those qualities?

G: I'm thinking. I've really always had them as a teacher. When I say I'm flexible, I mean I am *truly* flexible. Things that make other people angry just don't bother me. I mean, you know, it just doesn't matter. I guess that's just in my nature, though. You know, I can't think of anything in particular [that might have contributed to those qualities in me], unless it was being able to do student teaching in the university kindergarten where you had so much support and the materials that you needed to try your ideas and plenty of people to help you. When I say support . . . you had financial support, you had parental support, you had professional support, and then you had student teachers in your classroom . . . so you had everything you needed to make it an ideal situation. And I got to do that first before I ever taught anywhere else, so all the things that we learned in the classroom, became meaningful . . . they had meaning because I saw it work in the classroom. So it was easier for me to go out into the public school and be that kind of teacher because I had already seen it work somewhere else.

(First interview, 8/22/1992)

Gloria wishes she were more organized. Partly this is because she feels overwhelmed by the demands children place on her. She is bombarded by the children and their enthusiasm:

G: They're always telling me something and showing me something and I try to let them show me and I try to let them tell me, so I'm busy all the time. You know, I don't sit behind my desk and because I'm up in my room, working with my children all day, I don't have time to keep things as organized as I'd like them. That's my big problem.

H: Could you again describe yourself as a teacher? If somebody else described you, what do you think they'd say?

G: Um, do you mean as far as methods or . . .

H: Or just what kind of teacher you are? If they were trying to describe five different teachers, what would your description be like?

G: Well, I know the first thing that they would say about me is that I don't put a lot of pressure on my children. And even though I do expect them to do well, I don't peck on their desk and point to their paper and say you did not do that right, I don't put that kind of pressure on them. I'm very supportive. I give them lots of help and I hate giving grades, especially in first grade like until after Christmas really . . . That's another thing, like I have to really make a conscious effort to put grades down because we do have to quote average grades and give a grade and I really have to struggle and make a conscious effort to put things in the grade book and a lot of times I just do something to get a grade to go in the grade book . . . I'm also very subjective in my teaching. Teacher evaluation is much more important to me than what they do on a piece of paper . . .

H: In other words your professional judgment of what's going on . . .

G: I rely more on that than I do anything else. And one reason, I think if I taught older children that might not be as important to me. But when they're only 6 and 7 years old, anything you teach them is more than they knew, and they've got eleven more years to learn everything else . . . to me it's not crucial that they have to do x, x, and x . . . My children don't have to sit in their desks and do worksheets.

(First interview, 8/22/1991)

Apparent in this and other wishes the teachers have for the profession is a need to be trusted professionally by the general public, by parents and administrators. The mandates in education and specific skill-oriented, positivistically-based teaching limit or hinder the trust that teachers and students need and deserve in a classroom situation (Smith, 1986; Garrison, 1988).

Gloria is a very spontaneous teacher. She wants to leave room for changes and ideas that come from the children in any given situation. Again our teacher-researcher journal reveals this:

H: The discussion of trash cans in various places of the childrens' houses was long and involved. Did you plan it in advance or did it evolve in the situation?

G: No, I didn't plan it. I was thinking it was getting long myself. I like to pick up on children's comments and teach from them.

H: You used Thomas Moore's 'I've got a pocket' song. You ended with your own pocket riddle: 'It's round and hard and I use it to get my lunch.' Was this preplanned?

G: No, I am a very spontaneous teacher.

(T-R journal, 10/22)

The first-graders she got in August have puzzled her all fall. Every time we met or talked on the phone (including a three-hour drive to a conference) we seemed to be discussing the problems in that group and things that might possibly be done to alleviate them. The collective spirit of the group is still taking form. There are no individuals that actually disrupt the class, but the majority of the children in her class are extremely active and talkative. As of this writing, she and Andrea and I together have yet to come up with a solution to her dilemma. Andrea gave her some readings and Gloria changed her classroom management system. In a subsequent teacher-researcher journal we shared some of these concerns:

H: Could you write to me about your feeling of frustration in deal-ing with this particular class you have? How are your mental and physical energies in coping with the situation? If you could do anything in the world with the class what would it be? Could you describe the image you have in your head of your class (How would they act at group time? What would they say?)

G: I feel frustrated because they can't work together without fuss-ing about markers etc. They are too loud and *usually* don't give me the quality end product I expect. However, if I ask about their work, I am often surprised because there is a 'story' there. I like what my children say — I just don't like what they do. My ideal class would be orderly, mannerly, caring, and sharing. They would be able to work independently and help each other. They would know that they could 'change' my directions as long as they were being productive. I start off fresh each morning but I am usually frustrated by 1 p.m. However, some days are better than others!

(T-R journal, 9/25)

Gloria's profile in the BrainMap reveals her to be a whole-brain thinker. A person with this brain frame brings amiability and a realistic sense of im-mediacy into the school organization. According to the BrainMap, Gloria is an accommodator who looks for emotional equilibrium, which is what Gloria is very much after with the group she has now. Accommodators dislike the unwillingness of others to move ahead and act. This profile can also signify that a person is in the midst of significant value changes. The MindMaker6 shows Gloria to be group- and future-oriented rather than self- and past-oriented. Gloria's MindMaker6 profile identifies her foremost as an involver, secondly as a loyalist and choice-seeker. Her concept of reality is grounded in the importance of harmony, beauty, and awareness. Inner growth is an important criterion for assessing new situations.

Change

Gloria's change in her teaching was radical. Andrea was instrumental in encouraging Gloria to make changes in her teaching. She describes her change in our first interview (8/22/1991) like this:

G: Let me tell you what happened. When I taught at the University kindergarten I was happy and I loved it. I thought I did a good job, but I also knew how to teach kindergarten because we had done our practical experience, a lot of it, in the kindergarten and I worked closely with the professors and I knew what to do. I felt confident in what I was doing and then I got a job teaching fifth grade. I only had eight students but they ranged from a genius to a child that had a learning disability. And I really struggled that year . . . I taught only language arts and I only taught half a day and I was scared. I had never taught before and I pretty much went by the teacher's edition. But at the same time . . . I tried to do those creative types of things but I still did not have the confidence that I needed for that job . . . I remember thinking, *what's the big deal about being a teacher? because you can be absent and anybody could come in and do what the teacher was supposed to do because it was written out for you in the teacher's edition.* And then, when I went to public school, where you get thrown into a situation where nobody's teaching the way you were taught to teach when you were in college . . . what do you do? . . . everybody's so nice to share and they share their worksheets, and their units with you and . . . you've never taught that grade before and you don't want your children to miss out on something. And I suppose that was part of my nature too — to be a little bit insecure . . . It took me a couple of years to find myself and then I thought I was a poor teacher because I hated doing the flash cards in reading. I hated doing the vocabulary test on Friday. And the workbooks at the end of the year, I had to throw them away because I didn't want the parents to see how many pages we hadn't done. So I couldn't let the kids go home and play school with their leftover workbooks because I was afraid I'd get in trouble because I didn't do the workbook pages. So then through the whole language, and through . . . Andrea coming back into my classroom again, after having been out there on my own and kind of tasting the different methods of teaching, I kind of found myself again and then I was so excited and so proud to be a teacher and I *loved* it and I could hold my head up and say . . . I'm a teacher 'cause I was excited about being a teacher . . . So I really did a complete circle.

H: When did this happen, when did your excitement start bubbling over?

G: Well, if you really want to know the truth, it was really just two years ago, whenever Andrea got back into our classrooms, really, and we got that grant, because up until then, I kept changing grades.

(First interview, 8/22/1991) [Italics added for emphasis reflecting Gloria's tone of voice]

The change was inevitable because Gloria felt there was no excitement in teaching. The big question — 'What's the big deal about being a teacher?' — bothered her and took away from the professional pride that she thought she ought to have had. She was unable to let go of the restrictions that held her in her stagnant state till

the second year I taught second grade . . . Andrea came in and said: 'We can do something different, you know you don't have to do that. I can help you get materials and you can teach it a different way.' And that's when we changed and that's when I fell in love with teaching, really.

(First interview, 8/22/1992)

It is interesting that she is saying 'that's when *we* changed,' indicating how the change integrates Gloria into a community of learners, teachers, educators.

The extent of her enthusiasm and exuberance about teaching shows in her discussions with colleagues, workshops and on the videotape that was put together to describe the effects of the nationally funded program where she was interviewed to describe the changes in her teaching.

I can see my children learning. I feel good about what they're doing. I feel good about what I'm doing. We're all so excited and we are just thrilled that we're getting to do this. And it's made me a better teacher. It's made me develop confidence in myself and last year I was saying 'Am I doing this right, am I doing this right?' But now I know and I can see that I'm doing it right and I'm ready to go.

(*Collaborations in Oxford*, 1991)

Gloria now enjoys teaching, although the group she has this year causes her to question many of her assumptions about classroom management and her own philosophy. The best part about teaching for her is:

G: the children. I mean, I love it when they come and hug me and come back the next year and tell me hello. And it's silly, you know, I think: Are we that desperate for attention? But I just love it when the kids come and talk to me . . . When they put their arms around me and they say 'I loved that story. Will you read that one again?' or 'Can we do that again?'

H: That makes you feel that you really made a difference.

(First interview, 8/22/1992)

Through the changes that Gloria has made, she has loosened up and learned to hand more decisions and choice back to the children in her room. She says that 'as long as they're learning' (First interview, 8/22/1991) she is not all that concerned about what they do in the classroom.

I want them to be doing something on their own that's constructive, while I work with another group. And I like it when they can do it on their own. And I *hate* the process of going through teaching those routines. I don't like that. I like to be able to just jump in, and then be able to know what to do.

(First interview, 8/22/1991)

Philosophy

Gloria believes that good teaching is always a two-way street:

G: I don't know if this is the right word, but it's almost like a reciprocal relationship — that as I am teaching, I am constantly learning. My children teach me things, about them as individuals and how they learn, I learn by watching them, and then at the same time, I feel like I am teaching because I'm imparting knowledge to them, so we, in our classroom, I think we just have a circle going, and we are just constantly teaching each other.

H: Okay.

G: And we study things that I don't always know about. I have the basic knowledge in a lot of things, but they ask so many questions about things I don't know that we learn together. We go look it up together.

H: If you think about yourself when you first started teaching, would you have felt intimidated then if you had to teach something that you really didn't know about?

G: A little bit, because for one thing, I taught older children, and I don't think they are always as accepting of your saying 'Let's look it up.' But also I presented it in a different way, I presented information like I was the authority and this is what you need to know. And now, you know, we all come up with all the things we want to know, and then we go learn. And then we go find it. So it's not a big deal. You know, I don't always tell them 'I don't know.' We just go find out together. And then I make sure that I point out the answers to the things that they've asked me . . . I have an excitement for learning. There for a while I was so busy with the things I thought I had to teach that I didn't have time to learn anything else. So now my attitude towards learning has changed in that I'm more interested and aware of life. I mean this is silly, but we're really into the Discovery channel now because I might learn some things that I could go back to school and use. It used to be I didn't have time for the Discovery channel. And I still don't have any more time than I did then, but it's more important to me now — I guess that's the answer. It's more important to me now. And I read a lot and if it's something I'm interested in, then I'm going to learn it, one way or another, I'm going to keep on until I find out what I want to know. Some teachers are afraid to admit that they don't know the answers or that they might be wrong, I'm not that kind of teacher. I don't mind going around asking everybody until I find out what I want to know. That doesn't bother me. So . . . I think I'm probably a humble learner, in that . . . I don't mind saying: 'I don't know, I don't understand that, can you tell me again.'

(First interview, 8/22/1992)

Here Gloria unwittingly echoes Freire, who speaks of the humility of liberating or empowering dialogue: 'The naming of the world, through which people constantly recreate the world, cannot be an act of arrogance' (1970:79; translation slightly modified). The empowering teacher surrenders not only the arrogance of superiority, but that of self-consciousness as well: in becoming a humble learner, Gloria — like the other teachers in the study — loses all sense of her own superiority to the children in her class. 'At the point of encounter', as Freire says (1970:79; translation slightly modified), 'there are neither utter ignoramuses nor perfect sages; there are only people who are attempting, together, to learn more than they now know.' This is because, as Buber (1970:67) says and Gloria seconds, the teacher and learner positions in the classroom are interchangeable, reciprocal. Teacher arrogance is only possible when the teacher-learner hierarchy remains rigidly stable.

Self-esteem

For Gloria self-esteem is

how you feel about yourself, and I know that it's also how you think other people feel about you. I suppose that's true. I was going to say

I don't know if that is what I usually think of, but really, even if they perceive you in a different way you are still stuck with what you think. So you know, it's what you think about yourself and what you think other people think about you.

(Second interview, 1/20/1992)

Self-esteem is not an unchanging thing. It is not the static property of a self. It changes in different contexts depending on the dialogical relationships engaged at the time. With her group of children Gloria's self-esteem is constantly shifting, especially in the large-group contexts in the classroom. In the individual and small-group encounters Gloria has a strong sense of herself as a 'warm teacher', 'a positive teacher'. (First interview, 8/22/1992).

Reflection on participant-observation

When I talked to Gloria over the phone in the summer about the possibility of her being in my study, she was excited about the chance. I interviewed her in mid-August, discussed the details of the study and how and when we would start. Initially I visited the class without the video camera:

Gloria introduced me to the children, saying I was going to be coming to their classroom every once in a while to learn with them. She asked if I wanted to say something to the kids. I suggested they read to me the book they had looked at. They did so, reading altogether. After five pages some of the children start getting restless and talking. Gloria attempts to refocus children. In one of these instances she turns to me and mouths: 'See what I mean.'

(P-O journal, 8/27/1991)

We did a good deal of talking about Gloria's children bonding into a caring community. This was a very important issue for Gloria because she feels that is one of her strengths as a teacher.

Gloria feels that she is not doing a good job of creating a caring classroom atmosphere. After reading she comes to me: 'See what I mean?' I told her that maybe her perception of how she is doing is much worse than what actually is going on. I don't know what she is comparing it to. 'Maybe I am thinking about the class last spring and we are not there yet with these children.'
At the end of this participant-observation I felt very irritated at the length of time the children have to be paying attention, the openness of the school building where teachers have to whisper and always keep a lid on every response! My subjective feelings about all

this, especially the classroom time frame, are certainly going to be surfacing here.

(P-O journal, 9/4/1991)

In this entry my own biased lens can be seen very clearly. Partly this is just me getting started, getting the routine of participant-observation going, but partly also it is my deep frustration with classrooms where 'teachers . . . always keep a lid on every response.' It is easy to say, with many administrators, that the necessity of keeping this lid on is natural in a building where one group's overexcitement could potentially lead to chaos. Something like this scenario — either total silence or the collapse of all order in the school building — continues to motivate the strict monitoring of all speech and activity in the classroom. Partly on the basis of childhood expectations and experiences about learning and school, many people (administrators, teachers, parents) think that everyone learns best in silence, despite research showing that discussion, cooperative learning, and more active, hands-on experiences result in learning faster and more meaningfully (Hart, 1986; Glasser, 1990). The school in which Gloria teaches is only one of thousands across the country that constantly fight the open space concept architecture of the 1970s by shushing children 330 minutes a day.

I participated in Gloria's room by working with individual children and groups; I also went to lunch with them and joined them at recess, teaching them some outside games. The adults in the room were always uncomfortably aware of the group's hyperactivity. Especially large-group time, when Gloria felt least empowered, was potentially the moment where things would start getting uneasy:

Gloria expressed her frustration at the children's activeness. She said: 'See what I mean about them on the carpet. I want to have them feel that they can discuss without raising their hands each time but it makes me feel I am losing them.' I asked her if she felt that her sense of frustration might be picked up by the children during large group time. She didn't think so but was clearly falling short of her ideal image of how she would have liked to have the group interact. Her frustration was shown by looking at me with a 'this is what I mean look' on her face during the period of observation. She shows affection to her students by touching, hugging, smiling, and eye-contact.

Gloria suggested I work in one of the centers, which I did. We (Candace, Jake, Larry, Paul, Mary, Lisa, and I) worked in a center drawing something that we can do with our hands. The children discussed each others' pictures.

The videocamera did not cause as much commotion as I would have expected. Since I was sitting down with them and had been coming in and out of their classroom, helping with their journals, etc., they seemed to adjust to it quickly. Toward the end of the observation some children (especially Jake) went to make faces in front of the camera.

(P-O journal, 9/25)

Early on, as this observation shows, Gloria was worried that I would get an unfavorable impression of her classroom presence, because she was experiencing so many difficulties with her active group. Over the course of the semester this fear began to dissipate:

Gloria and I drove down together to a conference. I think all those conversations helped her to feel more at ease in my presence. I have felt comfortable in Gloria's room from the beginning but today there seemed to be a relaxed feeling about it; fewer self-conscious sideways glances. After Gloria read a book *Cookie's Week* (Ward, 1988) to the children, we circled around the children to see who needed help getting started in their writing, with sounding out words. There seemed to be kind of a competition over who got to have me by their desk. I circled around, left those who were concentrating on their drawing and writing alone, focused on those who had a difficult time proceeding.

At the end Gloria and I talked about some of the children that I had some questions about. Seems like Gloria has a good share of children who need special help or attention.

(P-O journal, 10/22)

Gloria did point out to me that she probably notices the children's behavior more when I am there. She wrote: 'Unfortunately, they are probably not much different and I just notice their behavior more. They can be cooperative, but they are unpredictable. They aren't bad, they just all want to share their ideas and answers' (T-R journal, 10/22).

During the data gathering I kept thinking about how much more I might have gained if I had had fewer classrooms so I could have learned to know each child better. Interviewing the children separately was a good experience in this respect. I felt that I was getting real children behind the faces.

Today I felt like things were coming together. I participated and observed in Gloria's room and also interviewed children as they had pauses between their activities. Talking to each of the children separately gave me a much better sense of who they are and what they are about in the classroom community. I almost wish I had done this earlier to have gotten a better sense of the children earlier.

(P-O journal, 11/19)

In December there was a change in the way that Gloria thought about her classroom. She was taking her apple tree (behavior management chart) down and starting all over again with her children. She was unhappy with the assertive discipline system they were supposed to have in the building because 'I hate the consequences and rules because I'm not that kind of a person.' She had decided that her children did not have to learn everything in a few months.

> I suggested that her relaxing about it might bring the change in the group that she is hoping to achieve. I took some pictures of her bulletin boards since I am trying to come up with a picture album to give each teacher for Christmas.
>
> I asked Gloria when I could come in to have the children draw and write for me. We agreed on Thursday. I discussed the voice-activated tape recorder with her. She suggested she wear it tomorrow (12/10) when I am not there so I could see what kinds of things happen in the classroom when I am not present. I said it was a good idea and was very thankful of her excited response to it. She said: 'I can't wait to see what you put together about all this.'
>
> (P-O journal, 12/9)

Gloria was very supportive and excited all through the data collection. Despite her frustration with the class she continued being patient and flexible, and our discussions consistently filled me with enthusiasm and her response, 'I can't wait to see what you put together of all this', repeated her similar sentiments with the children's interviews.

At the second interview I asked her again how she had felt about participating in the whole process. She again voiced her wish that her children would take turns better and be more polite in sharing ideas. She did not think that the time involved in answering the journal entries and doing the interviews was too much, but the participant-observation could have been more involved. 'I always felt that you were not here long enough to see the good in them, how sweet they were and what good ideas they had, because it always seemed too hectic when you were in here' (Second interview, 1/20/1992). Tellingly, after using a voice-activated tape-recorder to tape one entire day without my presence, Gloria told me that this characterization (which she had been mentioning throughout the fall) was not quite true: things were every bit as hectic when I wasn't there. The underlying issue here seems to be that I felt more comfortable in her room than she did with my presence there. My perception of her classroom was considerably more positive than hers, or at least than she thought mine would be: because I am more interested in enthusiastic, empowered and empowering learning than in silence and politeness and turn-taking, I felt more comfortable than she with the hyperactive behavior that she feared was giving me the wrong impression. Her evaluation of my participant-observation, on the other hand — her wish that I had visited her classroom more frequently — coincides with my own. If I had it to do over again, I would choose one classroom, or possibly two, and spend all my time there — although choosing the classrooms would be difficult.

Jasmine

Jasmine shares a pod with Christine in school B. They have been teaching together for thirteen years, the fall of my data-collection being their fourteenth year together. Jasmine's side of the classroom has no desks because the two teachers share desks which are located in groups of four on Christine's side of the room. The pod is separated from the hallway by a long counter behind which Jasmine's side has work tables, the sand table, a block area, and a rug area in front of the bulletin board, which has the calendar, the clock, and room to hang materials.

Jasmine has 27 children, a racially mixed group. She has sixteen males and sixteen whites, eleven females and eleven African Americans in the class. There are eight children from one-parent homes and sixteen children are entitled to free or reduced lunches. Mrs. Durant, a teaching assistant, is assigned to Jasmine but she also works with Christine's children a few times a week. This is Mrs. Durant's first year; she is already changing her ideas about learning because she sees the children getting so excited (Phone conversation with Christine, 3/8/1992).

Jasmine is medium height, fair, and slender. Her voice is soft but pleasant. She is fun ('she has fun, fun things to do', says Charlotta, 12/6), likes to laugh, listens to the children, is very organized and a 'little absent minded'. She thinks children might characterize her teaching by saying that 'we do exciting things and I listen to them. I think they really understand that I will listen to them and that I will value what they say and that I make a point to let them know that' (First interview, 7/26/1991:4). In the interviews I asked the children how they felt about her and learning. Jasmine is well liked by her children: 'I love her', 'I feel happy', 'I feel very good' were the most typical answers. Kevin (11/21/1991) said 'I feel smart. I like being in school,' which could be interpreted to mean that the way his teacher treats him makes him feel good about himself and school. April (12/5/1991) said Jasmine is 'kind of fun and fine' and Quincy (12/16/1991) felt 'sad' — probably because at the time of the interview Jasmine had laryngitis. Only two children think learning is not enjoyable, all others think learning is fun. Sherry (12/15/1991) said she likes learning because 'I could be a teacher', which is another way of complimenting the teacher.

A sense of humor is important for a teacher. Sometimes Jasmine utilizes her sense of humor in managing the classroom:

> J: I think sometimes, for instance, I can go [makes a dragon sound] like that, and that sounds terrifying, but they also know that it

is kind of a letting off steam kind of thing and I do not think that I would frighten anyone when I do it . . .

H: And also you let them know that it is all right to feel this way. Some of the children were saying when I asked them if their teacher was ever angry, they were saying, well, sometimes she makes this face and she says: 'Steam is coming out of my ears and fire is coming out of my mouth' . . .

J: You know, I do use that lots of times, and sometimes I am angry when I do it and sometimes — it is a warning type thing, and they know it and yet they know there is no fire that is going to come out, and when I say those things and even if I am mad or angry about something, I can look at their faces and tell that they know that they better straighten up, it is kind of a joke and it has kind of a double meaning.

(Second interview, 1/13/1992)

Jasmine's self-assessment BrainMap shows her to be a strong preserver and explorer in her thinking. A person with 'preserver' as the primary BrainFrame guards tradition and values, and is mentally and emotionally committed to conserving caring and bonding to what she believes in (BrainMap, 1989). As an explorer, a thinker enjoys putting together new perspectives for viewing explaining and arranging things, which interpretation fits together with Jasmine's love for encouraging creative thinking in children. An explorer also deals in possibilities and is at home with complex functions thinking creatively.

The MindMaker6 instrument shows Jasmine as an involver, loyalist and choice-seeker. An involver is democratic, shares easily, is sensitive to people's rights, and open to learning and self-development. The loyalist is detailed and thorough, conservative and stabilizing, trustworthy — characteristics that choice-seekers look for and answer: 'Does this make sense?' Choice-seeker thinkers are often pragmatists who see systems as global, but with an emphasis on personal responsibility. Jasmine's MindMaker6 profile shows a group and future orientation as opposed to self and past orientation (MindMaker6, 1991).

Jasmine 'cannot imagine doing anything else' but teaching (First interview, 7/26/1991). She teaches math and science to both Christine's and her own children, all of whom, when I asked them about their favorite things to do in school, expressed great interest in their math activities.

Jasmine's class works a lot in cooperative groups. She gives tasks to each group and responsibility for thinking and figuring out what happens in the group. After they have finished their daily projects they take time sharing their findings and experiences. One group of children at a time comes in front of the class to share what they learned during their group time with the rest of the class. Here is Jean's illustration of center time:

Drawing 3: Jean's illustration of center time

Jasmine is interested not only in the end result in these groups but also the process of it all: how the children actually worked together, what they found easy and difficult to do, how they solved the problems they came across, how would they work in the future in a similar situation.

> *H:* You focused with one group on how they had been able to work together. 'If you had to work together tomorrow, what could you do not to have this problem?' (problem with chairs)
>
> 'Don't fight over the chairs!' one of the offered answers.
>
> 'If you just say that, is that going to take care of the problem?'
>
> 'I could use my voice', another child suggested. After a lengthy discussion the children agreed with you they had been able to work over some problems in the center. How important do you find it for the children to work out their own problems?
>
> *J:* It's almost overwhelming to think of the difference it could make in our society. Sometimes I wonder if I'm getting anywhere with using cooperative learning when I know that next year they (will) be working *individually* and *stationary* — I keep hoping that somehow before I retire (ha!) there will be some major changes in the way our children are taught.
>
> (T-R journal, 10/30/1991)

Jasmine's children enjoy many things in school: free centers, going outside to recess, working on art projects, constructing with blocks and omagles (plastic, coloured manipulatives), reading, writing, singing, math, and going to PE. What do the children think they actually learn in school? Very few children provided a subject matter answer to this question. They focused instead on the specific things that had just happened to them. 'I learn to count to a hundred' (Detrick, 12/16/1991). 'I learn how to spell. Be nice' (Johnny, 11/21/1991). 'I learn in case of real fire you go outside and we learned go to the other neighbor house and call nine-one-one. Stop! Drop! Roll!' (Schewanda, 12/5/1991, second interview). The unit on the olden days had the children really excited about the past of their family members. The two classes had grandmothers come in to tell about how life was long before they were born. Shewanda (11/21/1991) said she learned that 'In the olden days they be makin' clothes, boxes to put things. Sometimes they pick cotton in the garden.' When I asked them about what they would do if they got to be the teacher in the room or how they would teach, many of them said they would like to teach 'like they teach now' (Ian, 12/6/1991) or they'd like to teach the things they were taught: 'I would like to teach them how to write, I'd teach them how to spell, use the typewriter, learning how to count to a hundred' (Jean, 12/5/1991). 'I would teach them to learn Spanish, English, North, East, South, West' (Labotshy, 12/12/1991). Shewanda said she would teach 'like I was teaching kindergarten'. An interesting question arises. What difference does she see between kindergarten and first-grade teaching? Since I did not have a chance to find out, we can only make guesses. Eight children answered that they didn't know how they would teach, as if even the thought of being the teacher was beyond their reach.

Ian's answer 'like they teach now' expresses the feeling everybody in the pod has of being one classroom community (Ian, 12/9/1991). Although they have the two groups and two teachers, the children feel that it is the whole pod that does things together, belongs together and learns together. This is seen also in their answers regarding their friendships in the room. Half of the children in each class, Jasmine's and Christine's class, named children from the other class as people with whom they liked to spend time, work and play.

Jasmine has worked at all age levels from first grade through junior high and high school, and thinks that has been helpful for her because she can project to their future and see what she is preparing the children for. She says: 'I can see in the distance a far-reaching goal because I can start them off and see where they are going' (First interview, 7/26/1991).

First grade is enjoyable because she can utilize the role of a 'problem solver':

> that is a role for everybody, whether you are a teacher or not; I think it is important for me to set examples for the children to solve problems and to make decisions and to share some of my strategies about decision-making and problem-solving. I think a teacher role in being a decision-maker and problem-solver is to give them an opportunity to do those things. Give them a chance to verbalize their feelings about things.
>
> (Second interview, 1/13/1992)

On the basis of my participant-observations, problem-solving through modeling and encouraging reflective thinking in children is a scarlet thread that goes through all Jasmine's activities. 'Problem-solving and the co-operative learning groups . . . that's probably my favorite' (Second interview, 1/13/1992). She never did any hands-on activities as a child, or as a student preparing to be a teacher, which preparation was for secondary level, but she has learned how important it is to incorporate real experiences into everything she does:

> we never did any hands-on things at all. I think probably lack of equipment to do those kinds of things was probably the reason why we did not do it back then, and it is easier to pick up the teacher's manual and follow the teacher's manual than it is to do any kinds of hands-on things, I think a lot of administrators have the idea that if you walk in a classroom and the children are at their desk and are quiet then learning is going on and then too I think the pressure put on teachers for teaching skills has kept them away from hands-on things, where concepts are dealt [with].
>
> (First interview, 7/26/1991)

For example, homework is much more meaningful if the parents can get excited too, and it doesn't disrupt their daily lives:

> The way we do homework really gets our parents involved more than anything that we have ever done. It's the type of homework that they don't have to sit down with their child and drill and fill in the blanks but it's active homework, where like they make a graph of dogs they see in a week . . . find a tree in their yard and find out as much about that tree [as they can].
>
> (First interview, 7/26/1991)

In this way Jasmine incorporates children's normal life experiences into the flow of school. The worksheets that she used to use in great numbers have given way to more meaningful activities. I asked her why she felt that worksheets were harmful: 'Because they limit children. Limit you and limit children. There's no creativity involved at all in a workbook. And it's one right answer, boring. And this is from a teacher who's used a lot of workbooks.' (First interview, 7/26/1991).

Jasmine feels empowered with her children, with Christine, with the teachers to whom she gives workshops, despite her shyness about presenting (which an observer is not able to see but she feels); but there are relationships that she wishes could be changed. The excitement she feels about teaching cannot be shared with everyone, and that is a difficult thing for her:

> *H:* You feel pretty good about the community in school, you feel like everybody welcomes your ideas?

J: Not really. I have had some . . . I don't know. Not exactly hostility but a reluctance to share and to be involved, and maybe some people are just being completely turned off — that has been hard for me because I have always had the respect and the close relationships with my fellow teachers.

H: Do you think that it has become that way for some reason or is it something to do with you doing so many workshops outside the school?

J: I think it is more that they have a different philosophy and are not truly that interested in changing it.

H: If you were to compare their philosophy and your philosophy, could you put it in a couple thoughts?

J: I think they should look at the research that has been done and the way our children have performed after they have gotten out of school, and realize that we have got to make some changes.

H: You think that there are a lot of teachers that are unaware of this?

J: Yes, a good many.

(Second interview, 1/13/1992)

Jasmine is concerned about some of the things she sees happening in education. Fortunately in her own school 'we have many opportunities to be as creative as we want to be and to develop programs.' She continues: 'I would love to be involved in some kind of math program in developing', illustrating her responsiveness to the need of teachers to find new ideas and become empowered in their own classrooms (Second interview, 1/13/1992). Jasmine has been involved in doing workshops inside and outside her own school district.

J: I think, for instance, in workshops, I talk on a teacher's level; that I'm not so involved in theory and the philosophical aspect of it, so the teachers relate to me in a way that sometimes they would not to another teacher.

H: And with children, you have the same ability to understand their point of view.

(First interview, 7/26/1991)

Change

Jasmine's story of change reflects similar kinds of feelings of stagnation and plateauing as Christine's. Indeed both women changed simultaneously, as they could not have taught side-by-side without a mutual understanding of what they wanted to do.

We made some pretty dramatic changes in our classroom, we really did . . . We have made some changes from sitting in rows and doing independent work and worksheets to . . . doing so few worksheets and putting desks in groups, setting up cooperative learning groups. That was a big change and of course we made little changes to improve all the time. Any teacher does.

(First interview, 7/26/1991)

H: Well . . . if you think about teaching, what are the important things in teaching for you? Why do you enjoy it?

J: Well, most people think I have a different kind of desire to teach than I do, but I think most people would say that they love children, but that's really not the reason I teach. I love teaching. I like learning and I love the way we've been teaching the last three years. I love the excitement of it.

H: Can you describe the last three years, what happened? Why are those three years different from the ones . . .

J: I think the main thing, the main difference that, the thing that's made the most important change in my life is that I'm learning so much with the children and I never did before. I never got involved with them as before. And I don't feel like I have a real good background and I think in the last three years, I've probably learned more than I ever have in my entire lifetime.

H: So can you put your finger on . . . Was there a crisis or some sort of a . . . what was the turning point?

J: Just looking around and seeing children not excited. And even though I think I was a good teacher . . . I just felt like I wasn't growing and I think my children enjoyed the classroom, but there just wasn't excitement. I guess that would be the main thing, we were just kind of stagnant.

H: And now you feel a difference?

J: Definitely.

(First interview, 7/26/1991)

Philosophy

Jasmine believes that the ultimate goal of education is helping children to become lifelong learners. To facilitate learning in children is 'to be involved with the children', which she thinks she has learned to do more after her change (Second interview, 1/13/1992). She is working on changing her 'ideas about the teacher being an authoritative person, and I think that I still have work to do in that' (Second interview, 1/13/1992).

Rather than an authority, Jasmine says, a teacher needs to be a nurturer and to 'look beyond what [children's] behavior is and try to see why the child acts that way. I really truly believe that if we nurture children and understand them, and try to resolve some of their problems in elementary, then they are not lost' (Second interview, 1/13/1992).

H: Could you describe that philosophy in some way?

J: Well, I guess it's the whole-language philosophy that you start with the whole and you give children opportunity to learn and to create and to explore and you become a facilitator instead of an authoritative person. Instead of just spouting out knowledge, you're guiding them and helping them discover knowledge on their own, giving them the freedom to become learners and having them know that they will always be learning and that learning is fun and it's useful and purposeful.

(First interview, 7/26/1991)

Here Jasmine separates her teaching philosophy from the banking concept (Freire, 1970) which views children as passive recipients of knowledge. Freedom to learn and discover knowledge on their own is central to Jasmine's belief about educating children.

To understand teaching is to discover yourself as a learner. 'I know you can't teach without learning yourself. You can't teach, you can't reach your potential unless you're learning yourself . . .' (First interview, 7/26/1991). Learning thus becomes an important ingredient in self-esteem.

Jasmine's teaching philosophy views knowledge as dynamic (not one right answer), where it is important for children to discover things for themselves. She would like to teach the children to

value each other's opinions, to respect one another, to learn to work together. I'd like for them to have a sense of belonging, not only in the classroom but a sense of their family and the traditions of their family . . . and value for the traditions in the country. Even if they don't agree with them — to respect another person's traditions.

(First interview, 7/26/1991)

Self-esteem

For Jasmine self-esteem is 'feeling good about yourself, believing in yourself, having self-confidence that you do the things that you want to' (Second interview, 1/13/1992). Jasmine feels good about what she does. She believes that 'teachers can make the biggest difference' because they 'set the tone for the classroom' (First interview, 7/26/1991:9). Self-esteem plays a big role in teaching:

J: If you feel good about yourself, lots of times you're going to have that sense of humor, and a lot of the other essentials that you need for teaching will just come automatically.

H: What do you think is the source of your self-esteem?

J: I don't know. I really don't have a good self-esteem in a lot of areas. I've always felt self-conscious about my background. I come from a very rural area and I'm real self-conscious about my language and those are things I've tried to overcome, but I still . . . probably the grammar has been really difficult for me and especially if I'm nervous and . . .

H: And you find that when you are nervous, those things come up more easily . . .

J: Right . . .

H: I feel that same way too.

J: I can't imagine you feeling that way. . . And I know lots of times when we do these workshops, I'm *real* self conscious about it and I think that hinders my doing the best possible job, because that's in the back of my mind. I can't let go of it.

H: Has [your] thinking about your background always been the thing?

J: Right, a little country school and then I came to [the university] — it was like night and day. Not only because of the academics but my country talkin' and this sort of thing.

H: Did you suffer from it? Did others . . .

J: Yes.

(First interview, 7/26/1991)

As the participation-observations progressed we began to notice that the more we learned to know about each other, the more we discovered similar vulnerabilities.

Reflection on participant-observation

After my first participant-observation I asked Jasmine how she felt about me being there and taking notes. She responded: 'I really don't think much about your taking notes, we have so many people taking notes in our room I barely noticed and it didn't bother me' (T-R journal, 9/5/1991). I mostly observed in Jasmine's room, and occasionally participated by circling around as children were working in centers.

At the end of my teacher-researcher journal for 11/21 I had written: 'Any free response to my being in your class today . . .' to which Jasmine's entry was the following disclosure:

I was really upset with some of my children last week because I think a few of them 'show out' [off] when we have visitors or when someone puts a camera in the room. Maybe their behavior just becomes more obvious to me during those times. I want them to learn to respect each other, me and what we do in the classroom. We have had so many visitors in our room, sometimes I want to just have my room to enjoy and not worry about what someone else thinks about it.

(T-R journal, 11/21/1991)

This is when I began to think that Jasmine really felt my presence was something that forced her to 'worry about' what I was thinking. Although I had not thought of myself as judgmental in any way, I was still an extra person who had to be dealt with in the room.

J: You know, I do not like to be watched. I feel comfortable with the children.

H: And yet, Christine is watching you all the time.

J: Yes, but she is really not watching me. I just feel more comfortable when . . . I am not somebody that likes . . .

H: Have you always felt the same way?

J: Yes, it does not bother me all that much, but some days it does, but to be completely myself, I like to be with the children.

H: If you think about the way that you are when I have been here and when I have not, what sorts of things do you see changing in yourself when I walk in?

J: It is not so much you, it is the change that I see in the children when someone else is there observing in the room.

H: Do you feel the same kind of change?

J: Specially with the camera on them, for some reason, it changes their behavior.

H: How about when some other people come in like . . . the mathematics students come in.

J: Right, and if they stay for a short time, it is fine, but if they stay for a very long time, it really puts a strain on things.

H: When that one day I walked in and you were talking about that very thing, you know about the video camera, and the other adults said they did not think that [the children] changed so much and you thought that they did change. Did you discuss that afterwards?

J: I probably did, but I do not recall, more than likely I did.

H: I hate to have caused you this anxiety of not being able to be yourself.

J: I mean, it was not anxiety, there were other times when I am not myself, completely, myself when I am observed by Mr. Cole, I don't really think anybody is.

H: Yes that is true, it is different when you are with the children yourself and in a laid-back and relaxed environment.

(Second interview, 1/13/1992)

While talking about relationships with Jasmine and the children in the classroom we had a discussion that shows how I as a participant-observer did not hide my way of thinking and withdraw behind a mask of an objective researcher. We had been discussing learning to live together in the classroom and the ideal relationship between teacher and children:

J: I guess I always had a misconception that if we talked peace it would really give them freedom, and we opened up our classroom more . . . and when they came to the rug they would not feel the need to hit their neighbor or to push their neighbor or to say ugly things to their neighbor.

H: I have a theory about that.

J: What?

H: A lot of things I have seen in Mississippi schools, I think one of the hard things is that because of the schedule given . . . there really is not very much time for them to take care of their physical needs. They do need more physical exercise time and you do try to alleviate it . . . you get up, and a lot of teachers do not even do that. You are trying to do it but still they don't get enough.

J: So you think if we did more of that kind of thing, that it would help?

H: I think so, but it's just my background and ideas about it. Somebody else was starting to do that. I guess it was Emilie [Patricia's former student-teacher, now a colleague in another school] who told me and said that she noticed a difference.

J: What kinds of things would you do?

H: Just go outside more, and let them move, I guess. They do not have enough time for those freedom kinds of things [reference to Glasser's five basic needs] to really let go of their bodies, maybe play games outside . . .

J: We'll take a break, go outside for five minutes and have a quick game and come inside?

H: Yes, something like a total break from what you are doing and I guess I am so excited about it because I read about this thing on the brain, and the brain needs more oxygen and a total change of atmosphere to be able to grip and learn better.

(Second interview, 1/13/1992)

We also had a chance to share our feelings about how the research had gone and the feeling that Jasmine had of being scrutinized by me and being filmed by the videocamera, and of this changing her children's behavior and making things more cumbersome for her:

J: I do not feel like I am being a very good participant, I'm sorry. Last semester . . . [makes a sweeping gesture with eyes expressing the difficult demands placed on her]

H: Right. I realize that. I guess I was feeling a built-up frustration. Towards the end I just thought you were going to blow up and say: 'Oh, I'm not going to do this, get out of here.' And I noticed myself growing much more awkward about coming to talk to you because I was worried that I would . . .

J: I could have just hidden that fact and gone on, and you would have never found out, but . . .

(Second interview, 1/13/1992)

My presence in Jasmine's class caused her tension and when I was there she became much more aware of the kinds of things that she thought I would be noticing and perhaps placing judgment on her teaching, but she felt secure enough about our relationship to voice her response. She is also very reflective in pondering about the possibility of her perception of classroom relationships and activities changing when I come in, rather than changes in children. Since teaching is an interactive dynamic, probably both the children's behavior and Jasmine's perception of it changed.

Christine

Christine shares her pod with Jasmine. As you walk in the classroom your immediate response is: there is a lot of room in this place! There are no walls between the two classrooms; the pod looks airy and open. Christine has a red wooden rocking chair in her part of the room that she likes to use when she is reading to the children, which is one of her favorite things to do with them. She has written a book of her own about visiting her grandparents and shared it with the children when they were studying the olden days this fall. A blackboard is on the far wall with a colorful rug in front of it and the rocking chair on the right. Children's coats are in the far left corner and there is a work table in front of the coat racks divided by a board. Desks are organized in an area close to Christine's own desk as you walk in, in groups of three or four. Desks are mainly used for daily journal writing; the journals are kept

> in their desks so they would not have to look in every desk for their journal (as we did last year!). Each desk contains one of my student's journals and one of Jasmine's student's journals, thus the reason for two names on each desk. There was no systematic way of doing this. Since we keep our desks in groups, they often get switched around and are often in different places each day.
>
> (T-R journal, 9/5/1991)

Christine has twenty-eight children in her class with equal numbers of girls and boys. Over half of the class (sixteen) is entitled to free or reduced lunches. Christine has ten African American and eighteen white children.

Christine is average height, dark-haired, energetic, and friendly. She is flexible, patient, enthusiastic, and creative. She walks and stands a lot while she teaches, leans closer to the children and communicates excitement, makes contact with her posture and eyes. Since she likes to stand, she is often seen leaning over with one hand behind her back, getting in close to the children to get them ready for what comes next, or to help them visualize a moment in their lives that will give them a personal link to what is being talked about. Her use of visualization and other imagery exercises is extraordinary; it is something I have rarely seen in classrooms, and Christine uses it wonderfully. We exchanged responses on one of these occasions. I wrote: 'You had [children] stand up and visualize their grandparents. Children were concentrating hard. There was a touch of mystery in the air and I could feel it on their faces. What do you think is the role of anticipation, mystery, secrecy and the like in the classroom of first graders?' She responded: 'One of the greatest rewards of teaching is the built-in motivation and joy for learning that resides in my children. Their innocent wonder and desire to know more makes teaching so much more fun' (T-R journal, 11/20/1991).

Christine walks and talks in the classroom in a relaxed manner and has an interesting combination of being at once focused and organized and relaxed. She sits on the floor, on the table, in her rocking chair, and occasionally behind her desk. Occasionally she has the children get up and move around to a record, a song or a finger play. This she does more now that she is taking classes at the university herself: 'Being a student myself has helped me as much if not more than my experience in the classroom to become aware of children's need to move around' (T-R journal, 11/20/1991). Sue's drawing illustrates one of these moments of getting up and getting refreshed through moving around.

Drawing 4: Exercising in the classroom

Austin describes eloquently what he learns in the classroom: 'I learn how to read, how to be good, and how to count. Sometimes you learn the world [points at the globe]. Don't fight, don't hit each other, being good to people, being kind to them, sharing' (12/3, 1991). (Laneika, 12/3/1991) is learning 'Cutractions [subtraction], ABC's, patterns, read, write.' Austin also thinks that learning is important so 'I have my applications and get my job' (12/3). Is Austin really this career-oriented at age six? Do his parents continually stress the importance of school for career reasons? It may just be that a member of his family was applying for a job, or a student-teacher had talked about applications — something that he did not quite understand but wanted to try out. In any case, it was an experience that meant something to him, a complex pondering on his felt reality, and he made the connection in school. Learning is 'so fun' (Dustin, 12/9/1991) and 'it's good to learn' (Debra, 12/12/1991) for most children because 'I get to grow up and get a job' (Laneika, 12/3/1991) or because 'when you learn you might be a teacher when you grow up' (Nicole, 12/3).

There is only one child, Dean, who is angry at life, who does not express the loving, liking, and admiring that they feel for Christine because 'she is a good teacher' (Valerie, 12/6/1991), 'she teach me good and she's nice' (Beth, 12/3/1991), 'she let us learn, write our journals and draw and spell stuff and we can be second-graders' (Lamont, 12/6/1991). (I will be returning to Dean in the next chapter.) In these responses you can feel the trust that the children have for Christine. In the classroom community they have become convinced that they can learn and that it is enjoyable to do so, and more importantly, that learning is a meaningful activity and has its ramifications from first grade on up to the choosing of their life directions. Lamont's words 'she let us learn', letting the children feel acceptance and 'allowing the kids to be creative' (Christine's second interview, 1/14/1991), are the core of empowerment in the classroom.

Children in Christine's classroom especially like art projects, writing in their journals and reading. Free center time is one of their favorites because they can choose the activity they want:

> Free centers. At one time there were children working at Omagles (six children), watermelon puzzles that matched seeds with numbers (one), patterning with plastic blocks (five), one boy just observing Omagles group with his hand resting on his cheek, three boys at the block center, five working with Legos, one child working with flash cards with the assistant teacher's help, ten children writing about what they had learned about their home town and the university, one boy cutting his own drawing of a bus, three children working with Christine on the floor (flop and teach style) with *There's A Monster Under my Bed* (Howe, 1986) two children working with Play-Doh, five at the birdseed table and one child at sentence strips with a university student.
>
> (P-O journal, 10/28)

In an environment with this many choices given to the children it is fairly easy for them to find an activity that feels meaningful for them.

The dominant processing in Christine's thinking is verbal and sequential, left-brain functioning. She is also spontaneous but open to complexity as well. Her MindMaker6 world-view profile gives the loyalist the highest score, with involver and kins-person as the two other highest scores. Christine is sensitive to obeying the law and respecting authority, although in her own teaching she is working towards a more democratic and egalitarian decision-making process with the children. She says her close relationships have influenced her to believe how important the laws are in society, but sometimes she wonders how much others have influenced her thinking. As a kins-person she is bound more to the past than the future. Obligations to duty are primary, personal thoughts tend to be secondary. Like the other teachers, she is also more group- than self-oriented. The kins-person in her sees the significance of family traditions and she has a strong sense of group unity in the class-room. The involver sees the world as caring, cooperative, sharing, democratic, and striving for learning. Her awakening to the world of learning has been one of Christine's greatest discoveries in her change. Although the kins-person's limitation might be unwillingness to take risks, Christine's change story proves that she has had the courage to go against the grain in changing her classroom practices drastically (Cochran-Smith, 1991:279).

Christine has taught thirteen years, all in the same school, and for all thirteen years as Jasmine's partner. She decided to become a first-grade teacher when she herself was in the first grade. This is what she said when I asked about her choice of career and whether her first-grade teacher was instrumental in that choice:

C: No, I didn't like my first-grade teacher and I thought I could be a better teacher than she was. She was not very affectionate and I thought she should let me hug her and things like that. I didn't come from a very affectionate home but that was just what I thought. A teacher should be a surrogate mother or something like that, she should be more open and she was very cold.

H: So why do you think you decided to become a teacher in first grade?

C: I don't know, I always felt that way and a lot of times when I do workshops I'll say: 'I feel called to teach just like preachers feel called to preach.' I feel like it's kind of a mission for me. It was just always what I knew I had to do.

(First interview, 7/30/1991)

Christine's aunt was also a teacher who let her help do bulletin boards in her classroom, so she had a chance to gain insights to teaching early on in her life. Christine's perception of herself as a teacher is that she is patient, enthusiastic, and flexible. 'I make those kids feel loved most days.' The best reward in being a teacher is when children 'experience things for the first time' (First interview, 7/30/1991). Teaching is a hectic job. 'Sometimes I start the day cluttered with stuff. Not personal stuff, really, but sometimes I spread myself too thin and I'm doing too many things at one time.' She wishes she could focus more and be 'more thorough with everything I do in a classroom' (First interview, 7/30/1991). The problem of focusing gets more complex as teachers have to divide their days into taking children to Specials: physical education, music, and special services for children who need them.

Like the other teachers Christine feels empowered in her classroom, but teaching has its troublesome sides too. The public attitude toward teaching and teachers bothers Christine: 'They think that teachers are teachers because they have three months in the summer' (First interview, 7/30/1991). She would like people to see teachers 'as people who are really committed to the children' (First interview, 7/30/1991).

Teaching is Christine's calling and she believes that good teachers should be 'committed to what they do and committed to being lifelong learners as well as making the children lifelong learners' (First interview, 7/30/1991).

As professionals, teachers have to confront attitudes that question the value of their work. If it is hard for teachers to teach differently from the way they were taught (Jones, 1984), it is even harder for a person who has little knowledge of education outside his or her own school experiences — which were often humiliating and boring. Testing and grading are such issues:

H: Is there anything you'd like to change about the profession *per se*, being a teacher?

C: Yeah, I'd like first of all to be considered more professional. It bothers me when I do a workshop and they come up to me and say, 'How do you come up with the grade', and I say, 'I look at the notes I've made about their reading, I look at my notes about their writing and I make a decision' and they just go [gasps], you know, and they can't, they think that you have to have grades averaged together and have 97.2 which means nothing . . .

H: Well, besides you have to judge as you come up with these things.

C: Right, and you know, I gave a worksheet to a child and he made a hundred and couldn't read it at all. I asked him to read it for me and every word he'd picked for the blank was the wrong one. It was not the word he thought it was but he just guessed it right like 'Dog saw the people.' It really said the dog saw the puppy. He thought it said people. It still made sense and he guessed every answer right which told me nothing about what he knew.

H: Which told you something about the test.

C: Right, and that was just a worksheet that would end up being averaged together to tell you what grade, so that really is an empty decision, and people think that that is more objective if you do that, and that when you just do it on your notes and on your portfolio and the things that you see and the things that you know, that too much of your personality plays a part in it.

Well, I guess my dream with them would be for people to respect us like doctors. We trust those doctors' decisions, and what
do they take into account: our symptoms, what they've read,
what they know and how we've described ourselves to them and
what they've checked out themselves. And I guess I want the
public to know that we are that kind of a teacher and I know I
guess that there are teachers who don't do that well. But those
few teachers shouldn't change everybody's opinion.

H: Why do you think that people are so concerned about the . . .
objective testing?

C: I don't know unless there have been parents who feel like their
children have been mistreated or have had prejudice against them
by teachers . . . I think it all boils down to being caught — with
grades, what group we're in, how smart our children are.

(First interview, 7/30/1991)

Change

Although the changes in each teacher were radical, Christine's description of
her change is probably the most dramatic. The change brought more excitement to teaching, teaching became meaningful again, and she feels after the
change she is more able to support the children's emerging sense of self-worth:

C: Probably the way we [Jasmine and I] changed, the way we've
taught increased my enthusiasm for teaching. Teaching this way
I'm learning so much and I didn't really learn that much before.
And . . . I stayed with that basal reader and I had my nose in that
teacher's edition and I didn't learn if I did it right and I didn't
learn . . . about orange trees and the things . . . and so I'm really
learning things, I think that's really increased my enthusiasm.

H: What do you think changed you? What gave you the courage to
throw that basal reader out and open yourself up to . . .

C: Change . . . I kind of feel that if I'm not changing I'm not growing and I like to keep growing so . . . I was pretty tired of that
basal reader. It was kind of a combination of being tired of it and
then Andrea in our conversation about what's developmentally
appropriate asked me some pointed questions that made me really
wonder what I was doing. So it's a combination of, I guess,
people making me search why I'm doing what I'm doing and
being open enough to want to change, to *want* to change.

H: Are you saying that with the basal reader you might not have
been as aware of what you were doing as you are now?

C: It just didn't bring in world kinds of things. You know, it didn't
bring in general broad knowledge. But because we are teaching

through themes the literature relates to besides the social studies
across the curriculum . . .

(First interview, 7/30/1991)

In this quotation the dialogical relationship in change is seen: 'we changed.'
The change was an individual change but connected to the important relationships in the classroom and outside of it. What actually changed in Christine's
thinking and how did it happen? The story of her change is best heard in her
own voice:

H: You've been describing the changes made in your teaching. Was
there some sort of a crisis or did something drastic happen all of
a sudden?

C: You haven't heard my story, huh? I figured I'd told it so many
times. It was three years ago in the spring, two years ago in the
spring, maybe, when I went to the kindergarten teachers and
said: 'I can't do this any more! I'm supposed to get them through
five readers, five workbooks, you're not getting them through
any workbooks! I can't do it! And I'm having to retain these
children because you aren't getting them through any workbooks. If I'm going to get them through five workbooks, you
need to get them at least through one, and maybe two.' Because
that's the way I felt like our system was supposed to work,
'cause we as teachers had decided they gotta get through these
five readers because second grade teachers were breathing down
our necks, you know. And Helen [kindergarten teacher colleague]
panicked and she called Andrea and she said we're having a
meeting and Christine Scott's hot and you've got to come and be
there and she said: 'I'm on my way.' And at that meeting, I
repeated the same thing with Andrea there and I said: 'Y'all need
to do workbooks,' and she said: 'We're not going to,' she said.
'It's not developmentally appropriate and we're not going to.'
And I said, 'Well, I'm going to have to keep retaining kids and
I'm going to tell them it's because you won't do workbooks.'
And she said, 'You better not.' And it was just kinda like that.
My face was red, her face was red, and the principal finally piped
up and said, 'You don't have to do all those workbooks, do
you?' And I said, 'That's what I was told. These are the first-
grade readers. To go to the second grade they have to complete
them.' And she said, 'Well, I don't care if you use the basal
reader at all.' Well I had kinda backed myself in a corner at that
point 'cause I was being so loud and obnoxious and then she
said: 'You don't have to do it.' . . . And Andrea said some things
about what is developmentally appropriate which is a term I had
kinda shoved back when I was given all these steps to follow to

go through . . . and I went home and really started thinking, maybe I do need to do something different. And Shannon Clemens, our principal . . . kept asking us as teachers, why are kids not loving to read? Why don't they love to read? Why do they never read after they leave your room? And so that had kinda been going on in my mind. And I said to Andrea, 'My kids are excited about learning. They can't wait to get to the next reader.' And she said, 'Yeah, because they know that what's you want them to do. And at that age, they want to please their teacher, whatever it is.' And she just said some things like that, and I really started thinking, so I just called her back and said, 'I want to try something new, will you help me?' And she said, 'Yeah.' And she gave me books to read, and I read *Transitions* by Regie Routman [1988] and it really changed my life . . . She really told how she made the transition and you could read her enthusiasm in everything. I could, and it was just speaking right to me, so I decided to ditch my basals and I just went into that classroom with no basal readers the next year.

H: So how did you feel the first time that you didn't have them?

C: It's really scary and I told my parents, 'I'm trying something new, I'm reading about it, I'm trying to learn about it, but if your children aren't reading by second semester like I think they should, I'll switch back over and I promise I'll get 'em where they need to be, just trust me and let me try this.' Which was really a mistake, because I'm a very honest person and I just thought I would lay it on the table. But I had some children with learning disabilities in my room or that were not mentally mature enough for what was happening to them and they didn't do as well as their parents wanted them to do and instead of accepting their immaturity, they blamed it on my trying something new. But you learn as you go and this year I went in and I told those parents: 'We are doing something that is wonderful! And it works . . . and you're going to be excited about it.' So you learn from the things that you do. And I talked a little bit about invented spelling at first, but not enough and the parents were real concerned about that. I didn't really think about how much in teaching this way they memorized those predictable books and that really bothered parents . . . they were calling me, saying: 'They can't read this book, they've just memorized it, they think they can read it,' . . . so this year I went in and said: 'They're going to memorize for the first semester and that's okay because that's the first step in reading and you just brag on them and it'll happen,' . . . so I learned from that first meeting, the right things to say.

(First interview, 7/30/1991)

As this passage shows, Christine's change was instigated by a feeling of dissatisfaction and stagnation. In her dissatisfaction she was laying blame on those outside the classroom, the kindergarten teachers, wanting them to send better equipped children to first grade. This is known as the push-down phenomenon in education (Katz and Chard, 1989): the business world says, 'We are getting people who don't have the basic skills!', so people in higher education wring their hands and say 'That's because the material we get from the high schools is so poor.' And on it goes, till we have younger and younger children having to drill on the 'skills' as soon as they are available to the system.

Christine tried to convince the kindergarten teachers to change because what she was attempting to do didn't work. The idea of changing herself was not a possibility at first, because, as she said, 'My kids are excited about learning. They can't wait to get to the next reader.' Christine needed to think about the conversations and suggestions made to her before she could allow herself to think about a possibility of changing her own practices. As Fullan (1982) stresses, teachers must find meaning in change before change makes a difference. Christine's reflection, and dialogue with Andrea, along with the feelings of plateauing she was having, provided that meaning for her change.

And so the 'Ms. Scott's hot' attitude has caved in and made way for a more reflective approach and a wish to truly share the classroom not only with her children, but also with colleagues and parents. Very clearly, as Christine describes it, putting the basal reader at the focus of her teaching blocked her from seeing the contribution the children made in a classroom, and also hindered her from having to think about what she was doing. Her ideas are freer to flow now because she is not imprisoned by the structure that the basal reader brought to her classroom. She wishes she was able to let go more and create but fears that the training she got as a child and through the school years has made it difficult. Jasmine had children bring in materials for inventing things: screws, pipe cleaners and other little things with which the children created their own inventions. Christine says, 'These are the kinds of things I needed as a child so I wouldn't be so left-brained' (Second interview, 1/14/1992). Christine thinks that she 'cheated all those kids those thirteen years . . . because I really didn't know them. I was too caught up in their skills to know them' (Second interview, 1/14/1992).

Christine used to be a textbook case of a nondiscerning teacher, mechanically carrying out actions (Knape and Rosewell, 1980). The triumphs she has seen in the classroom 'when a child first sees it' have given her the courage to open up further to a more democratic, less authoritarian way of teaching (First interview, 7/30/1991). From non-discernment she has moved into intuitive discernment, where she has developed a working educational decision-making process. With her change she has discovered professional sharing and reading as important ways to develop herself. She reads about whole language and teachers' experiences and is increasingly getting more interested in discovering more about how and why she believes the way she does.

Philosophy

Christine believes in working to teach children 'as much as I can teach them, to help them as much as I can, to teach them how to learn when nobody else is there to teach them, and to teach them that love for reading and learning and to know that I can meet their individual needs and I can learn a whole lot about each child' (First interview, 7/30/1991). She thinks it is important to be open to children, to accept them as they are, and learn to know them as well as possible. Teaching does not mean that you tell children what the answers are, because the answers might be different at different times.

Christine is convinced that it is important for teachers to 'model lifelong learning and just facilitate learning. I don't know that you can teach learning.' She has discovered the power of learning through the change she has made in her teaching practices from traditional to whole language teaching. She is looking for ways of meeting the needs of the whole child rather than going about her business in a preconceived, linear, locked 'I had my nose in that basal reader' manner. She is also 'more aware of how the brain works, how children learn than I ever was before' (First interview, 7/30/1991).

Self-esteem

Self-esteem for Christine is 'exactly how you feel about yourself. If you are comfortable with yourself; if you like yourself or do not like yourself depends on your relationship with the people' (Second interview, 1/14/1992). Christine thinks her source of self-esteem is her family, where she feels loved and valued. She is the problem-solver and initiator in her family. Christine sees self-esteem as a cycle that is related to how people treat you and what you do: 'You do what you like and you end up liking yourself 'cause you like what you do' (First interview, 7/30/1991). It is the feeling of acceptance she feels among her family that Christine takes with her when she walks in her class-room to engage in interaction with her children and Jasmine.

'I'm a pretty confident teacher, but I'm not as confident about what I know about things' (First interview, 7/30/1991). Self-esteem is crucial: 'it's very important and I think it really affects how you respond to other people, to children, to parents, to the staff' (First interview, 7/30/1991).

Reflection on participant-observation

Went to Christine's room where she is chatting with a second-grade teacher. Children rest their heads on their desks and start free center time. The group is ready to play. CS flips the lights three times to remind children of playing with a 'whispering voice' so other classes don't get disturbed. No communication with the group's children. Christine says she enjoys giving children free centers because she feels she has not done everything to 'help children take responsibility of each other and be kind to each other'. On the bulletin board there is an experience chart on kindness. I suggested an article by Alfie Kohn and she asked me to get it for her. [Brought it the next day.]

(P-O journal, 8/27/1991)

I first observed both Christine and Jasmine at the same time. I wanted to do it simultaneously to observe the collaboration more closely. This proved to be very tedious and superficial in terms of really noticing details in either one of the rooms, so I started observing them separately in October:

I noticed how difficult it might be for me to pay attention to both of their activities and interactions simultaneously. I guess I need to write notes side-by-side since sometimes they coincide and what happens with one group is important to the other one. Maybe I can talk to Cindy about the best way of doing this. It will be very difficult to bring the videocamera there so that I can shoot both classes simultaneously. What to do? Two videocameras? Compared to yesterday I was much more an observer. What went on didn't lend itself to participating too much.

(P-O journal, 9/5/1991)

Gradually I began to interact with individual children, small groups, and the large group:

Drawing with children. The children gathered around me. I was sitting in the red rocking chair with an elf cap on my head, a straw goat and candles in a wooden candlestick and told them about Christmas in Finland. I said I wanted to do that because they had helped me in my research this fall. We then proceeded to draw something that they had learned with their teachers. All went to work right away except for Dean, who wrinkled his paper, drew scribbles on it and finally threw it on the floor after punching a hole in the paper.

(P-O journal, 12/15/1991)

We discussed my role in Christine's room after the data collection, and Christine's feelings about an extra person in the room:

H: Could you just describe how my coming to your classroom and being there made you feel and what you would have liked me to do in a different way?

C: I don't know. It didn't really bother me. There were a couple of days that you left with that camera and I regretted some of the things that I said. I know one day . . . Paul was dancing around and I thought, they're not going to understand why you are turning flips, they are going to think is he supposed to be in kindergarten not first grade. You know, I worry about that. Man! That is a terrible thing to say to a kid . . . I cannot believe that she said that to a kid! So maybe it made me more aware of . . .

H: Of what you are actually doing?

C: I'm actually saying, which is good for me I think. Most times, I didn't always go home feeling like this, but a couple of times when you walked out of the room, you know, and it was the people with discipline problems that made me feel that way, and, which goes back to maybe I need to learn to accept Paul turning flips, but I haven't gotten there yet!

H: Well, it is difficult! Well, I wonder why it is that we are so worried about the discipline ideas. Like you said, maybe it is just children being children.

C: Right, exactly. I mean, and that is probably why we worry about it. Sometimes you know Paul wanted to show off in front of the camera and that is a real natural thing for a first-grader to want to do. Why couldn't I accept that and not worry about it? And I think my bottom fear was that somebody would say she has no control over those kids, and just like you said, it has been put, that kind of pressure has been put in us so much as teachers to have good discipline in your classroom, and I haven't moved away from that any more than I have from 'I am going to paddle you if you don't stop', because that is the ultimate punishment in the South.

H: Yes, it is like the concept of teaching is somehow, it is so interlinked with the idea of disciplining the children. And some of the, I guess, in some of the answers that the children gave when I asked them you know: If you got to be the teacher for one day when you woke up and you would not be yourself, you would be the teacher, what would you do? Some of them had the idea that as teachers, that it is the disciplining that is the teaching part of teaching.

C: Isn't that funny. Because we try to make it such a classroom thing, you know, we still talk about what do you think the best thing would be to do when . . . but still, all our job, but I see what you are saying.

H: I don't know what we could do to make the feeling of the [school] like our home away from home.

C: And part of it is the noise level in our room, and the looks we get from outside; I think that bothers us, but it has just been built into us so much that control in your classroom means you are a real good teacher, that even though deep down we know that is not what it is.

H: And you know control from the outside, that goes [back] to the authority business. Do we want our children to be self-controlling or do we want them to think that we've got to behave because Ms. Scott wants us?

C: And that is probably the area that I need the most work in, how to make them self-controllable. You know, want to control themselves, more than wanting me to tell them what is right.

H: But you are doing, you have added a lot of fun things like self-control through music, those things are really nice.

C: I mean, probably if I picked one thing that was the best thing I have added this year, would be the music, and to teach through music.

(Second interview, 1/14/1992)

We discussed classroom problems and general educational problems openly. Although I can only make estimations of Christine's experience with me in the classroom in terms of empowerment, these discussions to me were an indication that she was also gaining from our dialogue. We discussed the social programming that limits us and the possibilities of looking and experiencing outside of the programming. In a phone conversation (2/8/92) Christine disclosed that she felt pretty good about the experience because I 'didn't come there in judgment'.

Jasmine's and Christine's collaboration

Jasmine's and Christine's situation is interesting. They have taught side by side nearly thirteen years. Christine was first Jasmine's intern when she was studying. They have a deep respect for each other (Jasmine's first interview, 7/26/1991). They share fifty-five students. They switch groups daily, yet their children know: 'Ms. Scott's my teacher', 'Ms. Barton is mine.' Their assistant teacher, Mrs. Durant, who is assigned to Jasmine, helps both teachers. The interaction between the two teachers interested me because it seemed so seamless. The years together have made them understand each other with very minute clues, at least from an observer's perspective: a lifted eye-brow or a glance seem to communicate a whole conversation. They are aware of what the other is doing. Flexibility is the key in close collaboration like this:

H: At 9:50 I saw your first interaction with Christine as you exchanged messages about the visitor [Officer Austin]. With very few words you communicated where you were, what needed to be done. Could you describe that moment of communication? Had you been able to share beforehand that he was coming? Was that the first communication about it? Later on when Officer A. didn't show up you said, 'We've got one more [group report].' Do you often try to make your activities match each other's timewise? What goes on in your mind as you are trying to end at the same time?

C: We don't usually have visitors Thursday — and I forgot he was coming. We usually stay on schedule, but we adjust as necessary. We may be too relaxed about it, but we very seldom have conflict about it. We do try to match each other timewise because we planned our schedule together and found what works best most of the time, so we try to achieve that, but we don't go bananas if we can't.

(T-R journal, 9/5/1991)

C: And another thing is like our teaching assistant told me, Friday I was not in school because there was a death in the family and I was out and she told me, she said: well, the substitute was real firm, that was her description of her. Jasmine said she was screaming and hollering. She was hateful sounding [inaudible] and she said she was very firm and she had no trouble with Dean, he did everything she told him to do, which made me very defensive, you know, it is like you are saying to me that I am not firm enough and that is why he goes. . . .

H: Did you say it to her or just thought about it?

C: No, I just thought it, but then later in front of . . . to Jasmine I said: I understand Dean was really good for the substitute, maybe it is because she was really firm. And Jasmine said he just had a good day, you know he has good days and bad days, and that was one of his good days.

H: That made you feel better.

(Second interview, 1/14/1992)

Usually Christine and I brainstorm ideas . . . every year we look what we've done that year and talk about improvements we need to make. And then before school starts we sit down and work on those.

(First interview, 7/26/1991:4)

Christine and Jasmine share each other's triumphs as well as worries and problems. Together with the children they create an atmosphere in their pod that radiates security, mystery, and warmth.

As I hope these profiles make clear, the overriding reality of pedagogy of empowerment is individual people: teachers, students, researchers, learners of all ages and sizes. We need systemic changes as well; we need large-scale changes in the institutional structures that currently block many empowering pedagogical practices; we need what Sarason calls 'second-order changes' (Fullan, 1991:29). But none of these large-scale changes can bring about empowering learning environments in classrooms without the life-transforming changes from within of people like Patricia, Jasmine, Christine, and Gloria — individual teachers becoming more than teachers, people becoming people, learners becoming more fully human.

Chapter 4

Empowering Classroom Practices

To be a real friend you have to make yourself vulnerable.
(Patricia, 7/17/1991)

This chapter will be devoted to the empowering classroom practices I observed, including reflective thinking, personal disclosures, sense of ownership in the classroom and interaction, both verbal and non-verbal. In the section on interaction I will be exploring different relationships: teacher-student, student-student, teacher-teacher, teacher-parent, teacher-researcher, and researcher-student relationships. The section on empowering nonverbal interaction covers touching, proximity, eye-contact and facial expressions, gestures, posture, appearance, environmental factors, and chronemics in the classroom.

Reflective Thinking

As John Dewey (1933) stresses, reflective action can replace routine action. The changes that Patricia, Gloria, Jasmine, and Christine have made in their teaching practices and philosophy — from non-discerning to intuitively discerning teachers, and increasingly moving toward educated discernment — illustrate Dewey's claim in powerfully suggestive ways.

Reflection means thinking, but it is *more* than thinking conceived as considering, pondering, contemplation, speculation, and reasoning (Cruickshank, 1987). For Dewey reflective thinking is 'relative, persistent, careful consideration of any belief or supposed form of knowledge in light of the grounds that support it and further conclusions to which it tends' (1933:9). Like the other empowering practices in this chapter, reflective 'thinking is not an exclusive activity, something we can do without anything else. We do not suspend learning, remembering, or other aspects of mental life in order to engage in thought. Rather, thought permeates everything we do — it is the business of the brain' (Smith, 1990:31). 'Learning to think is less a matter of instruction than of experience and opportunity. Experience must provide familiarity with the topics and subjects that thought should address and also the confidence that underlies the disposition and authority to think on particular matters' (Smith, 1990:124).

Examples of how the reflective thinking of empowering teachers makes learning exciting for children abound in my data. I asked Jasmine about their time at learning centers and she thought there were many benefits of reporting orally on their activities. She does this frequently, with children responsible for their group activity or free center time; the children will engage in an experience, then discuss and reflect on what they did. She responded:

> Reporting is a reflection of the learning (and teaching) that has taken place in that class period and all the other class periods. The purposes are to develop language, foster self-esteem, reinforce concepts, foster respect for each other, increase listening skills, discuss problems, promote a higher level of thinking, a time for self-evaluation, teacher evaluation, and I could go on and on. It does require lots of patience. The problems are having patience at the beginning to 'listen' to incomplete sentences, sign language (shoulder shrugs, blank stares etc.) and having enough time.
>
> (T-R journal, 9/26/1991)

I found Jasmine's way of handling these group report situations most interesting:

H: I am fascinated by your ability to provide children with situations that allow them to think, and think about their own thinking. If you think about your teaching career, can you remember always seeing the importance of doing so, or is it something that you have perfected over the years? How conscious are your attempts to force children to think?

J: I think I've always done it some, but I'm more conscious of it now. Sometimes when I plan I try to think of questions I can ask to encourage them to think.

(Jasmine, T-R journal, 10/30/1991)

She is well aware, reflectively aware, not only of what she is trying to facilitate in her children, but of her own responsibility as a teacher in pursuing this goal. Her own increased reflective awareness of this has made her better able to give children the freedom they yearn for to gather experiences through varied activities — experiences that can be used as the subject matter and food for thought that Smith (1990) talks about.

H: I observed you also giving value to the children's own experiences: 'You may learn something about this pumpkin that I've never noticed before,' you said as you were preparing children to work with the big pumpkin. Do you actively seek situations like this, plan them ahead of time or do they just naturally happen as the day goes by?

> *J:* Sometimes there is planning, sometimes it just happens naturally.
>
> (Jasmine, T-R journal, 10/30)

Thinking is a natural activity that the brain does 'effortlessly and remarkably well' (Smith, 1990:31). It requires, though, in order to function well — to prevent the neocortex, the organ for thinking, from down-shifting or shutting down — an atmosphere free of threat and anxiety (Nummela Caine and Caine, 1991; Hart, 1986). In order to make that possible the children need to feel that their feelings are not only permissible but welcomed and part of their human experience.

Does it sound strange to have to spell this out? Isn't it obvious that children's feelings are part of human experience? All too often the traditional classroom denies children's feelings, suppresses them, even teaches children to feel ashamed of them. Surprisingly, the empowering encouragement of reflective thinking in the four classrooms I studied simultaneously encouraged and welcomed feelings — a part of experience that has long been considered opposed to or unrelated to thinking. And the integration of feeling and thinking helps children learn better: 'We have the best research reminding us of healthy, happy, positive, holistic, active, interactive, playful, multifaceted ways children *best* learn,' Mimi Brodsky Chenfeld writes. 'Despite this wealth of knowledge, plus more powerful information from our own hearts, why are so many children still learning that learning is a grim, scary, closed-in, superstructured, silent process where failure, humiliation, alienation, and disappointment are present every day' (1992:89).

> *H:* At the end of the intense work period the children had with their journals, Edward sighed, 'No wonder we are so tired, we have been working so hard!' Have you discussed with them about how their work makes them feel?
>
> *P:* No. Not really. They've mentioned this several times. Maybe we should discuss it. Edward . . . usually spends a good bit of time daydreaming or 'thinking things through!'
>
> (Patricia, T-R journal, 10/23/1991)

Two weeks after this conversation took place Patricia wanted me to come and see how children were learning to evaluate their own writing. They were comparing two pieces of their writing — both from their journals — and writing about the differences in them. The children were able to see their progress in a very concrete way. No praise was needed; the satisfaction that shone from the children's eyes as they noticed their progress was intrinsically rewarding.

The teachers see the value of reflective thinking in helping the children discover their own strengths as learners and in becoming more self-directed and independent.

Teaching them, but also allowing them to be thinkers and doers, I think you've got to do that. I think that you have to set the tone very soon, as soon as you can, because they see you as such an authority figure at first and they always will see you that way to a certain extent, but through the period of the year you have to let them see that you are only one way they learn, and as soon as they realize, and you have to keep telling them that, that they will learn through books, through their parents, from each other, they learn all sorts of ways, and they should never, ever depend on their teacher to be the only person to teach them . . . we have a rule in our room here that when they are in their response groups that they have to ask three people before they can ask me.

(Patricia's second interview, 1/10/1992)

'Teachable moments' and spur-of-the-moment situations provide times where authentic and deep dialogues can be generated. These are moments when opening up to the whole child is crucial — to the child's pain, bewilderment, joy or uncertainty; the whole experience.

Today . . . this little boy came to me and said: 'My mother and I had to run out of the house last night; my daddy came in drunk and he had a gun.' Instead of just stopping and just going on and teaching the skill in that sentence I'd probably sit down and say, 'I know that it made you feel really frightened. What are some other times that we are scared?' And you know, talk about it being okay to be scared and what do we do for help when we are afraid. I think teachable moments are more important, so when things come up that I haven't planned for, it's easy for me to stop and focus on that and then just simply make a note that we didn't do what I intended to do, you know. I have red marks all over that we didn't do this and this and I put it in my plan book and do it another time and make notes about what we did do so that I have records of that.

(Christine's first interview, 7/30/1991)

Jasmine thinks that the changes they have made in their teaching have not only made it possible to accommodate the different backgrounds of the children but also help children think and become more autonomous learners while enjoying learning all along.

I feel like in the whole language and teaching across the curriculum, we do a better job of that [accommodating different backgrounds] than if we were teaching in a traditional type of classroom, because I think we give enough, open enough situations, where those who are from a background that would encourage a higher level thinking, that they can take the ball and run with it, but yet those who have not had the background, who are not used to any in-depth thinking, and you know have not communicated a lot, then they have room to contribute and to grow and lots of times, I have found those who are from that kind of background can see things that the others can not. I have been very surprised at that.

(Jasmine's first interview, 7/26/1991)

This also shows how important it is for every child to be validated in the classroom. On the basis of those valuable experiences that everyone brings to the group, children may feel like full contributing members in the classroom community. When the children's experiences are welcomed, the children become teachers in the classroom. Teachers become their students' students.

Reflective thinking is connected with taking responsibility and initiative — with becoming an independent learner. Learning to reflect on one's own actions is a valuable tool for people to grow up with in order to make independent decisions and become lifelong learners. Patricia says it is important for children to 'do things independently and not feel like they've got to wait on somebody to give them direction' (First interview, 7/17/1991). As independent thinkers the children will be free to utilize the experiences and materials available to them to make decisions that they can live with. The same goes for teachers and researchers. The freedom to inquire creatively even in a research project that is an academic exercise is important in terms of the professional growth of a researcher (Bargar and Duncan, 1990).

One part of being reflective in a classroom is modeling learning for the children. One day Gloria was reading to the children and accidentally read *cookie* instead of *curtain*. She then said, 'I didn't look carefully enough.' 'This is an important part of my teaching,' Gloria says. 'I try to model what to do when you make a mistake. The children are learning to draw from their own knowledge and evaluate their own performance' (T-R journal, 10/22/1991). Gloria wants children 'to come to understand there isn't always one way or one right answer' (T-R journal, 11/19/1991). Having to produce different solutions to problems helps children prepare for real-life situations. An example of a discussion after reading the book *Ten Apples Up on Top* (Le Sieg 1961) illustrates this: 'You asked the children if they could walk around with four apples on top of your head. Randall said, "If you tied a rope to the stems you could!" You encouraged him and noted how this is the way you would be able to do that' (T-R journal, 11/19/1991). Gloria emphasizes that she wants the 'children to think, solve their own problems and become independent learners' (T-R journal, 11/19/1991).

Due to their involvement in the FIRST Grant all four teachers, Patricia, Gloria, Jasmine and Christine, have done workshops for other teachers, which is one indication of their need and willingness to share professional concerns and ideas. Much of what goes on in these workshops consists of teachers' own reflections on what they did, what worked, and building on each others reflections to plan for another time.

Verbal Interaction

That is what we build our relationship on — communicating with each other.
(Christine, 1/14/1992)

'Interpersonal understanding is dynamic' (DeVries, Haney and Zan, 1991) —
and the dynamics of interpersonal understanding, or what I am calling interaction, is essential to empowering practices. People relating to each other,
people caring for each other, people feeling like part of a supportive group —
people empower each other, in interactive dialogue with each other. People
relating to each other tyrannize each other, too, use power-over to deprive
others of power-with (Kreisberg, 1992), oppress each other, stifle each other.
The best way to reverse the effects of such interpersonal tyranny is not to
depersonalize the classroom — not to replace the despotic teacher with the
teacher as bureaucrat, dispenser of worksheets. The only way to empower the
disempowered is to humanize interaction: to give caring, sharing and supporting pride of place in the classroom, and to allow each member of the community their voice.

> We talked about how they have started helping each other, for in-
> stance in spelling. I mentioned that I had seen some of that happening
> with the children and Patricia said: 'This is how it *has* to be! Teaching
> does not work unless there is caring between the children too.'
> We went back inside. There were a few drops of rain that speeded
> our departure, Ken found a Ninja Turtle in the gutter coming into
> the building. We all went in, I started the taping and Patricia told
> children about a choice they could make, namely write their journals
> or keep writing the draft they had started before recess. When Patricia
> asked who had made a choice, half the class excitedly shot their hands
> up. 'What is your choice?', Patricia asked everyone. They went to
> their tables to work on what they chose to do. I circled around,
> adjusted the video camera, and came to Lassandra's table. I sat down
> on one of the chairs and started talking to Lassandra about her writ-
> ing. She had a hard time thinking about what to say about her pets.
> Pretty soon Ken walked over with a mischievous grin on his face.
> 'May I have a hug?', I said. He hugged me and declared, 'This is my
> seat.' 'Do you think I should move somewhere else?' I moved to the
> absent Latasha's chair.
> Everyone works on their journals, I take my field notes and start
> writing down my observations. Matt has the globe on the table and
> is writing about that, Quinnus moves over to draw a map taking
> some names of the countries off the globe. Tim asks where I am
> from. I show on the map how I flew across the North Pole to the
> West coast and drove across the country. They ask me about the
> weather. Matt looks at me writing my field notes and turns to

Lassandra and says: 'When she goes back to her mother, she can tell her all that stuff' pointing at my field notes.

Tim: You are not really writing in a journal?

H: Yes, I am. I am writing about what I am learning and what I am thinking about.

Lassandra: I wish Latasha was here today (sigh) — she is my best friend.

Tim: We are all friends here.

Lassandra: Yes, we're all like sisters and brothers in this class.

(P-O journal, 10/15/91)

Teacher-student

Some days I feel like I communicate really, really well, and some days, if the day goes well, like yesterday, I feel like I haven't communicated as well, because I've been dealing too much with self-control with the children.

(Patricia's second interview, 1/10/1992)

The fluidity of constant, dynamic change and the little triumphs when connections are made are apparent in the story of Dean. He expresses a lot of anger in the classroom, especially towards adults (including me, who had no official authority over him, but who as an adult probably represented authority), which has gradually led Christine to suspect physical abuse in his home. For this reason, she has not contacted the young mother every time she or Jasmine would like to. But in an empowering teacher's care breakthroughs happen in small ways:

C: Today was a good day; he had a bad experience in Mr. Mullins' room [physical education], and usually when he does, it blows the rest of the day, because he goes there right after breakfast; but he came in and came to the carpet with all the children, and many days he just sits at his desk, and I decided after Christmas to try to coax him to be a part of the group, and so I have tried to get him to come to the carpet with everybody else. Some days it's a battle, and I say: 'Just forget it!' you know, but today I didn't say a word, I looked down and there he was, he was all excited, then he went to Mr. Mullins and when Mr. Mullins says it's time to go back, well, they'd already had a battle. He [Dean] had baseball cards, he [Mr. Mullins] wanted him to put them up and do one thing and then he could play with them, and he said, 'I'm not doing anything.' He said that he would not do any hitting, anything, and then he [Mr. Mullins] said, 'It's time to go back,' and he said, 'I'm not going back.' So, he just, I mean the kids were freezing outside waiting for Dean to make a decision and he [Mr. Mullins] just physically picked him up, he said, 'I will carry you in, because these kids are cold,' so he physically carried him. Dean was screaming and hollering, 'I can walk, I can walk,' he [Mr. Mullins] said, 'Fine,' so he put him down, he laid down on the cold concrete, so Mr. Mullins just picked him up again and got him inside, and he says, 'Dean, you cannot go on to Ms. Scott's room making this much noise because you are going to disrupt everybody else, and I'm going to take you to the office and when you settle down you can go to Ms. Scott's room.' He [Mr. Mullins] said he got ready to leave and he [Dean] stopped and said, 'I'm going to go back to my class.' 'Are you ready to go to Ms. Scott's class?' He said, 'Yes,' so he [Mr. Mullins] said 'Come on,' and he said: 'Oh, I can't go in there like this. Look at my face.' He [Mr. Mullins] said: 'Then go wash your face and then go.' 'I'm not just ready to go in there,' so he left and I knew that he was in the office . . . I'm not really sure when he re-entered the room, but he was very quiet and not mad, and he was OK, so then he was with Jasmine, and Jasmine let him work with Ms. Idries in the room one-on-one today, and they were counting by twos, and she had trouble at first to get him to do it, then he saw a book about whales, in one of Andrea's boxes, it was sticking out. He said, 'I want to see that book.' She said, 'You do this and in the free time we'll look at all the books you want.' He did it, but it was neat, he understood it, I mean you know, which tells us that he can do that if he can be focused, and away from what's bugging him so much.

H: Something important happened today.

C: Yes, and then he went outside with the kids, I mean Ms. Idries praised him and everybody, kids clapped for him, when he showed them his page, I mean automatically, nobody told them to, they broke out into applause and after recess, he came in and I just closed with storytelling and he just walked up, didn't make a sound, listened to every story.

(Second interview, 1/14/1992)

Interaction in the classrooms is complex. It is connected with classroom management, the way the teacher was brought up to believe things should be done, what a child should be like, the way she thinks about teaching, her role in the group, what she thinks her responsibility is, and so on. In other words, the values and beliefs that the teacher holds are crucial to the shape interactive dialogues take in a classroom community.

H: What do you think your strengths are [as a communicator and interactor]?

P: Well, I really want them to do well, I want them to be good readers. I want them to feel good about what they can learn that they write well and I want them to have self-control, too, and that has been the hardest thing with this class right here.

H: Yes, I just read one of your entries in the journal where you said 'I work so hard on self-control' (Laughter).

P: Well, some days it is so wonderful and they are so proud of themselves at the end of the day. They know.

H: I think it is kind of funny that they know the term so well.

P: Oh, yes, they certainly know the term very well. But that is, I think you have got to have self-control, you cannot tell them, I don't expect them to want me to turn around. That's teacher control. They know that. I say that is me controlling you, and I will not always be there to control you.

H: So motivation to learn and self-control are really very well interlinked.

P: Oh, yes, I think they have to be. They have to realize that they are in control of themselves. They are in control of their learning ultimately. I will be gone, there will be someone else, but every year the only permanent thing will be themselves. And so they have to take charge of themselves and in their learning they have to make choices and they've got to try to make good choices, and if they don't they have to be able to take the consequences and not think it's somebody else's fault . . . and that is hard to do.

(Second interview, 1/10/1992)

What Patricia is talking about here, although it is at first difficult to make the connection, is *classroom management*. The reason it is difficult to connect Patricia's concern for her children's ability to make choices with classroom management is that the latter is usually thought of as discipline, specifically as punishment — whether corporal or behavioral (what behaviorists euphemistically call *consequences*).

'So the teacher put him in the corner', Harry Chapin (1987) sings in *Flowers Are Red* of the little boy whose flowers were 'too colorful' — 'she said, "It's for your own good. And you won't come out till you get it right, and are responding like you should." ' This good behaviorist program, which works because 'finally he got lonely, frightened thoughts filled his head', is very different from the encouragement of personally responsible choices that Patricia practices in her classroom. Since she tends to empower children to make these choices primarily through nonverbal channels, I want to hold off discussing those channels until the nonverbal section; but it is important to note at this juncture that there is a significant difference between punishing children for bad behavior and rewarding them for good behavior, on the one hand, and providing an environment where they can feel good about themselves and the other people in the classroom. The former method sets up a mechanistic antecedents-consequences system that bureaucratizes discipline and mechanizes the child; the latter operates on the assumption that a child (or any person) feeling good about himself will feel good about others as well, and will naturally, through an ongoing process of trial and error, learn to integrate personal desires with group needs, the assertion of self with group accommodation.

Corporal punishment is allowed in Mississippi schools, as it is in twenty-two other in the United States (Newsletter of the Committee to End Violence against the Next Generation, 1993). Growing up and living under oppressive practices like this makes it difficult to move away from it. For many children — and certainly their parents — paddling and spanking are natural (Children's interviews), and the four teachers in my study are themselves not far from that reigning assumption either. School B, Christine's school, allows physical punishment, and her background is anchored in the authoritarian punishment mentality; she finds herself struggling, trying to break away from the legacy of that tradition. As she moves from power-over children toward power-with children in the classroom she carries the baggage of her experiences: 'In all my life it was said to me through authoritative figures, "If you don't stop, I'm going to paddle you." Or "if you don't do this, I'm going to do that" and she still finds herself doing this a lot, although she does not want to. It's hard to remove myself from that, even though I don't want it to be that way' (Second interview, 1/14/1992). These are the times when it is easiest to slip back to the way things used to be in the teacher's childhood. This is probably why it is easier for teachers to keep teaching the way they were taught rather than teaching the way they were taught to teach (Jones, 1984). The bottom fear, Christine admits, is that somebody can point to her and say, 'She has no control over those kids.' In other words, on the societal level she is expected to adhere to the rule: Control from the outside and do it by paddling (Saville-Troike, 1985). In her second interview (1/14/1992) Christine talks about paddling as *the ultimate punishment* that teachers and parents use because that is the way they have been programmed.

Gloria agrees that paddling solves nothing. 'It didn't do any good' and yet, since paddling is in the rules as an appropriate school procedure, teachers find even their own administrators paddling without really knowing why (Phone conversation, 3/12/1992). It is easier to keep doing what has been done before than stop and look at the reasons for doing things.

Paying attention, or the good discipline that Christine mentions, is frequently equated with silence in the classroom (Gilmore, 1985; Mattson, 1985). Silence is also what organizes our understanding of spoken language. Silence, respect, and bodily postures are connected in that sometimes silence is not thought of as acceptable if it is not accompanied by a body posture communicating respect for the authority (Gilmore, 1985).

The ingrained need for silence in the way teachers think is hard to uproot; before one can even begin to uproot it, it first needs to be noticed. I recently observed a student-teacher who seemed to be constantly shushing the children — so much that, five minutes into the lesson, I started tallying her shushes. After a twenty-minute lesson with a group of only six children, she had shushed the children into silence twenty-three times — although no disruptions whatsoever happened. Afterwards I asked her if she had noticed herself repeatedly quieting children down. 'I didn't hear myself do it!' was her embarrassed reply.

Controlling is in the vocabulary of most teachers. Some need it there, some want to be rid of it, but it is hard to eradicate, because the society and everything that teachers have been taught to believe goes against even becoming aware of their controlling, let alone making moves to change it.

> *H*: When the yellowjacket buzzed around you, including sitting on your belt, what were your thoughts? What did you think when you walked in the classroom with the commotion? Did you think the group responded to your absence with chaos (especially with me being there)? You also told me your class was showing off because I was there. How else besides the face-making in front of the camera, you think this came out in their behavior?
>
> *P*: I'm really not afraid of wasps, etc., because I've never had one to sting me if I just leave it alone. One will probably surprise me one day!
>
> I knew immediately it would be hard for them to settle down. I guess I was disappointed because I've worked on self-control. This has happened twice before when we had someone new in our room. I thought about it after I got home and I realized that my children were the same way last year at the beginning of the year. Later they became so accustomed to having visitors that they didn't even seem to notice. This group is just being normal. I just don't like to use so much time settling them down . . . There are many strong personalities in this room. Several seem to have never had to consider the rights of others. This week has been great, however! Ken still hurts others. But several children are really trying to help him. We have a new little boy and he told me he loves our school. The other children have been so good to him. When I see this and the excitement when we share and discuss I know things are moving along ok. They'll never be perfect nor will they ever have a perfect teacher. We'll just muddle along together!
>
> (T-R journal, 10/3/1991)

The muddling along together, the same experiences that are the greatest obstacles for changing for teachers, can also be 'one of our greatest assets if we reflect on our experience critically' (Kreisberg, 1992:202). Educators lack opportunities to express their thinking and feelings about learning and teaching. This lack of opportunity can lead into accepting school culture as it is, unchanging and stable rather than invest energy in challenging one's own beliefs and assumptions and working towards changing the routines that are not beneficial for anyone in the school community (Weissglass, 1990).

Exploring and supporting, as well as helping children discover meaningful learning situations, is seen in Henry's statement: 'Well, I guess I feel like she makes good stories. She can tell them out easy. She makes the story kind of real with her voice' (Henry, children's interview, 12/3/1991). If the child likes the teacher and wants to please her, is that discipline? If the child gets excited about learning, loves to read and find things out, and associates those loves with an exciting teacher who also loves to do those things, is that discipline? The more empowering teaching becomes, the more interested and involved in children's lives teachers become, the harder it is to talk about discipline. The empowering teacher-student relationship cannot be inherently disciplinary because, as Freire (1970) and Buber (1970) both insist, the hierarchical positions are constantly broken down by reciprocity, by role-interchangeability: when the teacher is capable of learning from students, especially of learning when she has violated their individuality and thus herself become a 'discipline problem', there is no question of the teacher being someone who is there to provide discipline, or of the student being someone in need of the teacher's discipline. Self-control is essential in groups, and in empowering groups everybody learns it from everybody else, including themselves.

The different personalities in every group make life interesting in a classroom: 'Everybody has their strong points, but everybody doesn't have all strong points' (Patricia, second interview, 1/10/1992). The individuality of children is inviolable in the empowering classroom. We talked about a child who was labeled rowdy before he ever got to Patricia's class. Patricia points out how easy it would be to use power-over on him and crush him for good. 'He is the worst kid in the room as far as behavior. But I absolutely love him . . . This kid feels good about himself. And there's no way I'm going to take that away from him, but I could. It would be very easy for me to do that to him this year. And that's what happens so much' (Second interview, 1/17/1992). Patricia is aware of her power as a teacher. She admits that there is a fine line between breaking the child's spirit and guiding him to learn how to live in a classroom community. This is the frightening part of teaching. Without a sense of responsibility and a strong ethical commitment to becoming fully human, a teacher can choose to destroy lives as well as support them.

Student-student

In the four classrooms children work together in groups, pairs and alone. Letitia describes her favorite things to do in school as

I like it when we get to have centers and stuff and we have groups. I like to do books. Me and my friend Hannah are doing a Christmas book and you see, we have white and red and white paper [motions with her hands how they are stacked together] and I drew paper and she drew the Christmas tree and we are going to staple it and we are collaborating.

(Interview, 12/4/1991)

As children have chances to spend time with each other and share experiences with each other, a genuine bond starts developing between them. When someone has a strong experience, others empathize and provide support:

Heather rushed over to me and said: 'Do you know that this is Thomas' *last* day in our classroom!' 'I didn't know that. Where is he going?' 'He is moving to Minnesota and we will be so sad!' Ryan, Quinnus, Amanda, and Charlotte come by too and all of them express their dismay at having to part with Thomas. Heather said, 'I asked Thomas if he cried when he heard that they were going to have to move. I would have!' Thomas came to see me, too. He just looked at me. I said, 'I heard you are going to move to Minnesota.' He looked at me with forlorn eyes and hurled himself at me. I hugged him long and tight while he was hanging onto me as if being chased. My throat was constricted. He did not say a word. Just looked at me. I said, 'I think you might get to know some new people where you are going to move and they will become your friends.' That didn't sound very convincing. He looked at me and said, 'They have this much snow over there' measuring the depth of snow with his hands. 'That's exciting,' I said, 'I like snow.' It was the one link that he and I would share since just the previous week I had been in their class telling them about Finland, showing pictures of snow, children skiing and sledding.
Later on when the children went outside for recess I asked Patricia about Thomas moving. 'Doesn't he look just absolutely crushed. He is so sad. This morning the children gave him cards and letters they had written to him. You should have seen his face. He was so happy when he got the pile of cards. It was all for *him*. I asked him if he was going to read them right away or save them till he got to Minnesota. He said he wasn't sure but maybe he would save them for later.' Mrs. Hawthorne said she thought the family moved quite a bit and it was hard for their son, who had this year felt like he was a part of a group that cared for him. Patricia told me that the children had suggested that they write to Thomas about what's going on in the classroom.

(P-O journal, 1/31/1992)

In February Thomas moved back. I heard about it as I visited Mary, the student-teacher in the classroom. 'Did you *know* Thomas is back in our class!' It was Heather again telling me the news. Patricia was apprehensive about him catching up with the rest of the class but Thomas seemed content at being in the class he knew so well and where he felt he was important.

In classrooms where empowering practices abound, children learn to care about each other in significant ways. Here is an example of how children independently take care of problems that show up within a classroom.

Dear Heather
I'm srry Heather   [I am sorry Heather]
I was so mad I'm   [I was so mad. I'm
srry iam   [sorry. I am.]
i will nevre   [I will never]
do that agin Do you acsept   [do that again. Do you accept}
my a pulchey yes or no   [my apology? Yes or no]
   to you
   I love you
   Hannah

The word *yes* had a circle around it, and Patricia found the letter on the floor some time in October. This illustrates not only how the children are capable of solving their interpersonal problems when they arise, but also how they have discovered that they can use their newly acquired talent of writing in taking care of such things. Here is another example of children's group work:

At Ken's table Letitia was the monitor, and she did a firm job of guiding her flock. Ken kept wanting to go sharpen his pencil. They all told me he wants to sharpen his pencil just to get up and do something else. Ken vehemently denied he was ever trying to do that. After a while of concentrated work effort by all children in the group, Ken very nicely asked if he could sharpen his pencil, as if the previous conversation had never occurred, which is when Amanda suggested that Leslie really check if Ken's pencil was dull enough to sharpen. Letitia gave permission after looking at the pencil, hesitating a little. After sharpening his pencil Ken came back, studied the pencil and fiddled with it and it broke. 'You just sat there and broke it,' said Letitia. 'I didn't sit there and break it!', countered Ken. Letitia took the pencil and walked over to sharpen it herself, brought it back, sat down and said in a very motherly voice, 'That's why I didn't want *you* to sharpen it. Oh, Ken, Ken, Ken,' she sighed and shook her head with each 'Ken'. It is at this point that Ken came to you [Patricia] to see if he could resharpen his pencil (which you did for him) because it was smearing things on his paper. Later on Ken had an urge to write about his mother's birthday instead of about pilgrims that didn't capture his interest very much. He asked Ms. Hawthorne who told him he would have to wait till journal writing time for that.

(P-O journal, 11/22/1991)

H: Observing this whole conversation seemed to me that the children are learning to trust themselves as decision-makers. Their conversation is not just back-and-forth yes-no type arguing but they are allowing more unpredictable, more complex and fruitful conversations to take place.

P: I think they have more confidence in themselves. They are more willing to state their opinion freely. They realize how much they have ignored [been unaware of] their reading and writing because they had a part in their evaluation. That also has given them confidence.

(T-R journal, 11/22/1991)

The four teachers are concerned about the future of the groups. Their classrooms, where children are engaged in work with partners or groups, are quickly forgotten or actively unlearned in later grades, where collaboration is seen as cheating (Smith, 1986). Patricia wishes that her children were allowed to stay together, to continue growing together and to develop further in understanding what it means to be in a community and share life with others (Second interview, 1/10/1992). 'True collaboration is like two people carrying a heavy object that neither of them could carry alone' (Smith, 1986:198).

I witnessed a conversation, very complex and argumentative but not hostile, between Michael and Heather. Heather was the leader of the day and said leaders could teach other children something. Daniel didn't like the idea and said, 'I'm not gonna learn anything from you! We probably already know everything you have to teach us — at least *I* know!' They kept giving reasons for their own positions about the validity of their personal knowledge and experiences till Michael uttered a line that totally amazed Heather, who just looked at him with her mouth open. This is what Michael, vigorously pointing with his index finger, said, 'You can't say that because you are you and I am me!' It occurred to me that by emphasizing how important everyone's own work is (sharing it, respecting by listening when others read their piece) you have helped them to find their own voice, and work towards a stronger sense of self-esteem and self-respect (This also reminds me of what one of your kids said to the librarian, 'I guess I like my friends better this year.')

(Patricia, T-R journal, 11/22/1991)

Perhaps Derek sums up classroom interaction best. I asked him what his favorite thing to do in school is. His answer was, 'When we have problems we solve them' (Interview, 12/3/1991). His answer reflects the acceptance of natural disagreements in the group, yet a feeling that despite those everyone is liked and welcomed into the classroom community.

It is significant, I think, that of all the subsections on interaction, this was the easiest to write. In an empowering classroom, relationships are between equals, and this makes the student-student relationship crucial. As Kreisberg writes:

Empowerment embodies the idea of self-determination, a process through which individuals and communities increasingly control their own destinies without imposing on others. The link between controlling one's own life and valued resources while simultaneously respecting others' rights to do the same is crucial to empowerment theory.

(Kreisberg, 1992:191)

When this works in practice, as it so clearly does in the four classrooms I studied, much of the collective self-determination is performed in and by groups of children.

Teacher-teacher

Relationships with colleagues are important for teachers. Since teaching can be a very lonely, isolated job (Troen and Boels, 1988) the support of people who understand what is involved in teaching is crucial:

they keep me going . . . we may not get the recognition that we sometimes think we deserve from other people, we do from our colleagues and when you're down or when you have a problem, we have a good working relationship at our school and there's always somebody that can say well you did this, or it will be better tomorrow and so they are important to me. They keep me up and going, you know, along with my children.

(Gloria, first interview, 8/22/1991)

Christine looked at my list of different teacher roles and responded to the collegial role in a way that surprised her:

C: I can see when I started looking over this how much I've changed just over the last couple of years. I probably would not have considered myself, my role as a colleague as very important several years ago, but now I think it is real important that as a colleague I share what's happening in my room as a whole language teacher.

133

H: You were timid to do that before?

C: No, I just — there just wasn't anything different that I was doing that anybody needed to know about then, I mean you're teaching basal readers, you don't want anybody to tell you how to do it (laughter) and I really think that in the last couple of years as a colleague I have influenced a lot of teachers and I am finding out myself the importance of having that camaraderie with other teachers.

H: You get support from sharing.

C: Right, and I will always learn something, and that is one of the reasons why I like to do the workshops, because I come away having learned something, too, new to me and in the sharing of ideas.

(Second interview, 1/14/1992)

The empowerment that transcends classroom walls allows teachers not only to feel pride in their work, which is denied them as they work by themselves in the loneliness of their own rooms; it also spreads empowerment, passes it on to other classrooms. The changes in the teachers' rooms are grassroot changes that empower others to share and learn from ideas. The teacher-teacher relationship is an invaluable forum for unlearning outdated teaching practices; as Kreisberg points out:

> Our own experience is one of the greatest obstacles to being empowering teachers. But our experience is also one of our greatest assets if we reflect on our experience critically — if we in fact commit ourselves to *unlearning* our experience of what it means to be a teacher in this culture so that we can *relearn* what it means to be a teacher. This is no easy task, since we are all in a sense trapped within experiences — prospective teachers, experienced teachers, and teacher educators alike. I think the implication is that we must commit ourselves to a process of transformation, critical reflection, and risk taking in our educational practice and in our lives.
>
> (Kreisberg, 1992:202)

Weissglass (1990) agrees with Kreisberg but laments that there are so few opportunities for educators to think and work through feelings about teaching and learning and because of this lack of opportunity they are led into accepting the existing practices in school culture. Some of these practices and routines may be harmful or counterproductive but hard to change because they require the changing of assumptions and beliefs (Weissglass, 1990).

However, relationships with colleagues are sometimes problematic as well, especially relationships that underline the difference between a non-discerning and an intuitively discerning teacher. The four teachers I studied find that they can be empowered in certain collegial relationships, but not in others. Because of their personal teaching philosophy and beliefs about education, and the recognition they have received through the grant and invitations to do workshops for other teachers, some colleagues are eager to point out deficiencies in their teaching styles.

For example, Christine (12/18/1991) told me a story about a second-grade teacher in her school who came to her to complain about a 'learning-disabled' child in her class who had been in Christine's class the year before. Christine was shocked at the teacher's use of the term learning-disabled about this boy, who was an avid reader and loved to learn, but the second-grade teacher pointed out that he was weak on phonics; he was unable to distinguish *tub* from *tube* on a worksheet. Why would a child need phonics if he already knows how to read? From Christine's holistic point of view, analytical skills like phonics are a means to the end of reading and writing, and only one means, and by far the least effective means; from the second-grade teacher's analytical point of view, holistic teaching is a shirking of pedagogical responsibilities, a failure to teach the basics.

Moving from a more holistically-oriented classroom to a skills-, seatwork-, and teacher-oriented classroom can be hard on a child. Patricia often plans and dreams with her colleagues about a situation where the children could stay in a classroom with similar philosophy behind it (whole child emphasis) so people could see what a difference it could make in the children's lives.

Jasmine's and Christine's close teaching partnership is an example of how teachers with supportive and innovative practices can ignite each other to work daily in understanding the intricacies of the teaching profession better. They have grown close, but also respect each other enough to allow disagreements. Some years ago when teachers in the district went on strike, Jasmine joined it but Christine did not. Despite differences like this they have managed to work side-by-side in their own idiosyncratic ways. They are not each other's clones.

Teacher-parent

Parents are partners in education (Heck and Williams, 1984). All four teachers feel that parent involvement and mutual support and understanding are crucial to the children in their classroom. Gloria says that 'it's an honor to have [a] child' in her classroom (Second interview, 1/20/1992).

A functioning parent-teacher relationship is where both parties feel comfortable enough to initiate contact whenever needed. Letters home about what is going on in the classroom and what children have learned are ways to add to the feeling of partnership. Parent conferences are important in establishing links between home and school but 'we do not have as many parent conferences as we really need' (Gloria, 1/20/1992). Parent nights with children or without them give teacher and parents time to reflect on what is going on in their child's life.

There were twelve parents participating. Patricia explained her philosophy to them. 'I do what I would do with my own children.' Explained writing, reading, talking, sharing processes as they applied to whole language learning in the classroom. Parents were very attentive, sitting at the edge of their seats, looking around the room for signs of their children's work. Patricia had examples of childrens' work, books published by them, and explained about various activities and homework. ['Everything I send home has a purpose,' she said.] Daily news, journal writing, group sharing, honor roll. Hardly any parents leave when it is over. They go to her and sign up for things to do in the room (book binding, snacks for Friday refreshments, books).

(Patricia, parent meeting, 9/9/1991)

In school B, parent-teacher contacts are sometimes difficult to create due to long driving distances, lack of transportation, sometimes lack of interest. Since parents' working hours and other reasons hinder parent participation in school activities, Christine is especially grateful for those times when connections are made.

C: I had a father come in and read a book for a child and then I had some come in as visitors, and I think probably they are not being involved enough although it's my fault, too. I have great goals every year to involve my parents and then it just seems we get busy doing other things and they don't make themselves readily available and I don't take time to be, or you know, to make the situation available so that they can come in. Or I might send one letter and they don't respond and then I just give up, kind of thing. So it's probably my fault, too. But I've had some parents involved and offer to do things at home like type their stories which I think have been real helpful. I . . . I guess, it kind of comes in cycles. You have a class with parents really interested and then next year there is nobody and we just finished a year when we really didn't have but maybe one or two . . .

(Christine, first interview, 7/30/1991)

Teacher-researcher

I began exploring the teacher-researcher relationship in Chapter 3, in my reflections on participant-observation in each teacher's portrait, and I don't propose to repeat everything I said there. It is important to note, however, that the teacher-researcher relationship is focal to the ethnography of empowerment, which moves beyond the pedagogy of empowerment precisely by taking what teachers and children do in the classroom to the larger academic community — by attempting to pass on pedagogical empowerment to university students in teacher training and other programs, to colleagues in faculty workshops and seminars, to audiences at academic conferences, and to the readers of academic books and articles.

Certainly, as I have said before, I came away from my fall semester in first-grade classrooms feeling excited, enthusiastic about teaching — feeling empowered as a researcher to convey some of that excitement to you, my reader, and also as a teacher to convey some of that excitement to my students (also, incidentally, as the mother of a kindergartener who will be entering first grade next year).

All too often, I think, we 'university people' go into classrooms thinking that we have to help these poor teachers, have to show them how to teach better, and as a result they frequently, and quite rightly, resent us. That feeling dissipates once the researcher relinquishes the notion of his or her superiority, his or her higher position on the academic hierarchy, and enters into a dialogue between equals in which it is equally as likely that the researcher will learn something from the teacher as the other way around. The empowering teacher-researcher relationship will replicate the empowering teacher-student relationship in dissolving hierarchies and distributing learner roles more evenly to all participants in the dialogue. After all, if first-grade teachers can learn from six-year-olds, how difficult can it be for professors of education to learn from exciting, innovative practitioners?

In the case of the four teachers I studied, the empowering dialogue between teacher and researcher was complicated in enormously fruitful ways by the fact that all four teachers had initially been encouraged (and partially funded) in their change by a university professor, Andrea, with whom I too had worked closely, and whose effect on me had been as empowering as it was on the four teachers. The dialogical empowerment between teacher and researcher flowed from Andrea through the teachers to me, and back to Andrea, and from the teachers to Andrea to me and back to the teachers, forming a kind of biofeedback loop of empowerment that is much more effective — to put it mildly — than, say, the teacher doing things on his or her own and being observed by some objective researcher eye.

Researcher-student

The children's unconditional expressions of delight made me feel welcome in their classrooms. They shared their experiences in the classroom and welcomed me to participate in their activities. At recess I would play games with them, or talk to them about what they had done or were going to do, and so on. They also let me know when I had not understood all the intricacies of their classroom life.

Kimberly walked to the group and asked me to help with a spelling of a word. I asked her what the problem was with it and helped her by telling her what the two vowels were. Ken turned to me and said, 'You're supposed to let them sound it out!' [I had been helping Lassandra at her table prior to this, encouraging her to say the words and figure out what she heard in them.] In addition to learning math, reading, writing, etc., your children also tell me they are 'learning not to fight, not to cuss and good manners at lunch'.

(T-R journal, 11/22/1991)

Children were curious about me as a person: did I have kids, what were their names, did they ride the bus, did I always wear glasses, why was my hair so thin and blonde, was I the newslady, why did I have a scarf around my neck, what games did I know, what television programs did I like to watch. I shared a lot about my background, since around Christmas time all four classes were talking about different customs, and in Patricia's room they were 'visiting' several countries around the world in their room by having visitors from those countries — including me, from Finland. The equipment I brought with me was a source of many more questions. Besides the video camera I carried miscellaneous other things (as all educators do): field notes, and my guitar.

Here is Herb's portrait of me in Gloria's classroom.

Drawing 5: Herb's portrait of the ethnographer

The individual child interviews were enjoyable, I believe, for most children as they were for me. After the interview was finished, many lingered on and wanted to just chat. Mack (11/19/1991) urged me to ask another question when I was through with the questions. I asked him what he wanted to be as he grew up: 'a paramedic' was his quick answer, as if he had guessed the right answer in one of the television game shows.

Being more familiar to the children than most visitors gave me many valuable glimpses of children's deeper thoughts about school. This conversation is from my interview with Dean, in December 9:

> I was interviewing Dean, who seemed really quiet to begin with. He wanted to withdraw from the group but really didn't want to have anything to do with me. The opening question was revealing. I asked him what he enjoyed doing in school? 'Nothing', he answered in a sullen voice, turning his body towards the wall so I couldn't see his face. After a few 'nothing' answers, I started getting the idea that he was really angry. I asked how he would teach the class if he got to be the teacher, 'I wouldn't teach them nothing. They are laughing at me. I want to be a fire fighter.' I asked about learning, which he answered another 'nothing' to. I suggested he might need to learn something if he wanted to be a fire fighter at which point he turned to look at me curiously. 'I think you might be angry because you don't want to look at me,' I said. 'That's right, I'm angry because they are always making fun of me!' I said, 'I think you feel that nobody likes you.' He nodded, looked at me and folded his arms protectively around himself. I asked about learning again — he provided another 'nothing' answer. I asked him if he wanted to learn how to take a picture. He immediately got interested and I showed him how to take a picture with my camera. As he left me after the interview and I interviewed other children, I noticed several times his eyes found me and we shared a secret smile with each other. Later on he came to ask if he could take a picture of me and Dustin whom I was interviewing. I let him do that and he left me with a smile on his face.
>
> (Interview with Dean, 12/9/1991)

Nonverbal Interaction

The use of space, the shifting of focus and interpersonal interactions, the constant, dynamic motion in the lives of the classrooms — all this shows up in an interesting way in the videotapes when rewinding or fast-forwarding the tape so that the pictures can be seen. This sometimes captures the feeling the teachers have after a day's work. They are not aware of everything they do, but 'I do know I am exhausted by the end of every week' (T-R journal, Christine, 9/25/1991). Perhaps the metaphor of an amoeba or an ocean best fits the way the group is constantly locating and relocating, making contact and withdrawing from contact.

> The videotape is running, I walk over to Patricia who waits by the blue table with stacks of children's writing. Patricia is sitting higher

on an adult size chair, I sit on a child's chair. We make eye-contact.
I adjust my hair, she moves her glasses on the bridge of her nose. I
glance at my watch. I lean closer to look at the papers she is pulling
out to illustrate some of the ways in which the children's writing has
improved. We share a laugh at some of the cute expressions children
write. We seem to be communicating through the student papers,
deciphering children's inventive spelling, the papers as the focal point
of our attention. The children's utterances become a bond between
us. She looks at them directly, I look at them from an angle, leaning
closer each time she points out another feature of a child's paper. My
posture communicates interest, her posture is almost regal. Patricia
initiates the discussions on a paper explaining the actual event of
writing, I continue to respond to add or point out an interesting
feature. Her tone of voice expresses excitement, her body less so. As
Patricia points out what the children learned she talks faster, her pitch
rises; she has a richly expressive voice, and when it fills with emotion
it is impossible not to be moved. Her eyes and facial features shine
with the same excitement. We discuss the nature of the activity today:
the children will be working on self-evaluations of their early and
later journal writing.

Children come in from recess, some walking, some skipping,
some in their coats, some without. Children find their seats at centers.
The camera is shooting directly at the table where Patricia sits with
nine children getting ready to tackle today's job. Getting the group
ready for work Patricia asks children if they remember the beginning
of their journal writing. They look at Hannah's early work. Some
children are still shifting and settling. She absent-mindedly tugs
Lassandra down into her chair from a standing position, uses gestures
and illustrators (raised hand, pointing) to get the attention of the
group. She makes eye-contact, she smiles. 'Look at both of these
writings,' she says, and explains how they get to look at their own
folders to compare their own journal writing. She hands out an early
work to everyone. 'Hannah is going to look through and find what
she likes' in the later journal. They discuss the importance of putting
down dates and commends them for being able to do so. 'Don't
forget to put the date down,' she reminds them, shaking her finger.
Patricia leans over to talk to Michael. I am sitting behind the tables
outside the circle of the nine children but I can see and hear what is
happening. The videotape picks up all of the sounds in the room.
'Shhh', shushes Patricia, raising her hand, wanting to be heard. She
shushes infrequently — only when the situation demands a little quiet.
The group is concentrating now. 'Who has an early write now?' Most
children raise their hands. She explains that the children will take
these two pieces of writing and put them side-by-side. She holds them
up in front of the children, asking them what kinds of differences

they notice in the two pieces of writing. 'Who is ready?', she asks.
'I'm ready' Michael says and stands up ready to go and others chime
in. 'Hannah is going to go out to the hallway *by herself* and she is
going to write down all the ways in which she thinks she's improved.'
Hannah goes out. Edward comes in to interrupt, Patricia tells him
she'll talk to him in a minute. 'Really look at your papers carefully
and write down everything that you notice.' She holds up Michael's
paper. As children wonder what he is going to do because he has
writing on both sides of his paper Patricia explains that Michael wanted
to conserve trees and a way to do that was to write on both sides of
the paper. Michael gets instructions to go outside in the hallway —
Patricia uses gestures to make sure he understands where. Patricia
asks me to work in the hallway, with Rita. 'Sure,' I say, and Rita and
I go in the hallway, moving the camera as well.

Michael is working on his evaluation lying down, scrunched up
in a contorted position on the floor, and writing. I sit next to Rita,
who has a bad cold and sniffles constantly. Michael is tapping his foot
and rests his leg bent from the knee along the wall. Rita works to find
out differences, I ask an occasional question to help her along. Michael
crawls over to ask me to check if he spelled *illustrations* right. I write
in my field notes. Another class marches by.

(Videotaping, 10/4/1991)

Patricia's class is in perpetual motion, children move, shift, and change
position. Through all this there is no sense of panic in Patricia — though I feel
a little as I watch the scene on videotape later. She assumes that everyone in
the classroom is a responsible person, and they act accordingly. Children are
not immobile or frozen, their natural ways of moving are not blocked. Patricia
does not have a generalized need for silence but a situational need. When she
needs to say something that has an important link to what is being done, she
uses gestures, facial expressions and direct eye-contact to reach her goal.
She does not need to be in control of her space. She is not setting boundaries
that would distinguish her rights from the children's in the classroom. There
is a workshop-type atmosphere in the classroom: responsible individuals going
about their work, sharing ideas, experiences, and planning how they want
to accomplish a goal. This is what Patricia means by teaching children self-
control.

Through body language teachers teach unintentionally. Sometimes nonverbal and verbal interactions are opposed and send conflicting messages to
children. I asked the teachers how they thought their verbal and nonverbal
interaction were related:

P: I would not probably be aware if that was happening. It would
     probably be unconscious that I would be feeling that way. I know
     that there've been times that I would be teaching something and

I did not want to teach it at that time and it was not coming out well at all. I just have to stop and say I'll do that another day.

H: You allow yourself to do that and make that decision.

P: I do now, because I realize that I am just spinning my wheels. In the first place, it is obvious that nobody is paying attention anyway, because I don't want to do it or whatever. There are some things that I like to teach better than others. Plus there are some things that I like to teach in one day rather than I do another day; it just seems some days I love to do a certain thing, the day before that I would not have enjoyed doing that as much. I do not know what it is.

H: Atmosphere.

P: The time is right for certain things and sometimes the time will just be right for something and you have to be flexible enough to go and do it or lose it.

(Patricia, second interview, 1/17/1992)

Christine says this about conflicts between verbal and nonverbal cues:

C: I think that probably happens a good deal when we are so bombarded with so many children, like when five kids come to me and say: Look what I brought to school or see the story that I wrote and they are all telling me at the same time, I say: 'Oh, that's so good, that's so good' and I am turning around and walking off at the same time . . .

H: So which message do you think they will believe? Verbal or non-verbal?

C: I don't know. I think they probably believe the verbal more, because well, I don't know, because they continue until they get nonverbally what they want, maybe that's what it is. [The child thinks:] 'She said she liked it, but she did not even really look at it or . . . until she does, maybe that kind of thing.'

(Christine, second interview, 1/14/1992)

This is an example of *pretend listening* (Weisglass, 1990), which teachers often find themselves doing as they attempt to cope with their many daily interactions — estimated, as I mentioned earlier, as high as 1500 in number (Berliner, 1984). Christine's first impulse to answer this question is to say how important verbal interaction is, which coincides with the banking concept of teaching where the teacher simply pours out the knowledge to the students, who receive it passively. This kind of teacher talk becomes *verbalism*, 'an alienating and alienated "blah", an empty word for the children who are ready for the real connection — renaming the world together' (Freire, 1970:76). After thinking about her response she changes her mind. Maybe the children are not happy till they get confirmation from the teacher's body language, too. Since the majority of human communication is channeled through nonverbal encounters (Bennett, 1990; Ross, 1989), it is crucial that teachers be aware of the effects of their nonverbal behavior.

This, however, is difficult because much of the teacher's nonverbal interaction is spontaneous, unconscious, as Argyle (1988) points out and Patricia confirms, 'If I was televised all day, I probably would see a lot of things that I do automatically, this [makes a gesture with her hand], just a lot of signals that you give them' (Patricia, second interview, 1/10/1992).

Touch

Verbal interchanges are important in creating the atmosphere in the classroom. They cannot replace physical contact, however.

'I can't *not* touch the children. I need to touch the children because that's how I operate. I'll rather have the lice than not touch the children' (Christine, 12/1991).

In the four classrooms there is a lot of hugging, patting, and stroking. Teachers ruffle hair, touch on the shoulder, hold hands. Children do the same. In conflict situations there is also poking, pinching, shoving and kicking each other, usually in situations where they are not interested in what they are doing. Lunch room is an example of this. The space in both schools is large and has many classes eating simultaneously, an atmosphere that Husen (1989) calls the educational factory. In this physical environment the children's individuality seems to drown into the huge space that is disempowering them. The shoving and poking which are aggressive, dominating ways of touching (Argyle, 1988) become a way to create personal space and a voice in the classroom.

> When I walked in the classroom I had a rush of arms go around me as Edward, Letitia, Hannah, and Lassandra came to greet me. They were very excited. They had been writing their first draft of their first real book. They got ready to go out to recess (I had told Patricia that I wanted to go out with them so I would have some free time to interact with them freely and learn to know them better). As we walked outside (Lassandra holding my hand and wanting to walk next to me in line) the children rushed off to play.
>
> (P-O journal, 10/15/1991)

Excitement, sharing, vulnerability, concern, and happiness are portrayed in the classroom through touching. In communicating to others touching can strengthen the connection between people and the message of the interaction (Argyle, 1988). Children's answers of whether their teachers hug them vary from 'every day' to 'she hugs me to make me feel better' (Mack, 12/6/1991). Hugging is a way of showing liking. Occasionally children just walk to the teacher to be hugged as if reaffirming the connection between the teacher and them. Reciprocity is important. Hannah answered to my question of if she got hugged by the teacher, 'Uh huh, and I hug her too. This morning at recess I did' (12/3/1991).

> H: Did you make a special effort to give time for one-on-one on Thursday (I am thinking of the children coming to you as you were sitting in the rocking chair to hug you).
> C: I think one of the easiest and best things I can do is to hug the children. Many do not get hugs and I know how important they are to me! I don't know if I was hugging Dean or not but he has no mother living with him. He clings to me and often tells me I smell good. I can still recall my mother's sweet smell as a child. It breaks my heart that he's missing a mother's love so I try to hug him each day.
>
> (Christine, T-R journal, 9/25/1991)

The teachers feel that hugging needs to be a natural thing in the classroom, otherwise it does not mean anything. Conscious efforts to hug and go through the motions of touching children in certain ways are artificial and not believable. Hugging 'has to be spontaneous. Always' (Patricia, second interview, 1/10/1992). Patricia encourages children to touch each other in loving ways: 'I encourage my boys and girls to hug each other' — although she realizes that some parents 'may not appreciate that' (Second interview, 1/10/1992). In her classroom it is a way of feeling like sisters and brothers, like a community that sticks together.

Proximity

All four teachers are very flexible in using the space in their room. There is no teacher's area where the children are locked out. For example, Gloria has a hard time even getting to her own desk during the day because she is so busy being wherever the children are. In the wish to get to her desk she is probably struggling between the disempowering teacher behavior that says 'I am an authority and my desk is where I reign from', and the empowering practice of being where the children are and where the life of the classroom is.

Patricia's class is a good example of flexible uses of proximity. Since manipulating distance is a form of social control (Argyle, 1988), the flexibile use of space signifies the breaking barriers of that social control. The flexible uses of intimate, personal and social distances (Hall, 1965) in Patricia's classroom show in her habit of sending the children out into the hallway to work by themselves, into the loft with a suggestion to find a good space where they want to go. There is a sense that each member of the classroom community owns the space — it is shared. Everybody knows where everything is, and children can go to it and know what to do with it. Patricia especially seems to own the space in her classroom, and feels utterly comfortable letting children share it.

In School B the flexible use of space may be limited by the fact that two classrooms share it, and that everything is spatially connected to the rest of the school. Jasmine and Christine like the open space, 'I really like the openness of our classroom and do not prefer four walls' (T-R journal, 10/29/1991). The children seem to flow naturally from one side to the other but they also have a clear sense of their space at any given time.

When using public space it is typical that people raise their voices to be heard by a large group (Ross, 1989). In both schools the teachers typically use public space during the playground times and in the cafeteria.

Eye-contact and facial expressions

Direct eye-contact is essential in letting others know how important their response is, how their contribution is valued. 'Eye-contact is just the most important' (Jasmine, second interview, 1/13/1992).

Jasmine uses her joking dragon image in her classroom to diffuse situations that are potentially leading to conflicts. As she describes that 'smoke's coming out of my eyes and fire's coming out of my mouth', she makes a dragon face that gives the children a clue of what is going wrong in the teacher's mind. Ian said (12/6/1991); 'She go [makes a dragon face]' as I asked him how his teacher gets angry. Lee (11/21/1991), described the same situation; 'She says, "Smoke comes out my ears and fire comes out of my eyes."'

Jasmine says that one of the hardest things to do in the classroom in terms of helping children think for themselves is to listen to their incomplete verbal messages linked with 'sign language, shoulder shrugs, blank stares, etc.' (T-R journal, 9/26/1991). A teacher who is open to the children's experience is able to see 'the blank stare' and interpret situations in ways that will help children understand themselves better.

Gestures

Emblems, which are conventional hand signals like raising a hand for silence, and *illustrators*, which are situational gestures to help clarify the verbal message (as in telling Michael where exactly to go work in the hallway, 10/4/1991) are in abundant use in the four classrooms. Raising hands is used for indicating a child has something to say although in small groups this becomes unnecessary. Using fingers for counting days of the week (Gloria, videotaping, 9/25/1991), encouraging a child to give himself a pat for doing a good job (Christine, videotaping, 11/20/1991) shrugging shoulders and spreading hands for emphasizing a question (Jasmine, videotaping, 11/21/1991) draw children's attention. Gloria says she is more of a verbal than nonverbal person (Second interview, 1/20/1992). Christine says, 'I do not think I communicate well physically with the children' (Second interview, 1/14/1992). These responses to nonverbal interaction indicate how unconscious our bodily communication is.

In the large group time, discussing a book they had read, Christine (videotaping, 10/10/1991) used a variety of gestures: pointing, shrugs, pressing lips together with her fingers, listening with hands in the back with head tilted to the side. Her body language communicated humor, excitement, surprise, anticipation, dominance and amazement. She evoked giggles in children, excitedly raised hands, and gazes directed to her and the book. Her tone of voice (higher pitch) expressing discovery was accompanied with body movements and gestures. She behaves almost like an actress without knowing it. There seemed to be a bond between the children and Christine through the deliberate use of melodramatic gestures which the children knew were exaggerated but which they enjoyed all the same.

Posture

In the four classrooms studied socially acceptable postures vary. Not all postures are acceptable but they seem to match with the context of the classroom activities. For example, lying down in Jasmine's and Patricia's room is acceptable. No rigid rules except at times when the teacher needs the group's attention or shows anger at what's going on. On 11/20 both teachers, Jasmine and Christine, sit on tables when talking to the children about the changed rules in using the school library. Since this was a grave situation (many children had many books at home and could not borrow others till they had brought the previous one back) it seemed natural to have the teachers sit higher to convey the importance of the discussion and what responsibility they expected of their children. Towards the end of this conversation Jasmine leaned down on the table putting her almost in a lying position with just feet hanging down which communicated to the children that a more informal discussion was in store. Both teachers simultaneously talked to individual children in front of them.

The four teachers use their bodies as a tool in the classroom. They seldom think about how it works as they go about their daily activities.

> H: Tell me about teaching sitting and standing. Are you aware of how much you stand, when you get tired, etc.?
> C: I never think about how much I stand. I do know I am exhausted by the end of every week.
>
> (T-R journal, 9/25/1991)

Understanding nonverbal cues is difficult and does not necessarily improve with more teaching experience (Jecker *et al.*, 1965). Teachers in my study had learned that observing postures is one of the hints to change the pace, content, environment or timing of an activity.

> *H:* I enjoyed doing *Circle, Circle Turning* with your children. They just wanted to do it over and over again in the playground (behind the trailers — a place I had never been aware of before). Many children mentioned that playground and recess time is the best part of school for them. I guess because of my cultural background and experiences as a child in school myself, I wish all children had more chances to satisfy their physical needs and go out more often. What do you think about this? Am I seeing a problem in the schedule when there is none? You and Jasmine both try to alleviate this problem by doing physical activities or creative movement in the classroom, stretching, etc. during transitions to 'get the wiggles out' (to use your words of today). Are these exercises spontaneous that you just do when you notice children needing a change of pace, or do you try to think of some to do every day? If you think of yourself as a beginning teacher and now, how are transitions different to handle now than they were when you first started?
>
> *C:* I definitely feel that physical movement is important. I also enjoy visiting with the children on the playground. When we can't go outside I move with them inside. The stretching moments are spontaneous. We've tried to arrange our schedule so that they don't have to sit for a very long time. We've changed our schedule twice this year to accommodate this. Being a student myself has helped me as much if not more than my experience in the classroom to become aware of children's needs to move around. Sitting in class is hard for me. Through experience I have learned to help children move without their losing total control of themselves.
>
> (T-R journal, 9/25/1991)

Appearance

Although appearance was not something that I paid attention to extensively in the participant-observation, it did come out in dialogues with children. Megan (Interview, 12/4/1991) said she liked her teacher because 'I think she is nice and she is pretty.' Children are interested in how their peers and teachers look. Children are very perceptive about how everything looks and when changes have been made in the environment as well as in the appearance of other people. A missing tooth, a leg in a cast, the signatures on it, clothing and jewelry provoke conversations and can lead to a teachable moment in the classroom. An example of such a teachable moment was Jeremy's tooth issue in Gloria's class:

H: As your reading proceeded children started to get restless be-
    cause of Jeremy's tooth problem. You stopped the reading, talked
    about the snaggle tooth-issue, had them graph all baby teeth left
    and teeth fallen — categories with their bodies. Had this been
    an issue before today? How do the children usually respond to
    losing teeth? Is there peer pressure to belong to one of the groups?
G: Not a major issue, but losing a tooth is very important and scary
    to a first grader. Some want to pull their teeth at school; some
    at home. Jeremy had been telling me for three days he had a
    loose tooth. When it started bleeding he went into a complete
    upset. Most seem to accept losing teeth, but Jeremy made it a
    major issue. Nicole teased him and made him angry. This has
    never happened before. I don't know if there is peer pressure. I
    know if they lose a tooth, they tell everyone and usually bring
    the money the tooth fairy left.

These four teachers often choose a dress that matches the topic, the sea-son, something that helps the children to see the connection with what they are talking about and what they are seeing. Children notice what their teach-ers wear and when they change their hairstyle. When Gloria changed her hairstyle, the children said they liked it (T-R journal, 9/25). Another day (10/22) Gloria was wearing checkered culottes. Lisa walked up to her and studied the garment by physically separating the two pantlegs. For some children this is a way to see certain kinds of clothes for the first time. Teacher earrings and bows ended up in the pictures children drew of their teachers (Jamila and Holly, 12/17/1991).

In the interview I asked Earl if he liked the way the classroom looked, to which he responded, 'I like the way my friends dress and look' (Earl, 11/19/1991). He could have understood my question wrong but as he was thinking about an answer he looked around the room and fixed his gaze on a group of children standing nearby. For him the physical classroom environment was not more important than the people in it.

Environmental factors

The physical classroom descriptions in the classroom profiles of Chapter 3 show that all teachers have somewhat non-traditional physical classroom en-vironments. Gloria is the only one who has desks in rows, but in her room, as in the others, a bulk of classroom work happens in centers—small groups work around the room. McPherson's (1984) discovery that row-and-column classrooms were more difficult to manage than more informally furnished rooms might be one explanation of the problem that Gloria is having with her group this year. Christine and Jasmine have free center time as well where the children may decide what they want to work with. 'We get to do anything we want' (Ian, videotaping, 11/20/1991) has come to mean that the tables used for free centers are representatives of their freedom of choice. This everyone liked except for one child who did not feel at home in free centers at all. Most children said they liked a place in the classroom because of the activity that was done in it: 'Place where you draw and color' (Derek, 12/3/1991). It seemed that they liked the tables because they got to work in free centers there and they liked the free centers because they got to move more freely in the room and do what they liked the best.

Shawn (12/6/1991) and Brenda (12/9/1991), who liked hearing the stories their teachers read, liked the carpet where they would typically listen to the story. Certain places had an association with a pleasant, exciting and satisfying activity. Carlotta said, 'Learning is my best part. I don't like my desk because Malcolm colors on my desk' (Interview, 12/12/1991). Here too, we can see that the children's associations with places in the classroom can color a portion of their school experience, and a place in school can become unpleasant because of something that happened there. Conversely, bulletin boards and work tables become pleasant places for those children who have exciting and satisfying experiences there.

The children's favorite parts of the rooms — the reading loft, the tables where the centers are and bulletin boards — are another way of children saying these are the places that make our classroom mine and the reason I like learning here.

The change from rigid rows to a more fluid and informal structure communicates to children that the room belongs to everybody (Palmer, 1971). The traditional arrangement, with the teacher here and the students over there, is broken in all the classrooms, just as the four teachers are all breaking the conception of the teacher as the ultimate authority in learning. As Christine puts it, 'I used to think that the kids needed to know that I was the authority figure . . . and I was the one with answers as far as discipline and everything . . . It's been good to have the children make their own rules' (First interview, 7/30/1991).

The floor is used several times daily for large group discussion, reading, visitor gatherings, and other sharing times. Children's work — writing, art work and projects usually linked with the theme or unit under study — is displayed. When studying the olden days Christine's and Jasmine's children brought in artifacts from home to show the class. They were displayed on a table where children could see them and touch them. Longer projects, like apple dolls and life-size human body studies stayed out in the open as long as the children were working on them and the time they were displayed for others to see. In Gloria's room she has a science table that has objects to touch and feel, and in Patricia's room children take care of an aquarium. Instead of a sterile school atmosphere the rooms of these four teachers have a sense of collaboration, of functional activity, and a feeling that the rooms belong to the children as well as the adults in the rooms.

Chronemics

All teachers have schedules that are synchronized with the activities and set times for the school community. Within the confines of these parameters (beginning and end of school, lunch, recess, specials) all four classrooms show flexibility to different degrees. Christine and Jasmine are dependent on each other's schedules as well as the school's schedule but, as described before, although they attempt to synchronize their activities, they don't get too upset within their pod if something gets out of order. If one needs to wait for the other, she starts a discussion, a short game with the children, such as word games or *Simon Says*, or a song.

Gloria is very flexible in the way she designs her day. Her flexibility is restricted by having to share the pod with a second-grade class, so that, for example, if they want to do extra music, they will wait till the second-graders are out of their portion of the pod.

Patricia's self-contained class has more freedom to shift and change activities according to the children's independent needs, for example, through the stretching activities mentioned above. The student teacher in Patricia's room said it was hard to give a schedule for a day because they change it depending on how the work proceeds and how long it takes for children to finish whatever they happen to be working on.

In allotting time to certain activities and children all teachers expressed some concern about having ample time for working with individual children and their idiosyncratic questions. Teachers need more time to interact with individual children, 'simply one-on-one to have a conversation with children about whatever they want to talk about' (Christine, second interview, 1/14/1992). This is hindered by the number of children in the classroom and the requirements laid down by the state or the school district for the teachers to meet. To be able to sit down at least once a week and interview each child in her room, talking about what they liked, how they would have changed things, and what they would like to do next, is Christine's hope for interaction in the classroom. This would be a time of 'socialization separate from learning about a particular topic' (Christine, 1/14/1992). This is difficult since decisions like this are also curricular and often school-wide decisions. What is considered academic learning time? If we enlarge the conception of academic learning time, the 330 daily instructional minutes, to include the importance of helping the whole child grow, including their physical, social and emotional development, these kinds of schedule adjustments should be possible.

Nonverbally empowering classrooms are like homes: people sitting, moving around, standing, lying, gesturing, looking at each other, touching.

The scene is shifting. An empowering teacher exhibits humor and shows feelings and enthusiasm by smiling, varying facial expressions, varying intonation and by touching children. He or she uses hand gestures creatively and naturally, nods and maintains eye-contact for connecting with children. Non-verbal and verbal communications support each other. The use of space is flexible for everyone in the classroom.

Personal Disclosures

For these teachers vulnerability comes as a result of a struggle to release control of the classroom, to let go of power-over *so that responsive relationships in which co-agency and empowerment can develop are achieved. Openness and vulnerability involve taking risks, sharing one's thoughts and one's feelings, and being willing to accept the thoughts and feelings of others. Being vulnerable means being willing to admit one is wrong, that a mistake was made. It means being willing to show that one cares, that one is excited, disappointed, or angry. It means being honest.*

(Kreisberg, 1992)

With the changes that the teachers have made they have become more aware of becoming real people for the children, and of making efforts to get to know their children. If teachers felt more able to make time adjustments, such as the ones mentioned above, empowering interaction in the classrooms could more easily become a part of everyday life. 'I know my children better now than before' (Christine, second interview, 1/14/1992). Instead of remaining authorities whose power is beyond question, the four women have started doing things like apologizing to children, showing their own vulnerability, sharing their personal lives (Patricia, first interview, 7/17/1991; Christine, second interview, 1/14/1992). In collaboration with last year's student teacher Emilie, Patricia was changed in terms of giving more of herself to the children in the room:

P: Oh, Emilie did something so great! I had always shared with my kids, but I saw her share an experience . . . and it had all of the children in the room with tears in their eyes.

H: Really?

P: Yeah, and me too. And I saw . . . it opened me up even more. They should see my vulnerability, too. You know, they should see that I had [feelings] and so . . . because of her I talk a lot more about things in my childhood now that were important to me or hurt me or that I really enjoyed or were just wonderful. And I want them to see that their feelings are not unique. That people have been feeling that way for a long time . . . And I tell them, you know, I talked too much when I was in first grade, too, and that's the reason I allow them to talk. But I also have

151

a rule that says you must speak softly. I said, you know, even though I understand that you want to talk cause I did too, I also understand that if someone else has a thought in their mind and you're talking so loud it's making that thought go out, then you're keeping that child from learning and you can't do that.

(First interview, 7/19/1991)

H: You shared your personal story of pumpkins rolling around in the back of your truck. How much of your personal life do you feel like sharing with your children? Do you find it important/ not important for a teacher to do so?

J: I try not to tell too many personal stories unless I am going to have time to listen to their personal stories, too. I do think they are interested in hearing about my family and life outside school. They are particularly interested in my college age boys who drop in for money from time to time.

(T-R journal, 10/30/1991)

In becoming a classroom community where everyone has a valid place and is respected for him/herself it is important for the teacher to become human to the children, to become a humble learner instead of remaining the authority that distances herself from the real thoughts and feelings of children. All four teachers thought it was important to be themselves in the classroom, although with certain things happening or people visiting they agreed it was harder than other times. Christine said she is 'pretty real' with the children because she realizes that

sharing myself, my personal life with the children is vital. I think they need to know that I am a real person, that we have cattle at home and that Jim [husband] and I feed the cows together, we are excited when they have a calf, and we ride motorcycles, what I look like in a motorcycle helmet, and what I like and I don't like, and like when my mother is sick and I am worried about her, or when somebody has died in my family, we talk about it . . .

H: So you allow the children in your personal [life]

C: Yes, and I think that that is real important, because they need to know me as a human, and I think that is hard for them, it is a hard concept. When they see me in the grocery store, they go: 'hhhhh, you're buying groceries!!'

H: You don't go to the bathroom, you don't sleep.

C: But, and I think if they realize that about me, then it is easier not to be an authority figure, it is easier to be a nurturer, because they know I have feelings and I can understand you because you can understand what I am going through right now.

(Christine's second interview, 1/14/1992)

Children in an atmosphere of trust share things about their lives as well. They share their thoughts about school, what they have done, learned, what they are concerned about, what they thought about during a TV show and so on. 'I go have lunch with the group. In line waiting for our turn I hear about new pants that have three pockets inside each other, we have a long conversation on the funniest, scariest and saddest parts of *Home Alone*, I hear about the slush machine being installed and hear about, "I've got my shoes on"' (P-O journal, 10/28/1991).

Occasionally children will tell about their thoughts indirectly, through an activity, in their drawings, the way they behave, or in their writing. Sometimes children express their inability to cope with difficult inner conflicts or inner pain through behavior that normally gets labelled deviant or misbehavior, as in Dean drawing a few squiggles on his paper, then piercing it with his pen and throwing it on the floor. Jake in Christine's class had an experience that only came out in his writing a story, otherwise he did not talk about it at all.

Jake's story:
1st page: D.D. [and] Hammond had a heart attack
2nd page: One day when I went Hammond and D.D.K. house she gave me some cookies.
3rd page: Lily told me Hammond died. I cried [coffin in the picture]
4th page: When I went to D.D.K. house she gave me cookies.
5th page: Lily told me D.D. died. I cried, too.
6th page: I remembered back when D.D. and Hammond were alive. D.D. died by a hospital, Hammond died by a heart attack.
7th page: They gave me cookies when they were alive. They were chocolate chip cookies [picture of a cookie]
8th page: I've never been to their grave. [picture of a grave stone]

Examples like this illustrate how valuable it is for a teacher to really listen to what the children are trying to say, either directly or indirectly through their actions and behavior. Goodman (1986) calls this kind of careful listening kid-watching. Part of kid-watching is being aware of teachable moments, and just as with teacher change, when children find meaning in what they are engaged in, learning takes off without extra effort.

Affection is shown verbally or nonverbally, through words or actions. Christine uses music to help children show they care about each other. Christine recently came up with an idea. 'Everybody take time every day to make one person feel wonderful somehow' (second interview, 1/14/1992). Her problem is that children typically do this by saying something nice to each other about their clothing, and that was not what Christine meant to happen at all.

'Because friendships, you can be hurt through friendships, you can be hurt through relationships, and with children, I just think you have to be willing to be open and if you hurt, you have to take that, that's part of it. But

I take more risks. I'm not as hard as I used to be' (Patricia, first interview, 7/17/1991).

Sense of Ownership

The teachers have made a commitment to trying to understand the children that come to their classrooms. Although often they feel that instead of having enough time with each individual child, they like to make the children feel part of the group and classroom community. Learning to know one another is important in becoming a community. The teachers try to facilitate in different ways, through talking to the parents, through listening to children looking at their records, doing the daily news, and through journal writing. Respect and caring in the classroom are tied with how well the teachers know their children. Erich Fromm writes:

> To respect a person is not possible without *knowing* him; care and responsibility would be blind if they were not guided by knowledge; the knowledge which is an aspect of love is one which does not stay at the periphery, but penetrates to the core. It is possible only when I can transcend the concern for myself and see the other person in his own terms. I may know, for instance, that a person is angry even when he does not show it overtly; but I may know him more deeply than that; then I know that he is anxious and worried; that he feels lonely, that he feels guilty. Then I know that his anger is only a manifestation of something deeper, and I see him as anxious and embarrassed, that is, as the suffering person, rather than an angry one.
>
> (Fromm, 1967:170)

Seeing a child or a colleague more in-depth emotionally, in a context of a whole life rather than as an entity with momentary behaviors, either nice or not nice, is as crucial in a classroom community as it is in other places where people work and co-exist. When there is trust that personal experiences count, children and teachers relax to be more themselves, and more willing to share their ideas, hardships and personal triumphs.

> Quinnus comes over again and I ask him about his journal which he is just starting. I comment on the beginning of the journal and he says, 'This is already my second journal, can I show you my first one?' 'Sure, I'd be happy to see it.' He brings it over and shows every page. I mentioned that on every page he seems to be having more to write about.
>
> (Patricia, P-O journal, 10/15/1991)

Ownership in a classroom — the children's feeling that the classroom is theirs too, not just the teacher's — is strengthened by allowing and encouraging choice in the classroom. Through their ownership of the class-room children get to engage in activities that are interesting to them, become more motivated; they even get to participate in decisions on what goes on what walls, how the furniture is arranged, and the like, all traditionally deci-sions the teacher makes about his or her room. Expanding ownership of the classroom to include everyone in it also gives the teacher energy and time for other focuses, for example, one-on-one work (Bonnett and Doddington, 1990). Providing choice in a classroom helps satisfy the children's need for freedom and power (Glasser, 1990) and adds to their sense that they are able to meet their needs on their terms — a feeling no human being can live long without.

The legacy of our historical background helps us ignore the significance of feelings in a school setting. Children come to school with notions of what is proper to do and what is not already drummed into their heads. The dom-inant culture values calm, and the impression of strength and this set of cul-tural expectations comes out in the classrooms in various ways: in classroom rules (the premium placed on silence), and especially in children's answers about showing emotion in the classroom (Weissglass, 1990). In every group I had children who showed amazement (enlarged eyes, shrugging shoulders) at my question of what they did in the classroom when they got angry. Many children (N=17) reported that it was not acceptable to show anger in the classroom, or elsewhere either: 'It just ain't OK to be angry' (Lucas, 11/18/1991). Some even claim, showing a rather astonishing (in six-year-olds!) in-ternalization of their parents' ideals, that they quite simply never get angry: 'I don't get angry' (Herb, 11/19/1991; Olivia, 12/16/1991); 'I don't ever get angry' (Nicole, 12/3/1991; Rita, 12/3/1991; Henry, 12/3/1991). Thirteen chil-dren reported they did nothing if they got angry or at least did not show it: 'I don't show it on my outside. My mommy taught me that' (Quinnus, 11/21/1991). Some children said they did not know what they did when getting mad or angry. On the other hand many children (N=27) have learned to talk about their feelings of anger and frustration to the teacher or child with whom they have gotten angry and have noticed that they do different things when doing so. Some put their head down, sit down, throw a fit, pout, 'put a face on my face' (Jake, 11/19/1991); 'I be sad, be mad, mad face' (Beth, 12/3/1991), tell the teacher, or start acting nicely. Some have learned to talk their anger out with the person who occasioned it: 'I would say "don't mess with me." I'd say that to the person. I'd say "gosh!" ' (Tim, 12/4/1991); 'I just go [makes a face] shriek at the people at the playground. She says: "What's wrong?" ' (Edward, 12/3/1991); 'I talk about it with whoever I'm angry with' (Lassandra, 11/21/1991).

'Learning is never divorced from feelings — and neither is failing to learn' (Smith, 1986:60). The research done on the human brain and learning stresses how important it is to provide an atmosphere in the classroom that allows the children to feel secure, liked and valued (Hart, 1986; Neve, 1985; Nummela Caine and Caine, 1991). A positive interaction situation where feeling is shown has a powerful impact on learning in terms of improved student achievement, greater motivation, growing self-esteem, and development of personality (Lindh, 1983). In all situations, even those situations requiring intellectual and cognitive achievement, the way people function depends on their emotional state (Lindh, 1983).

Empowering practices in the classroom acknowledge the fact that education is not only limited to intellectual and cognitive pursuits. The whole prism of human experience is valid in the classroom: the emotional, the social, the physical, the moral, the creative. Learning through themes or units where children's and teachers' experiences and interests are guiding curricular factors, rather than what someone else decides outside the classroom, is a global approach that has therapeutical effects as well (Lozanov, 1978). The teachers and children actively gravitate towards situations where these, often neglected sides of human development, are celebrated.

Sometimes these situations are preplanned, but the most empowering situations are those where direction in activities comes spontaneously from children themselves, from their experiences. They have a voice that a traditional power-over classroom did not allow them to have. In open dialogue with the teacher they feel they have the power to learn, their self-esteem grows, they feel that they are worthy of new, exciting experiences, they are able to think and are aware of that ability, they can make decisions, they believe and trust that life in the classroom is good. Teachers are emotionally available, teaching is more interesting because there is more with which they can make connections. They are born into understanding what being a professional really is — a caring, responsible, humble, vulnerable and creative learner who inhabits the same roles as the child does. Teaching and learning are not all that different: both involve openness to experience; welcoming life into the classroom; being alert in a relaxed way; allowing uniqueness and difference; welcoming the change and unpredictability that used to cause much anxiety.

Empowering practices bring people alive in the classrooms because the needs of belonging, power, freedom, and fun (Glasser, 1990) are met in meaningful ways. It spills out of the classrooms and into the hallways, playground, other classrooms through interaction with colleagues, support groups, and workshops. Dialogue spreads out. Empowering practices are meaningful and need-fulfilling for other teachers in the school, for parents and administrators, as well. All participants allow themselves and feel allowed by others to be more of who they are, and to keep growing and eventually becoming more fully human.

Chapter 5

The Dialogics of Empowerment

Dialogue can change the meaning of experience.

(Howe, 1963)

In Chapter 1 I cited Freire's (1970) list of attitudes and practices that characterize 'banking' education. As a way of beginning to tie together the loose ends of this study I would like to offer a counterlist of attitudes and practices that I have come to find central to empowerment:

- The teacher and students both teach and are taught by each other;
- The teacher is aware of not knowing everything and is open to the students' knowledge and experience, which are actively valued;
- The teacher and students all engage in critical, reflective, imaginative and collaborative thinking;
- The teacher talks and listens, the students talk and listen; they engage in dialogue;
- The teacher and student interact, striving to meet each other's needs instead of being the respective perpetrators and victims of discipline;
- The teacher and students make choices based on what is most meaningful for them with sensitivity to each other's verbal and nonverbal cues;
- The students are actively engaged in meaningful experiences that the teacher facilitates;
- The teacher and students together decide on program content and revise and change it as their interests and needs change;
- The teacher allows her/his personal charisma, vulnerability, and humility to create her/his authority based on mutual respect, discovery, and love for learning;
- The teacher and students form a collective Subject of the learning process, sharing joint ownership of the classroom life.

These attitudes and practices echo the importance of transforming education in the direction of greater democracy:

- The *reciprocity* of teacher and learner roles breaks down the educational hierarchies that perpetuate dehumanizing power-over in the classroom and in society.

- The *humility* of the teacher and other learners in the classroom means that no one assumes from the start that she or he possesses knowledge that must be imparted to the others, who lack it; everybody has important knowledge, but no one is in a position to force their knowledge on anyone else.
- The *critical awareness* fostered by empowering groups is an invaluable catalyst for change; by learning about themselves in the group, teachers and students learn about themselves in society and the social norms and values in themselves, and thus become better able to decide which norms and values they find functional and worth preserving, which they find dysfunctional and worth fighting.
- The transformative power of egalitarian *dialogue*, which satisfies individual and group needs through caring *interaction*, creates a space for every member of a group to participate, to have a say in the direction the group is heading, to express her or his desires and fears, impulses and qualms. As Freire (1970) says, dialogue is the forum in which people work together to 'rename' the world.
- The grounding of *choice* in meaningful activities and contexts charges all of education with relevance for the individual and collective lives of everyone involved, and banishes the dehumanizing effects of content isolated from real life.
- The *facilitative* role of the teacher is a recognition that the teacher has something unique to offer the group, but also that he or she does it from within the group, as a member of the group, not from a power position above the group.
- *Democratic* decision-making underscores the inherent value of every member of the group.
- The grounding of respect and authority in *power-with* involves an emptying-out of the teacher's traditional power-over children into deeply felt caring and sharing.
- The empowerment of the *group* as the body that learns expands the learning process from the isolated individual who memorizes inert facts and replicates them on objective tests to the interactive, self-transforming society.

Such a list suggests that the pedagogy of empowerment is dedicated to the improvement of everyone's quality of life; it seeks the qualitative transformation of society so as to maximize the humanizing effects of active participation in a caring, supportive, egalitarian group. Ira Shor writes:

In proposing a qualitative process instead of mechanical learning, I want to suggest a pedagogy that is participatory, critical, values-oriented, multicultural, student-oriented, experiential, research-minded and interdisciplinary. Such a pedagogy focuses on the quality of an activity, not on quantity of skills or facts memorized, or on the quantity of hours or credits spent on a task.

(1986:418)

To take that one step further, it also suggests that the ethnography of empowerment is a form of 'qualitative' research not merely because it seeks to *describe* the qualities of a given phenomenon, but because it seeks actively to *improve* the quality of life of everyone involved in it. I have insisted throughout this book upon the identity of the goals of the teacher-as-learner and the researcher-as-learner: both are engaged in learning and sharing their learning not only to expand their own and others' knowledge base, but to transform their own and others' lives. As Heaney (1982:24) emphasizes, 'It is everyone's role to teach, as it is everyone's role to learn and to act. It is also everyone's role to integrate what is taught and what is learned with what is done.'

These empowering practices in all learners children, teachers, and researchers alike, are in dynamic connection with a personal transformation in which all of the individuals in a group are engaged, involving becoming aware of the personal and social conditioning one has experienced (Kreisberg, 1992). Elizabeth Swart's (1990:317) claim that 'teaching is a trade that hasn't yet got the idea that it can transform and rejuvenate itself' might be true in the aggregate, but in the case of the four teachers in my study — and in my case as well, and I hope in yours — the practical application of that 'idea' of self-transformation and self-rejuvenation has released an inner power that has created excitement about learning both inside and outside the classroom. Patricia, Gloria, Jasmine, and Christine have 'entered the process of personal and institutional change' (Kreisberg, 1992:197). They are changing themselves, the way they view the teaching profession, the way they think about students and the purpose of school. Their practices and ideas are changing not only them but other colleagues as well. The isolation of their profession is broken.

Empowerment is marked by constructivist listening, a deep caring for the children in the classroom and acceptance as the persons they are. Empowerment is marked by control over one's own life and allowing the same to another person. Empowerment is marked by respect for each individual in the group, based not on a position of authority or the skills of each individual but on the sense that each person has a valuable contribution to make, each has a unique voice that echoes the unique experiences of the individual and joins in the voices of others in the classroom community.

The empowerment of teachers in my study is by no means complete or perfect in terms of every possible dialogical relationship. 'One is never purely empowered or disempowered,' Kreisberg (1992:194) points out. In relation to their colleagues or administrators, the teachers in my study find themselves disempowered, stranded on an island. This is very much the situation that Louden calls the teacher's inability to 'control the power of the living tradition outside her classroom' (1991:190). This is the link to the society of which the teachers and students are a part. We cannot separate ourselves from the power structures, seen and unseen, of our society.

In the ethnography of empowerment the researcher, instead of engaging in some 'ballet of concepts' (Shor and Freire, 1987:19) abstracted from reality, attempts to write by composing a dialogical fabric with the informants and the reader, while becoming a reader, teacher, student, and writer — and learning from the interchange.

Administrators often restrict teachers' abilities to expand their interactive base of empowerment. Similarly, dissertation committees and editorial staffs of university presses often work to thwart the empowerment of researchers through the parameters imposed by the institution.

The hours spent in the classrooms and at my computer making sense of my experiences empowered me; the details of what was going on intrigued me. It seemed that when I was able to feel that research was part of life instead of something rigorously cut off from my reality — which I had come to experience in earlier work with forcefully objective, quantitative research — something important happened.

My research progressed, from its initial formulation through the field work to the writing stage, in an ongoing dialogue between the internalized voices of the quantitative and the qualitative researcher. On the one hand I was drawn, like a good quantitative researcher, to the minute details of the classroom interactions I was studying; on the other, as a good qualitative researcher, particularly one interested in improving the quality of life, I was drawn to the holistic feel of empowering classroom practices. I continued to amass detailed knowledge of those practices; but at the same time the subjective experience of the time spent in the classrooms in contact with the children and teachers revealed a vision that cried out: this really works, it's not just in my head! Perhaps this was the crucial point that caused the focus of this study to shift some time in November of 1991, midway through my research. Somehow the concept of interaction remained static and unchanging in my mind until I started seeing connections between my experiences and the data that I had gathered. Empowerment was it. Empowering practices were happening in the classrooms, and in the interactive dialogical relationships. Not only between the teachers and children but among children as they made discoveries, parents and teachers, university professors and teachers, teachers and their colleagues in workshops, hallways and support group meetings.

The ethnography of empowerment engages theory and practice in constant dialogue. This dialogue is ongoing: 'through action theory is developed, through theory is in turn modified through further action' (Houser, 1990:58). With empowerment as a focus I was able to see the dynamism that was going on in the classrooms: a constant shifting of relationships, interests, activities, meanings, emotions and interactions, all unified and channeled by a powerful vision of life. Empowerment allowed me to feel alive.

Meaningfulness: this matters. This is about life. It *is* life. I was and am renaming the world with the children and teachers — and with my colleagues and other, future readers. The teachers' change from non-discernment to in-tuitive discernment was paralleled, reflected, and in many ways catalyzed my transformation as well. From doing what I was expected to do according to the training I had received in educational research methodology, I entered into a reflective critique of that training and my beliefs about how research 'ought' to be conducted. This process has pushed the boundaries of my thinking. The process has made me question the categories of theory and practice, teaching and learning, students and teachers. In defining them the way we do, we are also limiting ourselves, since seeing in a certain way may blind us to seeing in other ways.

Suggestions for Further Study

Perhaps this project has given me more questions than answers. One of the most interesting questions is the teacher transformation, the dramatic begin-ning of which I only witnessed secondhand, through the stories of the teachers. What really happens in a teacher's change? In the initial stages? Could we predict who is ready to change? How do non-discerning teachers move from mechanistic thinking to intuitive and even educated discernment?

The videotaping aspect of my experience raised another new and inter-esting field of questions for me. How could it be used in helping teachers become more aware of their nonverbal interactions with children? What can be done with the inevitable gap between a strong subjective perception of a situation (my sense while teaching a group that I had failed miserably, for instance) and the later, more detached and distanced perception when watch-ing the same event on tape (my sense that the class had gone fine)? Is this gap necessarily to the detriment of subjective experience, as quantitative researchers have often assumed? Can it be put to transformative use — and if so, how? I noticed that with each viewing my own personal experience got further and further away from what had been preserved on tape. As I was working on describing the nonverbal aspects of an experience while viewing Patricia and myself I was thinking about 'they' as if I had not been present at all.

Another fascinating question to explore might be the one that I asked the children in my study about how they would teach if they became the teacher in the classroom. The answers, which varied from 'like she does' to a shrug of the shoulders, piqued my interest in the teacher's (and child's!) own ex-periential base as the 'greatest obstacle' in becoming an empowered teacher (Kreisberg, 1992:202). What do children think about teaching? How does the concept of teaching develop in children?

Since some of the teachers in my study had the belief that they really were no good at nonverbal interaction, would there be some value in con-structing ways for teachers to develop their nonverbal communication? How might it be done best? Through an intensive unit of study? What would this kind of a workshop or course consist of? How much attention is paid to nonverbal interaction in teacher education? How would two groups of teacher education students compare in the classrooms — one with extensive exposure to nonverbal interaction, one without?

A strong wish came from the teachers to keep the children together and continue their education in classrooms with similar philosophies. What are the personal effects of this lack of continuity on children's self-esteem, on their ability to cooperate and work with others? Just how important is continuity in children's (and other people's) lives, and to what extent do we want to capitalize on that importance in school settings? What is the rationale behind the redistribution of children at the end of every year — breaking up friend-ships? Minimizing discipline problems by 'isolating' troublemakers? Does anybody really know why this happens, or is it just another ossified practice that no one questions?

The self-assessment instruments used in this study raised some questions. Would there be some value in filling out these instruments and discussing their results in a school community, in order to promote discussion of and interest in the ways we think and believe and to provide those opportunities that Weissglass (1990) says we are lacking to scrutinize our assumptions? Since traditional 'banking' education seems utterly indifferent to the effect of brain functions on human learning, it would be interesting to find out how much background knowledge teachers have about how the brain works and how children learn the best. Does this vary on different levels of education?

How could schools nourish the social competence and cooperative cap-abilities of its teachers and empower more people in the educational settings?

Conclusion

Educational ethnography has come a long way. In the context of my work and the boundaries I have personally pushed in connection with it I would suggest that perhaps the ethnography of empowerment might well transform the marginalized position of ethnographic studies. Through empowerment, and the conviction that the ethnography of empowerment is not only a valu-able but a transformative tool in conducting research about educational pro-cesses, educators at all levels may help each other to change their practices from within. My personal process of being a participant-observer and ethno-grapher in Patricia's, Jasmine's, Gloria's, and Christine's rooms not only forced me to challenge my existing beliefs about research, teaching, and learning but it enabled me to make startling connections. These connections reach beyond education to the questions of power and change in society, connect with the concerns about the future of the planet, cooperative capabilities of nations and peace.

Is this going too far? Yes and no. This research process has shown that in order to understand the details you have to be open to the whole, and in order to understand the whole you have to start from details, individuals, their lives and transformations.

In connection with our personal experiences and contacts with other people we can begin to change the attitude and position of education in the minds of the general public, in the academic institution and in politics as one of the most significant and cherished assets our society has to give our children, so that they might be increasingly able to build a harmonious, working world. The university as an institution exists for the education of students who attend it; but at the same time teacher education is often the least respected department in the university, the composition teachers that stress pedagogy over arcane knowledge are professionally the least respected colleagues in English departments, and so on, strongly suggesting that education is not important for anyone. In placing pedagogy at the bottom of the pole we are undermining the significance of all education, even in the fields generally thought of as tough, rigorous and respected, like medicine and engineering. But perhaps, given the anxieties Freire provokes in so many educators, this general dismissal of education is what a frightened society wants and needs, especially if education becomes a dialogical forum for the questioning of traditional values and the empowering of the disempowered, the desire to ridicule and restrict education is understandable.

The strongest asset for education can be its focus on the one subject matter Whitehead (1929:18) thought important: 'Life in all its manifestations.' This is a challenge and an invitation to share in an open, dynamic, ongoing dialogue that empowers people — the teachers, students, writers, readers, researchers, administrators, parents and others — to become learners, to discover our own strengths from within and with others, and to reach out to others to discover the vulnerabilities we share. In this discovery we become humble, but empowered to tackle the dilemmas we need to solve in the breakthrough change of becoming fully human.

Appendix A

Teacher Interview

Background and demographic questions:

1 How many years have you been teaching?
2 How many years at this school?
3 Have you always been teaching at this grade level?
4 Describe your teacher education.
5 What made you decide to go into teaching? Was there a teacher in your childhood whose image helped you make your decision?
6 What are the important things for you in teaching (pay, colleagues, interaction, recognition, challenge etc.)?

Professional growth and teaching

1 What do you see as your strengths in teaching? Please describe how these strengths have emerged.
2 What things would you like to change about your teaching? Why would you like to change these things?
3 What would you say is the emphasis in your teaching? Why?
4 Describe yourself as a teacher.
5 Has your perception of yourself as a teacher changed over the years? How? What has made it change? Describe the changes you have made in your thinking and teaching.
6 What are your long-term and short-term goals as a teacher?
7 What do you think is best/hardest in teaching?
8 What is the relationship between teaching and learning?
9 How do you perceive yourself as a learner? How does this perception influence your teaching?
10 How would you rate yourself on a scale from 1 to 10 (as teacher, learner, person)?
11 When you have feelings that you are not good enough in your job, how do you deal with them?
12 What do you think motivates you to teach? Has the source of motivation been the same throughout your career?
13 What are some of your thoughts as you begin a school year? Describe your thinking process as you get a group of new children in

your classroom. Do you have similar thoughts every time or have the feelings of anticipation changed during the course of your career?

14 Describe the decision-making process you go through while you teach. Does it work similarly in different situations?

15 What role in your opinion do parents play in their children's education? How do you involve the parents of your students in classroom activities? How do you maintain their interest and involvement? What do you do with parents that do not often participate or do not show interest in what goes on in your classroom?

16 What things do you value in your profession? What would you like to change? Why?

17 Describe your professional self-image. How do you see this self-image in relation to the general image of teachers?

18 How do you view the future of education?

19 What are some traditions and values you would like to pass on to the children in your classroom? Why are these important?

20 How would you like to develop yourself as a professional? Do you see possibilities for this? Are there any obstacles you would like to remove in order to develop professionally?

Self-esteem

1 What characteristics do you think are important for a teacher to have?

2 You have made changes in your teaching. Have there been changes in thinking about yourself as a person that accompanied your professional changes? Describe the changes. Do you see more changes coming? Why?

3 What role does self-esteem play in teaching?

4 How would you describe the source of your self-esteem? Has it always been the same?

5 How do the people in your family describe you as a person? Would you agree or disagree with them? How do your colleagues perceive you in the school community?

6 Describe your ideal self-image.

7 What are your ways of coping with stress and pressures of school life? Are there things you would like to do but cannot to reduce stress in your teaching situation? What would have to change in order for you to be able to reduce stress?

To be asked after the classroom observation.
Interaction

1 What role does knowing the children play in your teaching? Describe how you learn to know the children in your group.

2 Describe yourself as a communicator. What are your strengths? How would you like to become a more efficient communicator?

3 Have there been changes in thinking of yourself as a communicator in the classroom? Describe these changes.

4 What do you think is important in interacting with children in the classroom?

5 Please describe verbal and nonverbal interaction. How do verbal and nonverbal interaction relate to each other?

6 What is important to you in communicating with the children nonverbally?

7 What do you do in the classroom when you notice that your verbal and nonverbal messages conflict?

8 What relationship would you like between you and your children?

9 What is your most important role in facilitating students' learning?

10 Children always have a variety of personalities and backgrounds. How do you accommodate these in a classroom?

11 Are there aspects of interaction in your classroom that you would like to change? How could you change them?

12 Here are some roles for a teacher. Describe each one of them in terms of how you relate to them as a teacher:
- teacher as a partner with parents
- teacher as a person
- teacher as a colleague
- teacher as an authority
- teacher as a nurturer, as understander of the learner
- teacher as facilitator of learning, teacher as interactor
- teacher as a researcher
- teacher as a creator, program developer
- teacher as a planner and administrator
- teacher as a decision-maker and problem-solver
- teacher as a professional leader (Heck and Williams, 1984)

Other questions were formulated for each teacher for clarifying emerging themes, events, and observations after the classroom participant-observation was over. These had to do with the specific situation of each teacher's classroom.

Child Interview

1 What is the best part about school? What do you enjoy the most? What are your favorite things to do at school?
2 If you were the teacher what are some things you would do differently than your teacher does?
3 What are some of the things you learn in school?
4 Do you like learning?
5 How do you feel about your teacher?
6 Do you always understand your teacher? What do you do if your teacher does not understand you? Does your teacher understand you?
7 What kinds of things do you enjoy doing at home?
8 Which classmates do you like to be with?
9 When you get angry in the classroom, what do you do? What does the teacher do?
10 Do you like the way your classroom looks?
11 Why is learning important?
12 Does your teacher get angry? How? How do you know when he or she is angry?
13 Does your teacher hug you? How often? Do you hug him or her?
14 What is your favorite place in the classroom?

References

ARGYLE, M. (1988) *Bodily Communication*, New York: Methuen.

ATKINSON, P. (1990) *The Ethnographic Imagination: Textual Constructions of Reality*, London: Routledge.

ATKINSON, P. and DELAMONT, S. (1990) 'Writing about teachers: How British and American ethnographic texts describe teachers and teaching', *Teaching and Teacher Education*, 6(2), 11–125.

BARGAR, R.R. and DUNCAN, J.K. (1990) 'Creative endeavor in PhD Research: Principles, contexts and conceptions', *The Journal of Creative Behavior*, 24(1), 59–60.

BARROW, R. (1984) *Giving Teaching Back To Teachers: A Critical Introduction To Curriculum Theory*, Totowa New Jersey: Barnes and Noble Books.

BENNETT, C.I. (1990) *Comprehensive Multicultural Education: Theory and Practice*. Boston: Allyn and Bacon.

BERLINER, D.C. (1984) 'Making the right changes in preservice teacher education', *Phi Delta Kappan*, 66(2), 94–6.

BLASE, J. (1986) 'Socialization as humanization: One side of becoming a teacher', *Sociology of Education*, 59(4), 100–13.

BLUMER, H. (1969) *Symbolic Interactionism: Perspective and Method*, Englewood Cliffs, NJ: Prentice-Hall.

BONNETT, M. and DODDINGTON, C. (1990) 'Primary teaching: What has philosophy to offer?', *Cambridge Journal of Education*, 20(2), 115–21.

BOOTH, E.O. (1987) 'Researcher as participant: Collaborative evaluation in a primary school', *Education as Urban Society*, 29(1), 55–85.

BRAINMAP, THE (1989) *A Dolphin Think Self-assessment Profile*, Fort Collins, CO: Brain Technologies Corporation.

BROPHY, J. and GOOD, T. (1974) *Teacher-student Relationships: Causes and Consequences*, New York: Holt Rinehart and Winston.

BUBER, M. (1970) *I and Thou*, New York: Charles Scribner.

CAHN, D.D. (1990) 'Perceived understanding and interpersonal relationships', *Journal of Social and Personal Relationships*, 7, 231–44.

CAMBOURNE, B. (1988) *The Whole Story. Natural Learning and the Acquisition of Literacy in the Classroom*, New York: Ashton Scholastic.

CARBONE, P.F. JR. (1991) 'The teacher as a philosopher', *The Educational Forum*, 55(4), 319–31.

CARPENTER, F.I. (1955) *American Literature and the Dream*, New York: Philo-sophical Library.

CHAPIN, H. (1987) *A Legacy in Song*, New York: Cherry Lane Music.

CHENFELD, M.B. (1992) 'Teaching in the "Key of Life" ', *Educational Leader-ship*, **49**(5), 89–90.

CHISERI-STRATER, E. (1991) *Academic Literacies: The Public Discourse of Univer-sity Students*, Portsmouth, NH: Heinemann.

COCHRAN, M. (1988) *Keynote Address at the National Conference: A Decade of Developing Day Care*, Jyväskylä, Finland, Nov. 1988.

COCHRAN-SMITH, M. (1991) 'Learning to teach against the grain', *Harvard Educational Review*, **61**(3), 279–310.

CONNER, J.E. (1989) 'Cutting edge: Brain-compatible learning', *Journal of De-velopmental Education*, **13**(1), 26–7.

CRUICKSHANK, D.R. (1987) *Reflective Teaching: The Preparation of Students of Teaching*, Reston, VA: Association of Teacher Educators.

CURRIE, J.R. (1988) 'Affect in schools: A return to the most basic of basics', *Childhood Education*, **65**(2), 83–7.

DELAMONT, S. (1976) 'Interaction in the classroom', London: Methuen.

DENZIN, N.K. (1978) *The Research Act*, New York: McGraw-Hill.

DEVRIES, R., HANEY, J.P. and ZAN, B. (1991) 'Sociomoral atmosphere in direct-instruction, eclectic, and constructivist kindergartens: A study of teachers' enacted interpersonal understanding', *Early Childhood Research Quarterly*, **6**, 449–71.

DEWEY, J. (1933) *How We Think*, Boston, MA: Heath.

DEWEY, J. (1944) *Democracy and Education*, New York: MacMillan.

DUNN, K. and DUNN, R. (1987) 'Dispelling outmoded beliefs about student learning', *Educational Leadership*, **44**(6), 55–62.

EISNER, E.W. (1979) *The Educational Imagination*, New York: MacMillan.

EISNER, E.W. (1991) *The Enlightened Eye: Qualitative Inquiry and the Enhance-ment of Educational Practice*, New York: Macmillan.

EISNER, E.W. and PESKIN, A. (1990) (Eds) *Qualitative Inquiry in Education: The Continuing Debate*, New York: Teachers College Press.

EKMAN, P. and FRIESEN, W.V. (1982) 'Felt, false and miserable smiles', *Journal of Nonverbal Behavior*, **6**, 238–52.

ELLISON, L. (1990) 'What does the brain have to do with learning', *Holistic Education Review*, **3**(3), 41–46.

ERICKSON, F. and WILSON, J. (1982) *Sights and Sounds of Life in Schools: A Resource Guide to Film and Videotape for Research and Education*, (Research series No. 125). East Lansing, MI: Michigan State University, College of Education, Institute for Research on Teaching.

FAGAN, W.T. (1989) 'Empowered students: empowered teachers', *Reading Teacher*, **42**(8), 572–8.

FELDHUSEN, J.F. (1989) 'Why public schools will continue to neglect the gifted', *Gifted Child Today*, **12**(2), 55–60.

FLANDERS, N.A. (1970) *Analyzing Teaching Behavior*, Reading, MA: Addison-Wesley.

FOSTER, K. (1990) 'Small steps on the way to teacher empowerment', *Educational Leadership*, **47**(8), 38–40.

FRASER, B.J. (1989) 'Twenty years of classroom climate work: Progress and prospect', *Journal of Curriculum Studies*, **21**(4), 307–27.

FREIRE, P. (1970) *The Pedagogy of the Oppressed*, New York: Continuum.

FROMM, E. (1967) 'The theory of love', in MATSON, F.G. and MONTAGU, A. (Eds) *The Human Dialogue: Perspectives on Communication*, New York: The Free Press, 158–76.

FULLAN, M. (1982) *Meaning of Educational Change*, New York: Teachers College Press.

GARDNER, H. (1985) *The Frames of Mind: The Theory of Multiple Intelligences*, New York: Basic Books.

GARRISON, J.W. (1988) 'Democracy, scientific knowledge, and teacher empowerment', *Teachers College Record*, **89**(4), 487–504.

GILLESPIE, J.K. (1988) *Foreign and US Teaching Assistants: An Analysis of Verbal and Nonverbal Classroom Interaction*, Urbana-Champaign, IL: University of Illinois.

GILMORE, P. (1985) 'Silence and sulking: Emotional displays in the classroom', in TANNEN, D. and SAVILLE-TROIKE, M. (Eds) *Perspectives on Silence*, Norwood: Ablex Publishing Corporation.

GILMORE, A.A. and GLATTHORN, A.A. (1982) (Eds), *Children in and out of School: Ethnography and Education*, Washington DC: Center for Applied Linguistics.

GIROUX, H. (1987) 'Literacy and the pedagogy of political empowerment', in FREIRE, P. and MACEDO, D. *Literacy Reading the Word and the World*, South Hadley, MA: Bergin and Garvey.

GIROUX, H. (1988) 'Literacy and pedagogy of voice and political empowerment', *Educational Theory*, **38**(1), 61–75.

GITLIN, A. and PRICE, K. (1992) 'Teacher empowerment and the development of voice', *Supervision in Transition*, The ASCD Yearbook.

GLASSER, W. (1990) *Quality School*, New York: Harper and Row.

GLICKMAN, C.D. (1989) 'Has Sam and Samantha's time come at last?', *Educational Leadership*, **46**(8), 4–9.

GOETZ, J.P. and LECOMPTE, M.D. (1984) *Ethnographic and Qualitative Design in Educational Research*, New York: Academic Press.

GOODLAD, J. (1990) *Teachers for our Nation's Schools*, San Francisco, CA: Jossey Bass.

GOODLAD, J., SODER, R. and SIROTNIK, K.A. (1990) *Places where Teachers are Taught*, San Francisco, CA: Jossey-Bass.

GOODMAN, K. (1986) *What's Whole in Whole Language*, Portsmouth, NH: Heinemann.

GOODMAN, J. (1987) *Key Factors in Becoming (or not Becoming) an Empowered*

Elementary School Teacher: A Preliminary Study of Selected Novices, Eric Documents 280808.

HALL, E.T. (1965) *The Hidden Dimension*, New York: Doubleday.

HART, L.A. (1986) 'A response: All "thinking" paths lead to the brain', *Educational Leadership*, **43**(8), 45–8.

HART, L.A. (1990) 'Cognitive development: A quick tour of the brain', *The School Administrator*, **40**(1), 13–15.

HEANEY, T.W. (1982) 'Adult learning for empowerment: Towards a theory of liberatory education', Unpublished manuscript.

HECK, S. and WILLIAMS, R. (1984) *The Complex Roles of a Teacher*, New York: Teachers College Press.

HENJUM, A. (1983) 'Let's select "self-actualizing" teachers', *Education*, **104**(1), 51–5.

HILLS, P.J. (1986) *Teaching, Learning and Communication*, London: Croom Helm.

HIRSJÄRVI, S. and HURME, H. (1984) *Merkityksen Ongelma Haastattelututkimuk-sessa*, [The problem of meaning in the interview method], Jyväskylän yliopisto: Kasvatustieteen laitos. [The University of Jyväskylä: Department of Education.]

HOLLY, M.L. (1989) *Writing to Grow: Keeping a Personal-professional Journal*, Portsmouth, NH: Heinemann.

HOUSER, N.O. (1990) 'Teacher-researcher: The synthesis of roles for the empowerment', *Action in Teacher Education*, **12**(2), 55–60.

HOWE, J. (1986) *There's A Monster Under My Bed*, New York: Athenaeum.

HOWE, R. (1963) *The Miracle of Dialogue*, New York: The Seabury Press.

HUMPHREY, J.N. and HUMPHREY, J.H. (1986) *Coping with Stress in Teaching*, New York: AMS Press.

HUSEN, T. (1989) 'Schools for the 1990s', *Scandinavian Journal of Educational Research*, **33**(1), 3–13.

ITTELSON, W.H. and CANTRIL, H. (1967) 'The theory of communication. Perception: A transactional approach', in MATSON, F.M. and MONTAGU, A. (Eds) *The Human Dialogue: Perspectives on Communication*, New York: The Free Press.

JACOB, E. (1988) 'Clarifying qualitative research', *Educational Researcher*, **17**, 16–24.

JECKER, J.D., MACCOBY, N. and BREITROSE, H.S. (1965) 'Improving the accuracy in interpreting nonverbal cues of comprehension', *Psychology in School*, **2**(3), 239–244.

JOHNSON, S.M. (1990) *Teachers at Work: Achieving Success in our Schools*, New York: Basic Books.

JOHNSON, D.W. and JOHNSON, R.T. (1991) *Learning Together and Alone: Cooperative, Competetive and Individualistic Learning*, Englewood Cliffs, NJ: Prentice-Hall.

JONES, E. (1984) 'Perspectives on teacher education: Some relations between theory and practice', *Educational Research* 247029.

KANPOL, B. (1990) 'Empowerment: The institutional and cultural aspects for teachers and principals', *NASSP-Bulletin*, **74**(528), 104–7.

KATZ, L.G. and CHARD, S.C. (1989) *Engaging Children's Minds: The Project Approach*, Norwood, NJ: Alex Publishing Corporation.

KIEFFER, C.H. (1981) 'The emergence of empowerment: The development of participatory competence among individuals in citizen organizations', unpublished PhD dissertation, University of Michigan, Ann Arbor.

KIRK, D. (1986) 'Beyond the limits of theoretical discourse in teacher education: Towards a critical pedagogy', *Teaching and Teacher Education*, **2**(2), 155–67.

KNAPE, C. and ROSEWELL, P.T. (1980) 'The philosophically discerning classroom teacher', *Educational Studies*, **11**, 37–47.

KOHN, A. (1991) 'Caring kids: The role of the schools', *Phi Delta Kappan*, **72**(7), 496–506.

KOTTKAMP, R.B., PROVENZO, E.F. and COHN, M.M. (1986) 'Stability and change in a profession: Two decades of teacher attitudes', 1964–1984, *Phi Delta Kappan*, **67**, 559–67.

KREISBERG, S. (1992) *Transforming Power: Domination, Empowerment and Education*, New York: State University of New York.

LANGER, S. (1951) *Problems of Art*, New York: Charles Scribner's.

LERNER, B. (1985) 'Self-esteem and excellence: The choice and the paradox', *American Educator*, **Winter**, 10–16.

LESIEG, T. (1961) *Ten Apples Up on Top*, New York: Random House.

LEVINE, S. (1989) *Promoting Adult Growth in Schools: The Promise of Professional Development*, New York: Allyn & Bacon.

LEVINE, S. (1989) *Promoting Adult Growth in Schools: The Promise of Professional Development*, Boston, MA: Allyn and Bacon.

LINDH, R. (1983) *Mielikuvaoppiminen Suggestiopohjaisen Oppimisen Opas*, [Learning through imaging. A guide to learning based on suggestion.], Porvoo: Werner Söderström Osakeyhtiö.

LORTIE, D. (1975) *School Teacher: A Sociological Study*, Chicago, IL: University of Chicago Press.

LOUDEN, W. (1991) *Understanding Teaching*, New York: Teachers College Press.

LOZANOV, G. (1978) *Suggestology and Outlines of Suggestopedy*, New York: Gordon and Breach Science Publishers.

LYNCH, J. (1989) *Multicultural Education in a Global Society*, London: Falmer Press.

McCREARY JUHASZ, A. (1990) 'Teacher self-esteem: A triple role approach to this forgotten dimension', *Education*, **11**(2), 234–41.

McPHERSON, J.C. (1984) 'Environments and interaction in row-and-column classrooms', *Environments and Behavior*, **16**(4), 481–502.

MASLOW, A. (1968) *Toward the Psychology of Being*, New York: Van Nostrand Reinhold.

MATTSON, C. (1985) *Misfits in the Classroom: Creative Divergent Children*, Saratoga, CA: R.E. Publishers.

MEAD, M. (1973) 'The art and technology of fieldwork', in NARROL, R. and

COHEN, R. (Eds) *A Handbook of Method in Cultural Anthropology*, New York: Columbia University Press.

MERTENS, S. and YARGER, S.J. (1988) 'Teaching as a profession: Leadership, empowerment and involvement', *Journal of Teacher Education*, **39**(1), 32–7.

MILLER, P. (1988) *Nonverbal Communication: What Research Says to the Teacher*, National Education Association.

MILSTEIN, M. (1990) 'Plateauing: A growing problem for educators and educational organizations', *Teaching and Teacher Education*, **6**(2), 173–81.

MINDMAKER 6 (1991) *A Values and Beliefs Instrument for the Information Age*, Fort Collins, CO: Brain Technologies Corporation.

NEVE, C.D. (1985) 'Brain-compatible learning succeeds', *Educational Leadership*, **43**(2), 83–5.

NEWSLETTER OF THE COMMITTEE TO END VIOLENCE AGAINST THE NEXT GENERATION (1993) Berkley, CA: End Violence Against the Next Generation, Inc.

NIAS, J. (1986) *Teacher Socialization: The Individual in the System*, Victoria, Australia: Deakin University Press.

NIAS, J. (1987) 'Teaching and the self', *Cambridge Journal of Education*, **17**(3), 178–85.

NIGRO, K. (1984) *Developing Confidence and Self-motivation in Teachers: The Role of Administrator*, ED 269842.

NOBLIT, G.W. and HARE, R.D. (1988) *Meta-ethnography. Synthesizing Qualitative Studies*, Beverly Hills, CA: Sage.

NUMMELA, R.M. and ROSENGREN, T.M. (1986) 'What's happening in the students' brain may redefine teaching', *Educational Leadership*, **43**(8), 49–53.

NUMMELA CAINE, R. and CAINE, G. (1991) *Making connections: Teaching and the human brain*, Alexandria, VA: Association for Supervision and Curriculum Development.

OVERHALT, G.E. and STALLINGS, W.M. (1976) 'Ethnographic and experimental hypothesis in educational research', *Educational Researcher*, **5**(8), 12–14.

PALMER, R. (1971) *Space, Time and Grouping*, New York: Citation Press.

PATTERSON, M.L. (1983) *Nonverbal Behavior: A Functional Perspective*, New York: Springer.

PATTON, M.Q. (1980) *Qualitative Evaluation Methods*, Beverly Hills, CA: Sage.

PEIRCE, C.S. (1958) *Selected Writings: Values in a Universe of Chance*, New York: Dover.

PELTO, P.J. (1970) *Anthropological Research: The Structure of Inquiry*, New York: Harper & Row.

PESHKIN, A. (1985) 'Virtuous subjectivity: In the participant-observer's I's', in BERG, D. and SMITH, K.K. (Eds), *Exploring Clinical Methods for Sound Research*, Beverly Hills, CA: Sage.

RIEBER, R.W. and CARTON, A.S. (Eds) (1987) *The Collected Works of L.S. Vygotsky*, New York: Plenum Press.

ROGERS, C. (1961) *On Becoming a Person*, Boston, MA: Houghton-Mifflin.

ROHNER, R.P. (1986) *The Warmth Dimension*, Beverly Hills, CA: Sage.

ROSENTHAL, N. (1990) 'Active learning, empowered learning', *Adult Learning*, **1**(5), 16–18.

ROSS, R. (1989) *Small Groups in Organizational Settings*, New York: Prentice-Hall.

ROUTMAN, R. (1988) *Transitions: From Literature to Literacy*, Portsmouth, NH: Heinemann.

SARASON, S. (1971) *The Culture of School and the Problem of Change*, Boston, MA: Allyn & Bacon.

SAVILLE-TROIKE, M. (1982) *The Ethnography of Communication*, Oxford, GB: Basil Blackwell.

SAVILLE-TROIKE, M. (1985) 'An integrated theory of communication', in TANNEN, D. and SAVILLE-TROIKE, M. (Eds) *Perspectives on Silence*, Norwood, NJ: Ablex Publishing Corporation.

SCHWAB, R.L. (1983) 'Teacher burnout: Moving beyond "psychobabble"', *Theory into Practice*, **22**(1), 21–6.

SHOR, I. (1986) 'Equality is excellence: Transforming teacher education and the learning process', *Harvard Educational Review*, **56**(4), 406–26.

SHOR, I. and FREIRE, P. (1987) 'What is the "dialogical method" of teaching?', *Journal of Education*, **169**(3), 11–31.

SICKLER, J.L. (1988) 'Teachers in charge: Empowering the professionals', *Phi Delta Kappan*, **69**(5), 354–6.

SLAVIN, R.E. (1991) 'Synthesis on research on cooperative learning', *Educational Leadership*, **48**(5), 71–82.

SMITH, F. (1986) *Insult to Intelligence*, Portsmouth, NH: Heinemann.

SMITH, F. (1990) *To Think*, New York: Teachers College, Columbia University.

SPARKS-LANGER, G.M. and COLTON, B.A. (1991) 'Synthesis of research on teachers' reflective thinking', *Educational Leadership*, **48**(6), 37–44.

SUGAI, G. and LEWIS, T. (1989) 'Teacher/student interaction analysis', *Teacher Education and Special Education*, **12**(4), 131–8.

SWART, E. (1990) 'So, you want to be a professional?', *Phi Delta Kappan*, **72**(4), 315–18.

TOMKINS, S.S. and McCARTER, R. (1964) *Perceptual and Motor Skills*, **18**, 119–58.

TOMPKINS, J. (1991) 'Teaching like it matters', *Lingua Franca*, **1**(6), 24–7.

TONELSON, S. (1981) 'The importance of teacher self-concept to create a healthy psychological environment for learning', *Education*, **102**, 96–100.

TROEN, V. and BOELS, K. (1988) 'The teaching project: A model for teacher empowerment', *Language Arts*, **65**(1), 688–92.

VAN MAANEN, J. (1988) *Tales of the field: On writing ethnography*, Chicago, IL: The University of Chicago Press.

VERDERBER, K.S. and VERDERBER, R.F. (1986) *Interact: Using Interpersonal Communication Skills*, Belmont, MA: Wadsworth Publishing.

WARD, C. (1988) *Cookie's Week*, New York: Putnam.

WEISSGLASS, J. (1990) 'Constructivist listening for empowerment and change', *The Educational Forum*, **54**(4), 351–70.

WHITEHEAD, A.N. (1929) *The Aims of Education*, New York: Macmillan.

WIBEL, W.H. (1991) 'Reflection through writing', *Educational Leadership*, **48**(6), 45.

WIERSMA, W. (1991) 'Research methods in education', Boston, MA: Allyn & Bacon.

WOLCOTT, H.F. (1990) 'On seeking — and rejecting — validity in qualitative research', in EISNER, E.W. and PESHKIN, A. (Eds) *Qualitative Inquiry in Education: The Continuing Debate*, New York: Teachers College Press.

WOOLFOLK, A.E. and GALLOWAY, C.M. (1985) 'Nonverbal communication and the study of teaching', *Theory into Practice*, **24**(1), 77–84.

YOLEN, J. (1987) *Owl Moon*, New York: Philomel Books.

Index